BACK of the BOX COOKING 30-MINUTE MEALS

BACK of the BOX COOKING
30-MINUTE MEALS

500 QUICK AND EASY FAMILY RECIPES FROM AMERICA'S FAVORITE BRANDS

Edited by Barbara Greenman

Illustrations by Ken Krug

BLACK DOG
& LEVENTHAL
PUBLISHERS
NEW YORK

Published by
Black Dog & Leventhal Publishers, Inc.
151 West 19th Street
New York, NY 10011

Distributed by
Workman Publishing
225 Varick Street
New York, NY 10014

Designed by Kay Schuckhart/Blond on Pond
Manufactured in China

ISBN-13: 978-1-57912-812-8

Library of Congress Cataloging-in-Publication Data is available on file

g f e d c b a

Table of Contents

Introduction

To the fans of *Back of the Box Cooking*, thank you! Your feedback has been enthusiastic and helpful. You've told me about recipes you loved, and shared your nostalgia for childhood favorites. And you singled out the quick recipes—the hearty, main-dish salads; the stir-fries; the quick soups and breads and no-bake pies—and wanted more. We all know how important it is to save time and money by serving simple, inexpensive meals to the family at home. So here is a sequel, *Back of the Box 30-Minute Meals: 500 Quick and Easy Family Recipes from America's Favorite Brands*.

To put together this new collection, we revisited our friends and experts—the heads of test kitchens, recipe developers, brand managers, nutritionists, and food editors—at America's major food companies, big and small. We asked them to recommend both their own favorites and their highest-rated recipes that can be on your table in 30 minutes or less. More than 30 companies responded with recipes chosen from their "all-time classics," "viewer favorites," "top-20 hit lists," and "30-minute miracles." And all the recipes have earned four or five stars from companies that give consumer ratings.

We read hundreds of recipes and tested each one for preparation and cook times. Here is the final selection—500 great ideas for breakfast and brunch, soups and sandwiches, salads, main courses, side dishes, desserts, and kids' favorites. Time-honored brands, 136 in all, are featured, and you are sure to find your favorites. In addition, several recipes highlight new brands introduced only in the last year. You'll find frittatas, quesadillas, chilis and stews, pot pies, burgers, stir-fries, pizzas, risottos, pasta, paellas, parfaits, cakes, pies, cookies, ice cream, and puddings. Not including the time needed for marinating, cooling, or freezing, each recipe can be ready in 30 minutes or less, sometimes a lot less. You'll find some 10-minute wonders here, like Festive Fruit Ambrosia, Fusilli Fanfare (a salad ready in 5 minutes), and Easy Chocolate Peppermint Pie.

These recipes are meant to be liberating. You don't have to cook them right before dinnertime after a stressful day. Prepare them in a free half hour during the morning, or make a few over the weekend and put them in the freezer. But if you've had a busy day, rest assured—dinner is a mere 30 minutes away!

In a good recipe, each ingredient contributes to the final result. So it is with a team creating a book. First, thanks to the contributors from the food companies for your patient and willing help. I now think of you as friends, and I hope I have remembered everyone (see page 339). And thanks to my publisher, J.P. Leventhal; Liz Van Doren, editor; Elizabeth Matlin, recipe tester; Candie Frankel, copy editor; Allison Frascatore, editorial assistant; Ken Krug, illustrator; and Kay Schuckhart, designer.

Enjoy!

Barbara Greenman

Breakfast and Brunch

Sunrise Fruit Salad

½ cup seedless green grapes

½ cup cantaloupe balls

½ cup sliced strawberries

½ cup orange pieces
(cut segments in half)

¾ cup plain yogurt

½ teaspoon lemon juice

1 tablespoon honey

1 teaspoon **FRONTIER** dried peppermint leaf

2 tablespoons crystallized ginger, finely chopped

PREP: 10 minutes

YIELD: 2 servings

Combine fruit in a serving bowl. In a small mixing bowl, blend yogurt, lemon juice, honey, peppermint, and ginger. Pour the dressing over the fruit and mix gently.

Courtesy of Frontier Natural Products Co-op

Festive Fruit Ambrosia

PREP: 10 minutes

YIELD: 6 servings

Combine pineapple, oranges, banana, grapes and kiwifruit, if using, in bowl. Blend yogurt or crème fraîche with lime zest and lime juice, if using. Gently toss with fruit and sprinkle with coconut or almonds. Serve over lettuce and garnish with fresh mint, if desired.

Courtesy of Del Monte Foods

1 (15 ¼-oz.) can **DEL MONTE® Pineapple Chunks in Its Own Juice**, drained

1 (15-oz.) can **DEL MONTE Mandarin Oranges**, drained

1 banana, sliced

1 cup red seedless grapes

1 kiwifruit, peeled and sliced (optional)

1 ½ cups vanilla lowfat yogurt or crème fraîche

½ teaspoon grated lime zest (optional)

2 tablespoons fresh lime juice (optional)

¼ cup flaked coconut or sliced almonds, lightly toasted

Lettuce

Fresh mint leaves (optional)

Four-Star Citrus Ambrosia

2 eggs

½ cup sugar

Grated zest of ½ **SUNKIST® Lemon**

¼ cup freshly squeezed **SUNKIST® lemon juice**

¼ cup butter or margarine, melted

2 **SUNKIST® Oranges**, peeled and cut into half-cartwheel slices

1 **SUNKIST® Grapefruit**, peeled and sectioned

2 **SUNKIST® Tangerines**, peeled, segmented, and seeded

Toasted shredded or flaked coconut

Fresh mint leaves (optional)

PREP: 20 minutes, excluding chilling

COOK: 10 minutes

YIELD: 4 servings

To make the sauce, in a saucepan, beat the eggs well. Stir in the sugar, lemon zest, lemon juice, and butter. Cook over low heat, stirring constantly, until thickened, about 10 minutes. Cover and chill. Meanwhile, divide fruit into four individual dessert dishes and chill. Spoon the sauce over the fruit, sprinkle with coconut, and garnish with fresh mint, if desired.

Courtesy of Sunkist Growers, Inc.

NOTE

The American Egg Board recommends the following method for preparing recipes with raw or lightly cooked eggs: In a heavy saucepan, stir the sauce over low heat, stirring constantly, until the egg mixture coats a metal spoon with a thin film or reaches 160°F. Immediately place the saucepan in ice water and stir until the egg mixture is cool. Proceed with the recipe.

Fresh Fruit Salad with Pineapple Dressing

1 (8-oz.) can crushed pineapple, drained

⅔ cup sour cream

2 tablespoons honey

Grated zest of ½ **SUNKIST® Orange**

¼ cup chopped pecans or walnuts

3 **SUNKIST® Oranges**, peeled and cut into cartwheel slices

2 unpeeled red apples, sliced

2 bananas, sliced

Green and red grape clusters

Salad greens

PREP: 20 minutes, excluding chilling

YIELD: 4 servings

To make the salad dressing, combine the drained pineapple, sour cream, honey, and orange zest; chill. To serve, stir the nuts into the dressing. On four individual serving plates, arrange the fruit on the salad greens. Serve with the salad dressing.

VARIATIONS

• Substitute 1 (8-oz.) can crushed pineapple in unsweetened pineapple juice, well drained, for the regular pineapple.

• Substitute 1 (8-oz.) carton vanilla lowfat yogurt for the sour cream. Omit the honey.

Courtesy of Sunkist Growers, Inc.

Citrus Green Salad

PREP: 25 minutes

YIELD: 6 servings

Drain pineapple chunks; reserve ¼ cup juice. Combine pineapple chunks, salad blend, sliced orange, onion, nuts, and feta in large serving bowl; set aside. Stir together reserved juice, orange zest, oil, and vinegar in small bowl. Pour over salad just before serving; toss to evenly coat.

Courtesy of Dole Food Company

1 (20-oz.) can **DOLE® Pineapple Chunks**

1 (8- to 10-oz.) package **DOLE® European, Field Greens**, or other **DOLE® Salad Variety**

1 tablespoon grated orange zest

1 orange, peeled, halved, and sliced

½ cup halved and sliced **DOLE® Red Onion**

1 cup chopped nuts, toasted

½ cup crumbled feta

2 tablespoons vegetable oil

2 tablespoons balsamic or red wine vinegar

Grilled Apple, Bacon & Cheese Breakfast Sandwiches

2 tablespoons butter, softened

8 slices **NATURE'S OWN Cinnamon Raisin Swirl Bread**

4 slices American cheese

16 thin slices Granny Smith apple (about ½ large apple)

4 slices bacon, crisply cooked, cut in half

PREP: 15 minutes

COOK: 4 minutes

YIELD: 4 servings

Spread butter on one side of bread slices. Turn over 4 slices and top evenly with cheese, apple slices, and bacon. Place remaining bread slices, buttered sides out, on top. Cook sandwiches in a large nonstick skillet over medium heat 2 minutes on each side, or until browned and cheese is melted; cut in half to serve.

Courtesy of Flowers Foods

Creamy Fruit Toast

2 slices **NATURE'S OWN 100% Whole Wheat Bread**, toasted

3 tablespoons cream cheese spread (plain or flavored)

Assorted cut-up fresh fruit (such as strawberries, kiwifruit, mango, peaches, banana)

1 tablespoon shredded coconut or chopped pecans

PREP: 10 minutes

YIELD: 2 servings

Spread toasted bread slices evenly with cream cheese spread. Top with fruit and coconut.

Courtesy of Flowers Foods

Banagel

PREP: 10 minutes

YIELD: 2 servings

Cut bagels horizontally in half. Spread cream cheese and jam evenly over bagel halves. Sprinkle bottom half of bagels with raisins. Arrange banana slices over raisins; top with remaining bagel halves.

Courtesy of Dole Food Company

2 whole wheat or plain bagels

1 ½ oz. (½ of a 3-oz. package) cream cheese, softened

2 tablespoons strawberry or other fruit jam

½ cup **DOLE® Seedless or Golden Raisins**

1 medium **DOLE® Banana**, sliced

Perfect Buttermilk Biscuits

PREP: 15 minutes

BAKE: 14 minutes

YIELD: 8 biscuits, ⅔ cup fruit butter

FOR THE BISCUITS: Preheat oven to 450°F. Combine flour, baking powder, baking soda, and salt in large bowl; cut in ½ cup butter with fork or pastry blender until mixture resembles coarse crumbs. Stir in buttermilk just until moistened. Turn dough onto lightly floured surface; knead about 10 times or until smooth. Roll out dough to ¾-inch thickness. Cut with 2 ½-inch biscuit cutter. Place 1 inch apart on ungreased baking sheet. Brush biscuits with melted butter. Bake for 10 to 14 minutes, or until lightly browned.

FOR THE FRUIT BUTTER: Stir together softened butter and preserves in small bowl until well mixed. Serve with warm biscuits.

VARIATIONS

- **SAVORY HERB BISCUITS:** Omit salt. Prepare biscuits as directed above, adding ¼ to ½ teaspoon garlic salt. Stir in 1 tablespoon finely chopped fresh herbs or 1 teaspoon dried herbs (dillweed, chives, or rosemary).

- **CINNAMON RAISIN BISCUITS:** Omit salt. Prepare biscuits as directed above, stirring in 2 tablespoons sugar and ¾ teaspoon ground cinnamon with flour. Stir in ⅓ cup raisins with buttermilk. Brush with melted butter and sprinkle biscuits with sugar before baking.

Courtesy of Land O'Lakes, Inc.

BISCUITS

2 cups all-purpose flour

2 teaspoons baking powder

¼ teaspoon baking soda

¼ teaspoon salt

½ cup cold **LAND O LAKES® Butter**

¾ cup buttermilk*

1 tablespoon **LAND O LAKES® Butter**, melted

*Substitute 1 tablespoon vinegar or lemon juice plus enough milk to equal ¾ cup. Let stand 10 minutes.

FRUIT BUTTER

½ cup **LAND O LAKES® Butter**, softened

3 tablespoons fruit preserves (peach, strawberry, raspberry, etc.)

Buttery Biscuit Squares with Orange Butter

PREP: 15 minutes

BAKE: 14 minutes

YIELD: 9 biscuits, ¾ cup orange butter

FOR THE BISCUITS: Preheat oven to 450°F. Combine flour, sugar, baking powder, baking soda, and salt in large bowl; mix in ½ cup butter with fork until mixture resembles coarse crumbs. Stir in buttermilk just until flour is moistened. Turn dough onto lightly floured surface; knead about 10 times or until smooth. Press dough into 7-inch (¾-inch thick) square. Cut into 9 squares with sharp knife. Place biscuits 1 inch apart on ungreased baking sheet. Brush biscuits with melted butter. Bake for 10 to 14 minutes, or until lightly browned.

FOR THE ORANGE BUTTER: Beat all orange butter ingredients together in small bowl at medium speed until creamy. Serve on warm biscuits.

Courtesy of Land O'Lakes, Inc.

BISCUITS

2 cups all-purpose flour

1 tablespoon sugar

2 teaspoons baking powder

¼ teaspoon baking soda

¼ teaspoon salt

½ cup **LAND O LAKES®** **Unsalted Butter**, softened

¾ cup buttermilk*

1 tablespoon **LAND O LAKES®** **Unsalted Butter**, melted

*Substitute 1 tablespoon vinegar or lemon juice plus enough milk to equal ¾ cup. Let stand 10 minutes.

ORANGE BUTTER

½ cup **LAND O LAKES®** **Unsalted Butter**, softened

3 tablespoons orange marmalade

1 tablespoon confectioners' sugar

Rosemary Buttermilk Biscuits

3 cups white flour

1 cup whole wheat pastry flour

1 ½ tablespoons minced fresh rosemary

4 ¼ teaspoons baking powder

1 teaspoon baking soda

1 ½ teaspoons salt

12 tablespoons (1 ½ sticks) **ORGANIC VALLEY European Style Cultured Butter**, frozen

2 scant cups **ORGANIC VALLEY Cultured Lowfat Buttermilk**

PREP: 17 minutes

BAKE: 13 minutes

YIELD: 12 to 14 (3-inch) biscuits

Preheat oven to 425°F. Place flours, rosemary, baking powder, baking soda, and salt in a large bowl; whisk to mix them together thoroughly. Using the large holes of a hand held grater, grate the frozen butter directly into the flour mixture. Stir lightly and briefly to combine. (Alternatively, you can mix the dry ingredients in a food processor and use a large-holed grating disk to grate in the butter. Then transfer the flour-butter mixture to a bowl.) Make a well in the center of the flour-butter mixture, pour in the buttermilk, and stir with a meat fork until mixture just barely comes together as a dough. Transfer dough to a lightly floured surface and gently but briefly knead it 4 or 5 turns. Use a floured rolling pin or your fingers to roll or lightly press the dough out to a ¾-inch thickness. Use a floured 3-inch biscuit cutter to cut out rounds, taking care to slice straight down into the dough without twisting the cutter. (This will help the biscuits rise better.) Gather any dough scraps, press them together, and cut additional biscuits. Transfer biscuits to an ungreased baking pan (an inch or two apart for crusty exteriors or close together for soft-sided biscuits). Bake until high and golden brown, 10 to 13 minutes. Serve hot or warm.

COOK'S TIP

There's nothing like biscuits right out of the oven, but producing them can be a trick when you're in the last-minute throes of meal preparation. To make it easier, prepare the flour-butter mixture and measure out the buttermilk ahead of time, and then keep them both refrigerated. Reserve a corner of your counter for biscuit assembly: flour the work surface and arrange near it a rolling pin, a baking pan, and a cloth-lined basket for serving the biscuits. Then, about 15 minutes before serving time, add the buttermilk to the biscuit dough, cut out the biscuits, and bake them.

Copyright by Terese Allen; courtesy of Organic Valley Family of Farms

Tomato Basil Cheese Biscuits

PREP: 15 minutes

BAKE: 13 minutes

YIELD: 8 servings

Preheat oven to 400°F. In a large mixing bowl, combine flour, baking powder, cream of tartar, and Tomato Basil Spaghetti Sauce Mix. Cut shortening and cheese into mixture. Add milk and stir with large spoon or spatula, forming a ball. Add half of reserved flour to a clean surface. Roll dough in the remaining half. Place dough on floured surface and roll out to ¾-inch thick. Cut dough into 8 round biscuit shapes and place on ungreased baking sheet. Bake for 10 to 13 minutes.

COOK'S TIP

In the last few minutes of baking, top the biscuits with more shredded cheese.

Courtesy of Simply Organic

1 cup flour plus ½ cup reserve

1 tablespoon baking powder

½ teaspoon cream of tartar

1 (1.31-oz.) package **SIMPLY ORGANIC Tomato Basil Spaghetti Sauce Mix**

½ cup shortening

¾ cup shredded Cheddar cheese

½ cup milk

Drop Cornmeal Biscuits

1 ¾ cups all-purpose flour

⅔ cup cornmeal

2 tablespoons sugar

1 tablespoon baking powder

½ teaspoon salt

½ cup cold **LAND O LAKES® Butter**

1 cup buttermilk*

*Substitute 1 tablespoon lemon juice or vinegar plus enough milk to equal 1 cup. Let stand 5 minutes.

PREP: 10 minutes

BAKE: 14 minutes

YIELD: 1 dozen

Preheat oven to 450°F. Combine flour, cornmeal, sugar, baking powder, and salt in large bowl; cut in butter with pastry blender or fork until mixture resembles coarse crumbs. Add buttermilk; stir until mixture is just combined. (If batter is too thin, stir in 1 to 2 tablespoons flour.) Drop by ¼ cupfuls, 1 inch apart, onto greased baking sheet. Bake for 12 to 14 minutes or until golden brown.

COOK'S TIP

Tender biscuits result when the dough is not overmixed. Combine the wet and dry ingredients only until the mixture holds together to avoid a tough texture. To make softer, fluffier biscuits, place the dough closer together on the baking sheet. If you prefer crustier biscuits, place biscuits 2 inches apart on the baking sheet.

Courtesy of Land O'Lakes, Inc.

Date and Nut Scones

2 cups all-purpose flour

¼ cup sugar

2 teaspoons baking powder

½ teaspoon salt

¼ cup margarine

2 eggs

⅓ cup lowfat milk

1 ½ cups **DOLE® Pitted Dates**, snipped

⅓ cup natural sliced or slivered almonds, toasted

Vegetable cooking spray

PREP: 15 minutes

BAKE: 15 minutes

YIELD: 8 servings

Preheat oven to 400°F. Combine flour, sugar, baking powder, and salt in bowl. With pastry blender or two knives, cut margarine into flour mixture until crumbly. Make a well in center. Separate one egg; reserve egg white. Lightly beat egg yolk, whole egg, and milk in small bowl until blended; pour into well. Stir flour mixture until dough cleans sides of bowl. Stir in dates and almonds. Turn dough onto lightly floured surface; knead about 10 times. Pat dough into 6 ½-inch circle. Cut circle into 8 wedges. Place wedges 1 inch apart on baking sheet sprayed with vegetable cooking spray. Lightly beat reserved egg white; brush on dough. Bake 12 to 15 minutes or until lightly browned. Serve warm.

COOK'S TIP

Recipe may be doubled.

Courtesy of Dole Food Company

Chocolate Chip Sweet Cream Scones

PREP: 18 minutes

BAKE: 12 minutes

YIELD: 1 dozen scones

Preheat oven to 400°F. Combine flour, sugar, baking powder, and salt in medium bowl. Cut in butter with pastry blender or fork until mixture resembles coarse crumbs. Stir in chocolate chips, egg, and just enough half-and-half so dough leaves sides of bowl. Knead dough lightly 10 times on lightly floured surface. Roll into 9-inch circle; cut into 12 wedges. Place wedges onto ungreased baking sheet. Brush tops with remaining egg. Bake for 10 to 12 minutes, or until golden brown. Immediately remove from baking sheet.

Courtesy of Land O'Lakes, Inc.

1 ¾ cups all-purpose flour

3 tablespoons sugar

2 ½ teaspoons baking powder

½ teaspoon salt

⅓ cup cold **LAND O LAKES®
Butter**

½ cup semisweet chocolate chips

1 **LAND O LAKES™ All-Natural Farm-Fresh Egg**, slightly beaten

4 to 6 tablespoons **LAND O LAKES® Half & Half**

Lemon Cornmeal Scones

TOPPING

2 tablespoons sugar

1 teaspoon freshly grated lemon zest

SCONES

1 ½ cups all-purpose flour

½ cup yellow cornmeal

2 tablespoons sugar

4 teaspoons baking powder

½ teaspoon salt

6 tablespoons cold **LAND O LAKES® Butter**, cut into 6 pieces

⅓ cup **LAND O LAKES® Half & Half**

2 eggs

2 teaspoons freshly grated lemon zest

PREP: 10 minutes

BAKE: 20 minutes

YIELD: 8 scones

FOR THE TOPPING: Combine sugar and lemon zest in small bowl; set aside.

FOR THE SCONES: Preheat oven to 400°F. Combine flour, cornmeal, sugar, baking powder, and salt in large bowl; cut in butter with pastry blender or fork until mixture resembles coarse crumbs. Stir in half-and-half, eggs, and lemon zest just until moistened. Turn dough onto lightly floured surface; knead 5 to 8 times until smooth, adding only enough flour to keep dough from sticking to surface. Pat dough into 9-inch circle on greased baking sheet. Sprinkle topping evenly over dough. Score circle into 8 wedges with knife but do not separate. Bake for 15 to 20 minutes, or until lightly browned. Cool 10 minutes. Carefully separate scones.

VARIATION

Prepare scones as directed above, stirring in ½ cup sweetened dried cranberries, chopped dried apricots, or chopped pecans with flour.

Courtesy of Land O'Lakes, Inc.

Blueberry Ginger Muffin Tops

1 ½ cups **QUAKER® Oats** (quick or old-fashioned, uncooked)

½ cup sugar

⅓ cup (5 tablespoons plus 1 teaspoon) margarine or butter, melted

1 ⅓ cups all-purpose flour

1 tablespoon baking powder

¾ teaspoon ground ginger

⅔ cup milk

1 egg, slightly beaten

1 cup fresh or frozen blueberries

PREP: 10 minutes

BAKE: 22 minutes

YIELD: 12 servings

Preheat oven to 400°F. Grease large cookie sheet. Combine oats and sugar. For streusel topping, combine ¼ cup oat mixture and 1 tablespoon of melted margarine in small bowl; set aside. For muffins, add flour, baking powder, and ginger to remaining oat mixture; mix well. Combine milk, remaining melted margarine, and egg; add to dry ingredients and mix just until dry ingredients are moistened. Stir in blueberries. For each muffin top, drop batter by ¼ measuring cupfuls onto prepared cookie sheet. Sprinkle streusel topping evenly over batter, patting gently. Bake 20 to 22 minutes, or until golden brown. Serve warm.

COOK'S TIP

To freeze, wrap muffin tops securely in foil or place in freezer bag; label and freeze. To reheat, microwave at high about 30 seconds per muffin top.

Courtesy of The Quaker Oats Company

Apple Cheese Muffins

PREP: 7 minutes

BAKE: 20 minutes

YIELD: 10 to 12 muffins

Preheat oven to 400°F; grease muffin pan. Blend muffin mix, half of chopped apple, cheese, oats, milk, oil, and egg together well. Spoon batter into prepared muffin cups. Combine topping ingredients and add remaining chopped apple to mixture. Spread mixture on top of batter. Bake 18 to 20 minutes.

Courtesy of "JIFFY" mixes, Chelsea Milling Company

MUFFINS

1 package **"JIFFY" Apple Cinnamon Muffin Mix**

1 apple, chopped, reserve half for topping

⅓ cup shredded Cheddar cheese

⅓ cup quick oats

½ cup milk

2 tablespoons oil

1 egg

TOPPING

1 tablespoon sugar

¼ teaspoon cinnamon

Banana Chip Muffins

1 package **"JIFFY" Banana Muffin Mix**

1 small banana, mashed

1 tablespoon quick oats

1 egg

¼ cup milk

⅓ cup mini chocolate chips

PREP: 7 minutes

BAKE: 14 minutes

YIELD: 6 to 8 muffins

Preheat oven to 400°F; grease muffin pan or use paper liners. Mix ingredients together until blended. Pour batter evenly into prepared muffin pan. Bake 12 to 14 minutes or until lightly brown.

Courtesy of "JIFFY" mixes, Chelsea Milling Company

Blueberry Lemon Muffins

PREP: 10 minutes

BAKE: 20 minutes

YIELD: 1 dozen

Preheat oven to 425°F. Combine blueberries and 2 tablespoons Oatmeal Muffin Mix in small bowl; toss to coat. Combine remaining muffin mix and all remaining muffin ingredients in large bowl; mix well. Gently stir in blueberry mixture just until moistened. Spoon batter evenly into paper-lined or greased and floured 12-cup muffin pan. Combine all topping ingredients in small bowl; sprinkle evenly over batter. Bake for 17 to 20 minutes or until lightly browned. Let stand 5 minutes; remove from pan.

OATMEAL MUFFIN MIX: Combine 3 ¾ cups all-purpose flour, 3 cups old-fashioned or quick-cooking oats, 2 ¼ cups firmly packed brown sugar, and 2 tablespoons baking powder in large bowl. Store in container with tight-fitting lid up to 3 months. Stir thoroughly before measuring.

COOK'S TIPS

- For an easy topping alternative, just dip warm muffins in melted butter and then in cinnamon sugar.

- If using 2 ½ x 1 ⅛-inch muffin pan cups, yield will be 15 muffins.

Courtesy of Land O'Lakes, Inc.

MUFFINS

1 cup fresh or frozen blueberries

3 cups prepared Oatmeal Muffin Mix (at left)

1 cup **LAND O LAKES® Fat Free Half & Half or Half & Half**

½ cup **LAND O LAKES® Butter**, melted

1 egg

1 tablespoon freshly grated lemon zest

TOPPING

½ cup prepared Oatmeal Muffin Mix (recipe at left)

2 tablespoons **LAND O LAKES® Butter**, melted

1 teaspoon freshly grated lemon zest (optional)

Spiced Pumpkin Muffins

PREP: 10 minutes

BAKE: 20 minutes

YIELD: 1 dozen

Preheat oven to 400°F. Grease a 12-cup muffin pan or insert paper liners. Stir together all ingredients except butter, pumpkin, buttermilk, and eggs in large bowl. Stir together all remaining ingredients in medium bowl; stir into flour mixture just until moistened. Spoon into muffin pan. Bake for 15 to 20 minutes, or until lightly browned. Cool 5 minutes; remove from pan.

Courtesy of Land O'Lakes, Inc.

2 cups all-purpose flour

⅔ cup brown sugar, firmly packed

⅓ cup sugar

1 tablespoon baking powder

1 teaspoon salt

1 teaspoon ground cinnamon

¼ teaspoon baking soda

¼ teaspoon ground ginger

½ cup **LAND O LAKES® Butter**, melted

½ cup canned pumpkin*

⅓ cup buttermilk**

2 eggs, slightly beaten

*Substitute ½ cup cooked fresh sugar or pie pumpkin, mashed.

**Substitute 1 teaspoon vinegar or lemon juice plus enough milk to equal ⅓ cup. Let stand 10 minutes.

Bayou Broccoli Corn Muffins

1 red pepper, diced small

¾ cup cottage cheese

½ cup sour cream

1 stick butter, melted

2 eggs

1 tablespoon Creole seasoning

4 oz. pepper Jack cheese, shredded

1 (1-lb.) bag **BIRDS EYE® Tender Broccoli Cuts**, thawed

2 (8.5-oz.) boxes corn muffin mix

PREP: 10 minutes

BAKE: 20 minutes

YIELD: 1 ½ dozen

Preheat oven to 400°F. In large mixing bowl, combine all ingredients; do not overmix. Spoon into three 6-cup greased muffin pans. Bake 15 to 20 minutes.

Courtesy of Birds Eye Foods, Inc.

Doughnut Puffs

PREP: 10 minutes

BAKE: 20 minutes

YIELD: 1 dozen

FOR THE MUFFINS: Preheat oven to 375°F. Grease a 12-cup muffin pan. Combine milk, melted butter, and egg in small bowl. Set aside. Combine flour, sugar, baking powder, salt, and nutmeg in large bowl. Add egg mixture; stir just until combined. Stir in currants, if desired. Spoon batter into pan. Bake for 15 to 20 minutes or until toothpick inserted comes out clean.

FOR THE TOPPING: Place melted butter in small bowl. Combine sugar and cinnamon in another small bowl. Remove muffins from pan; let stand 2 minutes on wire cooling rack. Immediately dip top of each muffin into melted butter, then into cinnamon sugar mixture. Serve warm.

Courtesy of Land O'Lakes, Inc.

MUFFINS

½ cup milk

⅓ cup **LAND O LAKES® Butter**, melted

1 egg, beaten

1 ⅔ cups all-purpose flour

¾ cup sugar

1 ½ teaspoons baking powder

½ teaspoon salt

¼ teaspoon ground nutmeg

¼ cup currants (optional)

TOPPING

⅓ cup **LAND O LAKES® Butter**, melted

½ cup sugar

1 teaspoon ground cinnamon

Super Easy Cinnamon Buns

1 (16.3-oz.) package refrigerated large buttermilk biscuits

⅓ cup **SHEDD'S SPREAD COUNTRY CROCK® Calcium plus Vitamin D**

1 teaspoon ground cinnamon

½ cup confectioners' sugar

1 teaspoon milk

PREP: 10 minutes

BAKE: 20 minutes

YIELD: 8 servings

Preheat oven to 350°F. Grease a 9-inch round cake pan. Arrange biscuits in prepared pan. Combine **SHEDD'S SPREAD COUNTRY CROCK®** with cinnamon in small bowl. Evenly spread 1 tablespoon Spread mixture on biscuits. Bake 20 minutes or until lightly browned. Cool 10 minutes in pan on wire rack. Meanwhile, stir confectioners' sugar and milk into remaining Spread mixture until smooth. Evenly spread frosting on warm biscuits and serve immediately.

Courtesy of Unilever

Flavored Brunch Butters

PREP: 10 minutes

YIELD: ¾ cup

Combine all ingredients for desired flavored butter in small bowl. Beat at medium speed until fluffy and well mixed. Serve on muffins. Store refrigerated in container with tight-fitting lid up to 2 weeks.

Courtesy of Land O'Lakes, Inc.

STRAWBERRY BUTTER

½ cup **LAND O LAKES® Butter** or 1 stick **Fresh Buttery Taste® Spread**

¼ cup confectioners' sugar

¼ cup strawberry or your favorite flavor fruit preserves

ORANGE-CINNAMON BUTTER

½ cup **LAND O LAKES® Butter** or 1 stick **Fresh Buttery Taste® Spread**

1 tablespoon brown sugar, firmly packed

1 teaspoon freshly grated orange zest

½ teaspoon ground cinnamon

Seviche Olé

PREP: 30 minutes

MARINATE: 8 hours or overnight

CHILL: 30 minutes

COOK: 16 minutes

YIELD: 4 servings

With a sharp knife, cut fish on the diagonal into paper-thin slices. In a glass bowl, combine the fish, lemon zest, and lemon juice; cover. Marinate in refrigerator for 8 hours or overnight, until fish is opaque and has a "cooked" look; stir occasionally. (Or marinate in a tightly sealed plastic bag, turning occasionally.) Stir in remaining ingredients. Cover and chill for 30 minutes to blend flavors. Serve as an appetizer in cocktail glasses, garnishing each as desired with lettuce, avocado slices, lemon slices or cartwheel twists, cilantro, or parsley.

Courtesy of Sunkist Growers, Inc.

1 lb. fresh halibut, sea bass, or red snapper fillets

Grated zest of ½ **SUNKIST® Lemon**

¾ cup freshly squeezed **SUNKIST® Lemon Juice**

1 large tomato, diced and drained

1 medium onion, chopped

2 tablespoons chopped canned or fresh green chilies*

1 tablespoon vegetable oil

1 tablespoon bottled taco sauce or a few drops hot sauce, to taste

1 tablespoon cilantro, chopped

½ teaspoon salt

*Reduce amount if using hot chilies, such as serranos or jalapeños.

Smoked Salmon and Whipped Potato Patties

2 cups boned, flaked smoked salmon or other smoked fish

1 ½ cups cold mashed potatoes

3 tablespoons minced onion

2 tablespoons prepared horseradish (or to taste)

1 **ORGANIC VALLEY Egg white**, beaten

¼ teaspoon white pepper

2 to 3 tablespoons **ORGANIC VALLEY Butter**

ORGANIC VALLEY Sour Cream (Regular or Lowfat)

Chopped fresh parsley

PREP: 15 minutes

CHILL: 1 hour

COOK: 15 minutes

YIELD: 4 servings

Mash smoked fish with a fork and remove any stray bones. Combine fish with mashed potatoes, onions, horseradish, egg white, and pepper. Form into 8 to 10 (3-inch) patties. Chill 1 hour or longer. Heat butter in large, nonstick skillet until hot. Add patties and cook over medium heat until bottoms are lightly browned, 2 to 4 minutes. Carefully turn the patties and cook on other side until bottoms are lightly browned and patties are hot throughout, another 2 to 4 minutes. Handling the patties gently, serve them with small dollops of sour cream and a sprinkling of parsley.

Copyright by Terese Allen; courtesy of Organic Valley Family of Farms

Open-faced Salmon Tea Sandwiches

PREP: 20 minutes

YIELD: 1 dozen

Combine sour cream, cream cheese, dillweed, and lemon juice in small bowl; mix well. Spread sour cream mixture evenly onto bread slices. Top each with 2 slices cucumber and 1 piece salmon. Garnish with lemon zest and fresh dill.

COOK'S TIPS

• Make cream cheese mixture ahead, cover, and refrigerate until ready to assemble sandwiches.

• Score cucumber slices with the tines of a fork before slicing.

Courtesy of Land O'Lakes, Inc.

¼ cup sour cream

1 (3-oz.) package cream cheese, softened

2 teaspoons chopped fresh dillweed

1 teaspoon lemon juice

12 slices cocktail rye bread

1 medium cucumber, cut into 24 slices

1 (4-oz.) package smoked salmon, cut into 12 slices

Lemon zest curls

Fresh dill sprigs

Avocado & Baby Swiss Scramble

12 **ORGANIC VALLEY Grade A Extra Large Brown Eggs**

¼ cup **ORGANIC VALLEY Heavy Whipping Cream**

3 tablespoons **ORGANIC VALLEY Unsalted Cultured Butter**

Sea salt and freshly ground black pepper

3 oz. **ORGANIC VALLEY Baby Swiss Cheese** (thinly sliced)

3 ripe avocados, pitted and sliced

Fresh chives (for garnish)

PREP: 10 minutes

COOK: 10 minutes

YIELD: 8 servings

Crack the eggs into a medium-size mixing bowl. Add cream and whisk until the mixture becomes foamy and light. In a 10-inch skillet over medium heat, melt the butter until it foams, then turn down the heat to low and slowly pour in the egg mixture. Using a heat-resistant rubber spatula, slowly stir the eggs from the outside of the pan to the center. Once eggs begin to set, stirring slowly will create large, cloudlike curds. The cooking process takes about 10 minutes to create nice soft eggs. Season the eggs with freshly ground black pepper and sea salt. Serve with a few slices of avocado and Baby Swiss, and sprinkle with chopped fresh chives.

COOK'S TIP

Serve with a side of fresh organic grapes or slices of kiwifruit.

Courtesy of Organic Valley Family of Farms

Cheesy Denver Breakfast Skillet

PREP: 15 minutes

COOK: 12 minutes

YIELD: 8 servings

Melt 1 tablespoon butter in 10-inch nonstick skillet until sizzling; add onion and bell pepper. Cook over medium heat, stirring occasionally, for 1 minute. Add eggs. Cook, lifting and stirring slightly with spatula to allow uncooked portion to flow underneath, until eggs are set, 2 to 3 minutes. Remove eggs from skillet, cover, and keep warm.

Melt remaining butter in same skillet until sizzling; add hash browns. Cook, stirring occasionally, until lightly browned, 4 to 5 minutes. Add ham; continue cooking until ham is heated through, 1 minute. Spoon scrambled eggs over hash browns in skillet; sprinkle with cheese. Cover; cook until cheese is just melted, 1 minute.

Courtesy of Land O'Lakes, Inc.

2 tablespoons **LAND O LAKES® Butter**

2 tablespoons finely chopped onion

2 tablespoons finely chopped green and/or red bell pepper

4 **LAND O LAKES® All-Natural Farm-Fresh Eggs**, beaten

1 cup refrigerated hash browns

¼ cup finely chopped cooked ham

1 oz. (¼ cup) **LAND O LAKES® Deli White American Cheese**, shredded

Morning Melts

4 **NATURE'S OWN Honey Wheat English Muffins**, split

⅓ cup peach preserves

2 tablespoons honey mustard

8 slices Canadian bacon

8 eggs

½ cup cold water

½ teaspoon salt

¼ teaspoon pepper

2 teaspoons butter

8 slices Colby or Co-Jack cheese

Snipped fresh chives (optional)

PREP: 10 minutes

COOK: 12 minutes

YIELD: 4 servings

Place English muffin halves on foil-lined baking sheet. Broil until lightly toasted. Combine preserves and mustard in small bowl. Spread evenly over toasted English muffins; top each with 1 slice Canadian bacon. Broil 1 to 2 minutes or until heated through. Remove from oven; set aside. Whisk eggs, water, and salt and pepper in large bowl. Melt butter in large nonstick skillet over medium heat. Add egg mixture. Cook, stirring and lifting gently to allow uncooked eggs to flow under cooked portion. Eggs should be soft-set with no liquid remaining. Evenly divide scrambled eggs over Canadian bacon. Top each English muffin half with 1 cheese slice. Broil 2 minutes or until cheese is melted and lightly browned. Sprinkle with chives, if desired.

Courtesy of Flowers Foods

Bacon & Egg Bagel Pizzas

PREP: 13 minutes

COOK: 12 minutes

YIELD: 4 servings

Whisk eggs, water, salt, and pepper in large bowl. Melt butter in large nonstick skillet over medium heat. Add egg mixture. Cook, stirring and lifting gently to allow uncooked eggs to flow under cooked portion. Eggs should be soft-set with no liquid remaining in about 10 minutes. Meanwhile, toast bagels. Top bagel halves evenly with scrambled eggs, bacon bits, tomato, green onions, and cheese. Broil 2 minutes or until cheese is melted. Serve immediately.

Courtesy of Flowers Foods

8 eggs

½ cup cold water or milk

½ teaspoon salt

¼ teaspoon pepper

2 teaspoons butter

4 **NATURE'S OWN Plain Bagels**, split

½ cup real bacon bits

½ cup finely chopped tomato

4 green onions, sliced

½ cup shredded Cheddar cheese

Fajita Omelet

¼ cup sliced green pepper

¼ cup sliced onion

6 large eggs

1 cup milk

1 (1-oz.) package **SIMPLY ORGANIC Fajita Seasoning Mix**

½ cup shredded cheese

PREP: 5 minutes

COOK: 5 minutes

YIELD: 6 servings

Preheat skillet on medium. Add pepper and onion and sauté until tender, adding a little water if needed. In a medium mixing bowl, whisk eggs, milk, and **SIMPLY ORGANIC Fajita Seasoning Mix**. Pour over pepper and onion and cook until done. Top with shredded cheese.

COOK'S NOTE

Serve with guacamole on the side.

Courtesy of Simply Organic

Greek Omelet with Feta

PREP: 10 minutes

COOK: 13 minutes

YIELD: 2 servings (½ omelet each)

Spray small nonstick skillet with cooking spray. Add spinach, onion, and garlic; cook on medium heat, stirring frequently, until onions are tender, 4 minutes. Stir in tomatoes. Beat eggs and water with wire whisk until well blended. Pour evenly over spinach mixture; tilt skillet to evenly distribute eggs. As eggs set, lift edge slightly with spatula to allow uncooked portion to flow underneath. When eggs are almost set, sprinkle evenly with 2 tablespoons feta. Cook until eggs are set, an additional 1 to 2 minutes. Slip spatula underneath, tip skillet to loosen and gently fold omelet in half. Sprinkle with remaining feta. Remove from heat; let stand 2 minutes to allow cheese to melt slightly. Cut in half to serve.

Courtesy of Kraft Foods

1 cup fresh spinach leaves, cut into thin strips

2 tablespoons chopped red onion

½ teaspoon minced garlic

2 tablespoons chopped tomato

2 eggs

2 tablespoons water

¼ cup **ATHENOS Traditional Crumbled Feta Cheese**, divided

Anytime Ham and Cheese Frittata

PREP: 6 minutes

COOK: 24 minutes

YIELD: 8 servings

Preheat oven to 400°F. In a large mixing bowl, whisk eggs, milk, dry mustard, red pepper flakes, and salt. Add bread pieces, stirring to combine; set aside.

In a large 10-inch ovenproof skillet, heat olive oil over medium-high heat. Add potatoes and cook until golden and beginning to crisp. Add ham and cook, stirring often, 2 to 3 minutes more. Push ham and potatoes to the side of the skillet; pour egg mixture into skillet, stir over heat, and when the eggs begin to set, stir to combine the ham, potatoes, and eggs. Stir in cheese. Place in oven and cook for 10 to 15 minutes, until cheese is melted and eggs are set. Cut into wedges to serve.

SERVING SUGGESTIONS

Ham and cheese frittata works for weekend breakfast or brunch with muffins and juice. You can also serve it as a light lunch or supper with a green salad.

Courtesy of National Pork Board

6 eggs

½ cup milk

1 ½ teaspoons dry mustard

¾ teaspoon red pepper flakes

¼ teaspoon salt

2 cups bread torn into 1-inch pieces

1 tablespoon olive oil

2 cups hash brown potatoes with pepper and onion, refrigerated or frozen

2 cups chopped ham

1 cup cubed Cheddar cheese

So-Easy Skillet Frittata

6 eggs

4 oz. (½ of an 8-oz. tub) **PHILADELPHIA Cream Cheese Spread**

½ cup each chopped red and green pepper

6 slices **OSCAR MAYER Bacon**, crisply cooked, drained, and crumbled

1 cup **KRAFT Mexican Style Finely Shredded Four Cheese**, divided

3 tablespoons chopped fresh cilantro

PREP: 10 minutes

COOK: 15 minutes

YIELD: 6 servings

Preheat oven to 400°F. Beat eggs and cream cheese spread with wire whisk until well blended; set aside. Spray 10-inch ovenproof nonstick skillet with cooking spray. Add peppers to skillet; cook and stir 2 minutes or until crisp-tender. Add bacon to cream cheese mixture; add ¾ cup of the shredded cheese and the cilantro; stir until well blended. Add mixture to ingredients in skillet; stir. Cover skillet with lid. Reduce heat to low; cook 6 to 8 minutes or until egg mixture is almost set in center. Remove lid. Place skillet in oven. Bake 5 minutes or until center is set. Remove from oven. Top with remaining ¼ cup shredded cheese; cover with lid. Let stand 2 minutes. Loosen frittata from side of skillet with spatula; slide onto serving plate. Cut into wedges to serve.

Courtesy of Kraft Foods

Broccoli & Mushroom Frittata

PREP: 15 minutes

COOK: 10 minutes

YIELD: 6 servings

Melt butter in 10-inch skillet until sizzling; add mushrooms and onion. Cook over medium heat until tender, 3 to 4 minutes. Beat eggs and pepper in large bowl with wire whisk until well beaten. Pour into skillet. Cook over medium heat, lifting slightly with spatula to allow uncooked portion to flow underneath, until eggs are almost set, 3 to 4 minutes. Arrange red pepper strips and broccoli on top. Cover; continue cooking until eggs are set, 4 to 5 minutes. Sprinkle with cheese; cut into wedges.

Courtesy of Land O'Lakes, Inc.

3 tablespoons **LAND O LAKES® Butter**

1 cup sliced fresh mushrooms

1 medium onion, chopped (½ cup)

9 eggs

¼ teaspoon pepper

½ medium red bell pepper, cut into 1 x ¼-inch strips

1 cup frozen broccoli florets, thawed

4 oz. (1 cup) **LAND O LAKES® Cheddar Cheese**, shredded

Summer Vegetable Frittata

PREP: 10 minutes

COOK: 15 minutes

YIELD: 6 servings

Preheat oven to 375°F. Spray a large ovenproof skillet with nonstick cooking spray. Set over medium-high heat, add onion, and sauté for 1 minute. Add zucchini and pepper, and sauté for 2 minutes, until tender crisp. Stir in half of the basil. In a large bowl, beat together eggs, ½ cup cheese, and Worcestershire Sauce. Add sautéed vegetables and freshly ground pepper, if desired. Stir until well blended. Spray the same skillet with additional nonstick cooking spray. Add egg mixture and disperse vegetables evenly. Cook for 30 seconds over medium heat. Place skillet in center of oven and bake for 10 to 12 minutes, or until eggs are set and toothpick inserted in center comes out clean. In a small bowl, mix together Marinade and tomatoes. Cut frittata into 6 wedges and top each wedge with 2 ½ tablespoons tomato mixture. Sprinkle with remaining ½ cup cheese and remaining basil.

COOK'S TIP

Add ¼ to ½ cup light cream to eggs for a slightly creamy and richer frittata.

Courtesy of H.J. Heinz Company, L.P.

1 cup diced red onion

1 cup diced zucchini

1 cup diced red pepper

2 to 3 tablespoons chopped fresh basil, divided

8 to 10 eggs

1 cup grated Parmesan, divided

2 tablespoons **LEA & PERRINS® Worcestershire Sauce**

Freshly ground black pepper (optional)

¼ cup **LEA & PERRINS® Marinade for Chicken**

1 cup diced fresh tomato

Mini Brunch Quiches

12 slices **NATURE'S OWN Honey Wheat Bread**

2 tablespoons butter, melted

⅓ cup ricotta

1 egg

¼ cup chopped Canadian bacon

2 tablespoons grated Parmesan

½ teaspoon dried basil leaves

½ teaspoon instant minced onion

¼ teaspoon salt

⅛ teaspoon pepper

PREP: 17 minutes

COOK: 10 minutes

YIELD: 1 dozen

Preheat oven to 400°F. Roll bread slices thin using rolling pin; cut 3-inch circle from each slice. Brush one side of each circle with butter. Press circles, buttered sides down, into muffin cups. Bake 3 minutes; remove from oven. Reduce oven temperature to 350°F. Meanwhile combine remaining ingredients in small bowl. Divide mixture evenly among bread shells. Bake at 350°F for 10 minutes or until filling is set. Remove quiches from cups with tip of a knife.

COOK'S TIP

Save the bread scraps for fresh bread crumbs. Tear bread into pieces; place in food processor or blender container. Cover; pulse on and off to form fine crumbs. Freeze bread crumbs in airtight container and remove as needed to use in other recipes.

Courtesy of Flowers Foods

Linguine Carbonara with Turkey Bacon

1 teaspoon olive oil

3 slices (about 3 oz.) **Organic Prairie Turkey Bacon**

1 (9-oz.) package fresh linguine

2 extra-large **ORGANIC VALLEY Eggs**, at room temperature

6 tablespoons **ORGANIC VALLEY Shredded Parmesan**, divided

1 tablespoon minced fresh chives

Freshly ground black pepper

PREP: 5 minutes

COOK: 20 minutes

YIELD: 3 servings

Place a large bowl and serving plates or shallow soup plates in the oven. Set oven to 200°F to warm the plates. Place a large pot of salted water over high flame. Meanwhile, heat olive oil in a skillet over a medium-high flame. Lay the turkey bacon in the hot oil and fry it until crispy on both sides. Drain on paper towels and slice each piece of bacon crosswise into ¼-inch strips. When water comes to a rolling boil, stir in the linguine and cook following package directions. While the linguine cooks, beat the eggs in a bowl with half the Parmesan, the chives, and pepper to taste (be generous with the pepper). Beat in 1 tablespoon of the pasta water. When the pasta is cooked—that is, barely tender—remove the bowls from the oven. Drain the pasta and dump it into the large bowl. Immediately add bacon strips and egg mixture and toss well. Keep stirring until the egg mixture sets and clings to the pasta. (If the pasta cools off too quickly, you can finish the dish in the skillet over a low flame.) Divide pasta onto serving plates, sprinkle with remaining Parmesan, and serve immediately.

Copyright by Terese Allen; courtesy of Organic Valley Family of Farms

Nell's Guacamole

PREP: 25 minutes

YIELD: About 4 cups

Remove pits and mash avocado in bowl. Add the remaining ingredients and mix well. Add salt and pepper to taste. If you don't like it hot, you can either omit the jalapeño or add it in smaller quantities. Serve with pretzels or soy crisps.

COOK'S TIP

Another very tasty option is an ingredient called *chiles en adobo*, found in Hispanic markets. These are smoked jalapeños packed in a tomato chili paste. If you like your guacamole really hot, you can substitute one of the *chilies en adobo* for the jalapeño. Add a few teaspoons of the paste for less heat and a great smoky flavor.

Courtesy of Nell Newman, Co-Founder and President, Newman's Own Organics

4 large avocados

4 teaspoons fresh lemon juice

1 ripe medium tomato, chopped

1 medium white onion, finely chopped

3 cloves garlic, minced

1 jalapeño, minced (wear gloves to remove seeds and inner ribs)

¼ cup fresh chopped cilantro

1 teaspoon mild chili powder

½ teaspoon coriander

¼ teaspoon cumin

Salt and pepper to taste

NEWMAN'S OWN ORGANICS Pretzels or **Soy Crisps**

Turkey and Bean Burritos

1 tablespoon canola oil

1 medium onion, chopped

2 cloves garlic, minced

1 jalapeño, seeded and diced

1 cup shredded turkey

1 (14-oz.) can diced fire-roasted tomatoes, drained

Juice of 1 lime

1 teaspoon cumin

¼ teaspoon cayenne pepper

½ cup chopped cilantro

1 (16-oz.) can black beans, rinsed and drained

1 cup cooked brown rice

1 cup **STONYFIELD FARM Plain Yogurt**

6 (10-inch) flour tortillas

2 cups shredded Cheddar cheese

PREP: 19 minutes

COOK: 11 minutes

YIELD: 6 servings

Heat oil in skillet to medium-high. Add onion, garlic, and jalapeño and sauté until onion is clear, about 5 minutes. Reduce heat to medium and add turkey, tomatoes, lime juice, cumin, cayenne, and cilantro. Let simmer for 5 minutes. In small bowl, combine black beans, brown rice, and yogurt; set aside. On flat surface, place ½ cup turkey mixture in center of tortilla and ½ cup of yogurt, bean, and rice mixture. Add ⅓ cup cheese to each burrito. Fold left and then right side of tortilla over filling. Roll up unfolded sides. Cut in half and serve with salsa.

Courtesy of Stonyfield Farm

Veggie Breakfast Burritos

PREP: 5 minutes

COOK: 10 minutes

YIELD: 4 servings

Melt butter in a skillet over medium heat. Add eggs and cook just until they start to set, about 2 minutes. Add cooked vegetables (cut down any large potatoes) and scramble with eggs until just cooked through, about 2 minutes. Season with salt and pepper. Equally divide egg mixture between tortillas, sprinkle with cheese, roll up, and serve.

Courtesy of Birds Eye Foods, Inc.

1 tablespoon butter

4 eggs, beaten

1 (12-oz.) package **BIRDS EYE® STEAMFRESH® Baby Potato Blend**, cooked according to package directions

Salt and pepper

4 (8-inch) burrito-size flour tortillas

½ cup shredded Cheddar cheese

Breakfast Burritos

PREP: 10 minutes

COOK: 10 minutes

YIELD: 4 servings

In nonstick skillet, melt butter and oil. Add broccoli, onion, and tomatoes. Cook over medium heat 3 to 4 minutes until tender. In a bowl whisk together eggs, milk, salt, and pepper. Add egg mixture to the skillet and cook, stirring with wooden spoon, until eggs are just set. Sprinkle with cheese, remove from heat, and let stand until cheese melts. Divide mixture down the center of each tortilla. Roll up tortilla and serve with salsa and chopped cilantro.

Courtesy of Birds Eye Foods, Inc.

1 teaspoon butter

1 tablespoon oil

1 (1-lb.) bag **BIRDS EYE® Tender Broccoli Cuts**, thawed (2 cups)

2 tablespoons chopped onion

¾ cup chopped tomato

6 large eggs

2 tablespoons milk

¾ teaspoon salt

½ teaspoon pepper

½ cup shredded Cheddar Jack cheese

4 (8-inch) flour tortillas, warmed

Salsa

Chopped cilantro

Goat Cheese & Spicy Walnut Quesadillas

1 tablespoon **HAIN PURE FOODS® Canola Oil**

1 ½ teaspoon chili powder

½ teaspoon **HAIN PURE FOODS® Iodized Sea Salt**

¾ cup chopped walnuts

12 oz. goat cheese

6 (6 ½ -7 ½-inch) whole wheat tortillas

6 tablespoons thinly sliced green onion

PREP: 15 minutes

COOK: 15 minutes

YIELD: 6 snack-size servings

Preheat oven to 400°F. In a small skillet, over medium heat, heat oil. Stir in chili powder and salt. Add walnuts and stir well to coat. Stir until nuts are lightly toasted. Remove from heat and set aside. Spread 2 oz. goat cheese onto each tortilla. Sprinkle with 2 tablespoons walnuts and 1 tablespoon green onion. Fold each tortilla in half, pressing together slightly. Place folded tortillas on an ungreased baking sheet and bake until heated through, turning over once, about 10 minutes. Cut each tortilla into three triangles. Serve warm.

Courtesy of Hain Celestial Group

Zesty Corn Quesadillas with Spinach Salad

QUESADILLAS

4 (7- to 8-inch) tortillas

1 cup shredded lowfat Monterey Jack

1 cup **DEL MONTE® Whole Kernel White Sweet Corn**

¼ cup salsa

1 tablespoon chopped cilantro

SPINACH SALAD

3 cups washed baby spinach leaves

2 cups **DEL MONTE Mandarin Orange Segments**, drained; reserve syrup

½ cup chopped red onion

2 tablespoons olive oil

2 tablespoons white wine vinegar

PREP: 10 minutes

COOK: 15 minutes

YIELD: 4 servings

FOR THE QUESADILLAS: Heat a 10-inch ungreased skillet over medium heat. Place one tortilla in skillet and cook until it starts to brown; turn. Fill one side of tortilla with ¼ cup cheese, ¼ cup corn, 1 tablespoon salsa, and some cilantro. Fold other half over cheese mixture. Continue cooking until tortilla is golden brown and cheese is melted.

FOR THE SPINACH SALAD: Combine spinach, oranges, and red onion in bowl. Combine oil, vinegar, and reserved syrup. Toss dressing with salad.

Courtesy of Del Monte Foods

Chicken and Artichoke Quesadilla

PREP: 12 minutes

COOK: 13 minutes

YIELD: 6 servings

In a medium bowl, combine artichokes, yogurt, cheese, and garlic. Evenly spread mixture on 3 tortillas and top each with chicken and mozzarella and remaining tortillas. Spray a 12-inch nonstick skillet with nonstick cooking spray. Cook quesadillas over medium-high heat for 2 to 3 minutes until tortilla is golden brown. Turn once and cook for 1 to 2 minutes until second side is golden brown and cheese is melted. Cut into wedges. Serve with a dollop of plain yogurt and salsa or guacamole.

Courtesy of Stonyfield Farm

1 (14-oz.) can artichoke hearts, drained and chopped

½ cup **STONYFIELD FARM Plain Yogurt**, plus more for topping

1 cup grated Monterey Jack

1 clove garlic, finely chopped

6 (10-inch) burrito-size tortillas

1 cup (about 4 oz.) cooked chicken, thinly sliced

½ cup shredded mozzarella

Salsa or guacamole

Chicken Quesadillas with **SHORT CUTS**

4 large (8- or 9-inch) flour tortillas

1 (4-oz.) can chopped green chilies

1 (9-oz.) package **PERDUE® SHORT CUTS® Carved Chicken Breast, Original Roasted**

1 (2-oz.) can sliced black olives, drained

3 green onions, coarsely chopped

3 tablespoons coarsley chopped fresh cilantro

1 (8-oz.) package shredded Mexican-style cheese blend with taco seasoning (about 2 cups)

Sour cream, salsa, and fresh cilantro sprigs for garnish (optional)

PREP: 10 minutes

COOK: 15 minutes

YIELD: 4 servings

Preheat oven to 375°F. Place tortillas in a single layer on baking sheets and toast for 5 minutes. Evenly spread two tortillas with chilies. Top with chicken, olives, green onions, cilantro, cheese, and another tortilla. Bake for 8 minutes or until cheese is melted and the tortillas are toasted. To serve cut each quesadilla into 6 wedges.

Courtesy of Perdue Farms, Inc.

Southwestern Scramble

PREP: 10 minutes

COOK: 15 minutes

YIELD: 4 servings

Combine eggs, evaporated milk, ½ cup cheese, chilies, and pepper in medium bowl. Spray large skillet with nonstick cooking spray. Place tortilla strips in skillet and heat over medium heat, stirring occasionally, until strips are lightly browned. Pour egg mixture into skillet. Cook, stirring frequently, until eggs are cooked. Sprinkle with remaining ½ cup cheese. Top with salsa, avocado, and/or green onions, if desired. Serve with beans, if using.

Courtesy of Nestlé USA

8 large eggs, well beaten

1 (5-fl. oz.) can **NESTLÉ® CARNATION® Evaporated Milk** (⅔ cup)

1 cup (4-oz.) shredded Mexican-blend cheese, divided

2 tablespoons diced green chilies

⅛ teaspoon ground black pepper

Nonstick cooking spray

2 medium (8-inch) or 3 small (6-inch) corn tortillas, cut into thin strips

Mild salsa, chopped avocado, and/or sliced green onions (optional)

1 (15-oz.) can black beans, rinsed and drained (optional)

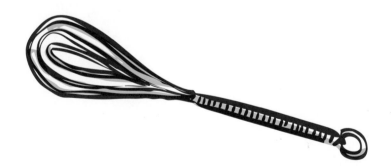

Mexican Omelet

6 eggs

¼ cup cream

2 tablespoons **FRONTIER Mexican Seasoning**

2 tablespoons oil, divided

2 tablespoons butter, divided

¼ cup onion flakes

3 sweet banana peppers, chopped

1 sliced red chili pepper, seeds and stem removed

1 cup grated cheese (Cheddar, Swiss, or other favorite)

¼ cup picante or tomato-chili sauce

¼ cup plain yogurt

PREP: 7 minutes

COOK: 15 minutes

YIELD: 2 servings

Blend together eggs, cream, and Mexican Seasoning. In small skillet, melt 1 tablespoon oil and 1 tablespoon butter. Sauté onion flakes and sweet peppers until soft. Remove from heat. In a large skillet, melt remaining oil and butter. Pour egg mixture into large skillet and cook over low heat. With spatula, loosen edge of omelet and let uncooked egg run under. When nearly cooked through, sprinkle onion, sweet peppers, chili peppers, and cheese on half of the eggs. Fold in half and cover until cheese is melted. Top with sauce and yogurt.

Courtesy of Frontier Natural Products Co-op

Nutty Breakfast Rolls

PREP: 15 minutes

YIELD: 4 servings

Evenly spread **SKIPPY®** peanut butter on hot pancakes, then top with bananas; roll up. Cut in pieces and serve with maple syrup, if desired.

VARIATIONS

- **APPLE CINNAMON:** Stir ¼ cup applesauce and ½ teaspoon ground cinnamon into peanut butter.

- **CINNAMON:** Stir ½ teaspoon ground cinnamon into peanut butter.

- **CHOCOLATE CHIP:** Stir ¼ cup semisweet chocolate chips into peanut butter.

- **CINNAMON RAISIN:** Stir ½ teaspoon ground cinnamon and ¼ cup raisins into peanut butter.

Courtesy of Unilever

½ cup **SKIPPY® Creamy, SUPER CHUNK®**, or **Roasted Honey Nut Peanut Butter**

8 hot cooked pancakes

2 medium bananas, halved lengthwise, then crosswise

Maple syrup (optional)

Orange "Puff" Pancake

PREP: 10 minutes

BAKE: 20 minutes

YIELD: 4 servings

Preheat oven to 425°F. In a bowl, beat the eggs with an electric mixer until foamy. Gradually add the biscuit mix alternately with the milk; beat until smooth. In a 9-inch glass pie plate or a 9- or 10-inch ovenproof skillet, melt the butter in the preheated oven. Meanwhile, continue beating the egg mixture at high speed for 3 minutes more; stir in orange zest. Carefully remove hot pie plate from oven; pour in batter. Bake for 17 to 20 minutes or until pancake is puffed and browned. Meanwhile, combine orange pieces and brown sugar. Spoon fruit into warm pancake. Top with sour cream and sprinkle with nutmeg. Cut into pieces to make 4 servings.

Courtesy of Sunkist Growers, Inc.

3 eggs

½ cup buttermilk biscuit or pancake mix

½ cup milk

2 tablespoons butter or margarine

Grated zest of 1 **SUNKIST® Orange**

4 **SUNKIST® Oranges**, peeled, cut into bite-size pieces, and drained

⅓ cup light brown sugar

Sour cream

Sunrise Pancakes

1 cup **ARROWHEAD MILLS® All Purpose Flour**

1 cup **HAIN PURE FOODS® Organic Brown Sugar**

1 tablespoon baking powder

1 teaspoon cinnamon

1½ cups **HAIN PURE FOODS® Carrot Juice**

2 tablespoons **HAIN PURE FOODS® Canola Oil**

1 egg

1 very ripe banana, mashed

PREP: 10 minutes

COOK: 20 minutes

YIELD: 12 pancakes

In medium bowl, combine flour, brown sugar, baking powder, and cinnamon. In small bowl, combine carrot juice, oil, egg, and banana. Stir into flour mixture just until moistened. For each pancake, pour ¼ cup mixture onto preheated 400°F nonstick electric skillet. Turn when bubbles form on surface. Cook until lightly browned.

Courtesy of Hain Celestial Group

Heavenly Heart-Shaped Pancakes

2 ½ cups all-purpose flour

1 cup (6 ounces) **NESTLÉ® TOLL HOUSE® Semi-Sweet Chocolate Mini Morsels**

1 tablespoon baking powder

½ teaspoon salt

1 ¾ cups milk

2 large eggs

⅓ cup vegetable oil, plus more for the griddle and cookie cutters

⅓ cup brown sugar, packed

Confectioners' sugar

PREP: 10 minutes

COOK: 20 minutes

YIELD: 18 (3-inch) pancakes

Combine flour, morsels, baking powder, and salt in large bowl. Combine milk, eggs, oil, and brown sugar in medium bowl; add to flour mixture. Stir just until moistened (batter may be lumpy). Heat griddle or skillet over medium heat; brush lightly with oil. Pour ¼ cup batter onto hot griddle into the shape of a heart; cook until bubbles begin to burst. Turn; continue to cook about 1 minute longer or until golden. Repeat with remaining batter. Sprinkle with confectioners' sugar before serving.

COOK'S TIP

For perfectly shaped heart pancakes, brush the inside of 3-inch heart-shaped cookie cutters with oil and place on griddle. Pour about ¼ cup batter into each cookie cutter and cook until bubbles begin to burst. Remove cookie cutters. Turn; continue to cook about 1 minute longer or until golden.

Courtesy of Nestlé USA

Pumpkin Pancakes

PREP: 10 minutes

COOK: 18 minutes

YIELD: 12 (4-inch) pancakes

In a large bowl, whisk together the flour, sugar, salt, baking powder, baking soda, and spices. In a separate bowl, beat the eggs, adding vanilla, yogurt, milk, and pumpkin purée. Mix well. Pour the egg mixture into the flour mixture and stir until just blended. Spoon the batter onto a preheated, oiled griddle, using ¼ cup batter for each pancake. Cook pancakes slowly over a low-medium heat for 4 to 6 minutes, flipping after 3 minutes.

Courtesy of Stonyfield Farm

2 cups unbleached all-purpose flour

½ cup sugar

½ teaspoon salt

2 teaspoons baking powder

2 teaspoons baking soda

½ teaspoon cinnamon

3 eggs

½ teaspoon vanilla extract

1 cup **STONYFIELD FARM Plain Yogurt**

¾ cup **STONYFIELD FARM Milk**

1 cup canned pumpkin purée

Crispy Marmalade French Toast

2 eggs, beaten

½ cup **LAND O LAKES® Fat Free Half & Half**

3 cups cornflakes, crushed

8 slices sandwich bread

¼ cup orange marmalade

4 (1-oz.) slices **LAND O LAKES® Deli American Cheese**

4 slices Canadian bacon or deli ham

¼ cup **LAND O LAKES® Butter**, melted

Maple syrup (optional)

PREP: 15 minutes

BAKE: 10 minutes

YIELD: 4 servings

Preheat oven to 425°F. Spray a 15 x 10 x 1-inch baking pan with no-stick cooking spray. Set aside. Combine eggs and half-and-half in shallow dish with wire whisk until well mixed. Place cornflakes in another shallow dish. Spread one side of 4 slices bread with 1 tablespoon orange marmalade each. Top each with 1 slice cheese, 1 slice Canadian bacon, and 1 slice bread. Dip both sides of each sandwich into egg mixture, then into cornflake crumbs. Place sandwiches into prepared pan. Drizzle with melted butter. Bake for 10 to 15 minutes or until lightly browned. Serve with maple syrup, if desired.

COOK'S TIP

Marmalade is a preserve made from the peel and the flesh of citrus fruits cooked with sugar until thick and intensely flavored. It can be used alone or as a flavor complement to savory ingredients.

Courtesy of Land O'Lakes, Inc.

Cinnamon-Buttermilk French Toast with Strawberries

PREP: 5 minutes

COOK: 25 minutes

YIELD: 4 servings

Whisk buttermilk, eggs, orange zest, and vanilla in shallow dish. (Mixture will be thicker than traditional French toast batter.) Melt 1 tablespoon butter in large nonstick skillet over medium heat. Dip bread slices, one at a time, briefly in egg mixture, turning over to allow egg mixture to coat both sides. Place 3 dipped bread slices at a time in skillet. Cook 3 minutes on each side or until golden brown. Repeat with remaining bread slices, adding more butter to skillet as needed for each batch. For each serving, top 3 slices French toast with ¼ cup strawberries. Sprinkle with confectioners' sugar, if desired. Serve with maple syrup.

COOK'S TIPS

• Citrus zest is the colored part of the peel; do not grate the white pith, which is bitter. To easily grate zest, use a fine rasp grater or the smallest holes on a box grater.

• To keep French toast warm while cooking remaining batches, preheat large heatproof platter or baking sheet in 200°F oven. Place French toast in single layer on platter or baking sheet in oven until ready to serve.

Courtesy of Flowers Foods

1 ¼ cups lowfat buttermilk

2 eggs

1 teaspoon grated orange zest

¼ teaspoon vanilla extract

2 to 3 tablespoons butter

12 slices **NATURE'S OWN Cinnamon Raisin Breakfast Bread**

1 cup sliced strawberries

Confectioners' sugar (optional)

Maple syrup

Cinnamon French Muffin Toast

2 eggs

½ cup milk

½ teaspoon cinnamon

¼ teaspoon salt

4 **NATURE'S OWN Original English Muffins**, split

2 teaspoons butter, divided

Confectioners' sugar

Maple syrup

PREP: 8 minutes

COOK: 12 minutes

YIELD: 4 servings

Whisk eggs, milk, cinnamon, and salt in a 9-inch pie plate. Soak 4 muffin halves in egg mixture 1 minute on each side. Melt 1 teaspoon butter in large nonstick skillet or on a griddle over medium heat. Cook soaked muffin halves 3 minutes on each side or until golden brown. Cover; keep warm. Meanwhile soak remaining 4 muffin halves in remaining egg mixture. Repeat cooking as directed above with remaining 1 teaspoon butter. Serve topped with confectioners' sugar and maple syrup.

Courtesy of Flowers Foods

Orange Waffles with **SUNKIST®** Citrus Syrup

PREP: 10 minutes

COOK: 20 minutes

YIELD: 4 servings

In a small 1-quart saucepan, combine the orange juice, grapefruit juice, maple syrup, and cinnamon. Bring to a boil, reduce heat to medium, and cook for 18 to 20 minutes, until the mixture thickens and reduces by half. You should end up with about a ½ cup of syrup. To assemble, top each waffle with orange pieces and drizzle with 2 tablespoons syrup. Top each waffle with 1 tablespoon of slivered almonds.

Courtesy of Sunkist Growers, Inc.

2 **SUNKIST® Oranges**, juiced (about ¾ cup)

½ **SUNKIST® Grapefruit**, juiced (about ½ cup)

2 tablespoons maple syrup

Pinch of cinnamon

4 whole grain toaster waffles, toasted

2 **SUNKIST® Oranges**, peeled, cut into quarters, and then cut into bite-size pieces

4 tablespoons slivered almonds (optional)

Tropical Waffles

4 lowfat waffles

2 cups **DEL MONTE® SunFresh® Tropical Mixed Fruit**, drained

1 cup sliced banana

¼ cup warm maple syrup

¼ cup lowfat plain yogurt

PREP: 5 minutes

COOK: 10 minutes

YIELD: 2 servings

Prepare waffles according to package directions. Place 2 waffles on each dish. Combine Tropical Mixed Fruit with banana slices; spoon fruit over waffles. Drizzle with maple syrup and spoon yogurt over fruit.

Courtesy of Del Monte Foods

Brown Sugared Bacon

PREP: 10 minutes

BAKE: 16 minutes

YIELD: 6 servings

Preheat oven to 350°F. Line 15 x 10 x 1-inch jelly roll pan with kitchen parchment paper. Combine brown sugar and allspice in small bowl. Coat bacon slices with brown sugar mixture. Place coated bacon onto prepared pan. Bake 14 to 16 minutes or until crisp. Place cooked bacon on clean parchment paper; let stand until slightly cooled, 3 to 5 minutes. Serve warm or at room temperature.

COOK'S TIP

Prepare this recipe ahead and refrigerate until serving time. Reheat bacon or serve at room temperature.

Courtesy of Land O'Lakes, Inc.

⅓ cup brown sugar, firmly packed

1 teaspoon ground allspice

½ lb. (6 to 8 slices) bacon, cut in half

Soups, Stews & Chilis

Fabulous Fruit Soup

2 cups **ORGANIC VALLEY Orange Juice**

2 cups plain, vanilla, or berry-flavored yogurt

1 tablespoon lemon juice

1 teaspoon flax oil

Honey to taste (add more if using plain yogurt)

Cinnamon to taste

Nutmeg to taste

1 large banana

1 pint berries (seasonal choice)

Slivered almonds (optional)

Blood oranges, peeled and cut into sections or slices (for garnish)

Fresh mint sprigs (for garnish)

PREP: 10 minutes

YIELD: 6 servings

Whisk together orange juice, yogurt, lemon juice, flax oil, honey, cinnamon, and nutmeg. Slice banana and add it and the berries to the mixture. For a crunchy version, add slivered almonds. Garnish with blood oranges and mint.

Courtesy of Organic Valley Family of Farms

Cantaloupe Soup with Lemon and Ginger

PREP: 15 minutes

CHILL: 4+ hours

YIELD: 8 servings

Place butter, honey, ginger root, and lemon zest in a small bowl. Microwave until butter is fully melted, about 45 seconds. Stir to blend mixture. Use a rubber spatula to scrape mixture into a food processor or blender. Add melon chunks and puree until as smooth as possible. Stir in milk. Transfer to a bowl, cover, and chill thoroughly, 4 or more hours. Garnish each serving with a mint sprig and some finely diced melon.

VARIATION

For a dessert version, increase the amount of honey and use **ORGANIC VALLEY Half & Half** or **Vanilla Soy Milk** instead of the milk.

Copyright by Terese Allen; courtesy of Organic Valley Family of Farms

2 tablespoons **ORGANIC VALLEY Butter**

2 tablespoons honey (or to taste)

1 tablespoon finely grated fresh ginger root

1 heaping tablespoon finely grated lemon zest

6 to 7 cups coarsely chopped fully ripe cantaloupe or muskmelon

1 ½ to 2 cups **ORGANIC VALLEY Milk**

8 sprigs fresh mint (for garnish)

1 cup finely diced cantaloupe or melon (for garnish)

Refreshing Melon Soup with Assorted Berries

2 cantaloupes

1 cup strawberries, halved

1 cup raspberries

1 cup blueberries

1 cup blackberries

1 (16-oz.) container **BREAKSTONE'S** or **KNUDSEN 2% Milkfat Low Fat Cottage Cheese**

PREP: 15 minutes

YIELD: 6 servings

Cut cantaloupes into quarters; remove seeds and rind. Place in blender or food processor container; cover. Blend until pureed. Pour cantaloupe purée into six large soup bowls. Top with berries and cottage cheese.

Courtesy of Kraft Foods

Pineapple Gazpacho

3 cups fresh **DOLE® Tropical Gold® Pineapple**, cut into chunks or 1 (20-oz.) can **DOLE Pineapple Chunks**, drained, divided

1 medium cucumber, peeled, seeded, and chopped, divided

1 cup chopped **DOLE Yellow Bell Pepper**, divided

⅔ cup chopped **DOLE Red Onion**, divided

1 ¼ cups **DOLE Pineapple Juice**

2 tablespoons Italian salad dressing

2 tablespoons sugar

2 tablespoons chopped fresh **DOLE Cilantro**

1 teaspoon chopped jalapeño

PREP: 25 minutes

CHILL: 2 hours

YIELD: 5 servings

Combine 1 cup of the pineapple chunks, ½ cup cucumber, ½ cup bell pepper, and ⅓ cup onion in medium bowl; set aside. Combine remaining pineapple chunks, cucumber, bell pepper, onion, pineapple juice, Italian dressing, sugar, cilantro, and jalapeño in blender or food processor container. Cover; blend until smooth. Stir into reserved pineapple mixture. Cover; refrigerate 2 hours or until chilled. Serve.

Courtesy of Dole Food Company

White Gazpacho

GARNISH

3 tablespoons olive oil, divided

12 slices stale white bread, cut into crouton-size pieces

1 bunch seedless green grapes

SOUP

8 to 10 slices stale white bread

2 cups blanched slivered almonds

5 to 10 cloves garlic (more or less to taste)

2 teaspoons salt

¾ cup olive oil

6 tablespoons red wine vinegar

2 cups chicken broth

2 cups ice water

PREP: 30 minutes

YIELD: 8 servings

FOR THE GARNISH: Drizzle the bottom of a large baking sheet with 1 tablespoon of the olive oil. Toss the bread cubes with the remaining olive oil and place them on the baking sheet. Bake in a preheated 350°F oven for about 30 minutes, until the cubes are crisp and light golden brown.

FOR THE SOUP: Combine the 8 to 10 slices stale white bread and cold water to cover in a small bowl. Let sit until bread is soaked, 5 to 10 minutes. Squeeze water from bread, set bread aside, and discard water. Combine the almonds, garlic, and salt in a large-size food processor. Process until the almonds are completely ground. Add the soaked bread; process till smooth. With the motor running, gradually add the oil, then the vinegar. Process, stopping to scrape the sides of the bowl occasionally, until the mixture is smooth. Add the broth and blend again until smooth. Pour the mixture into a large bowl, and stir in the cold water, adding more for a thinner soup, if desired. Store in the refrigerator until ready to serve. To serve, stir soup a few times to make sure all the elements are combined, ladle it into bowls, and top with generous amounts of croutons and green grapes.

Courtesy of King Arthur Flour

Quick Black Bean Soup

PREP: 10 minutes

COOK: 10 minutes

YIELD: 5 servings

Place all ingredients except the parsley in a saucepan. Season with sea salt, cover, and simmer for 10 minutes. Turn off flame and stir in the parsley before serving.

Courtesy of Eden Foods

2 (15-oz.) cans **EDEN ORGANIC Black Beans**, do not drain

1 cup water

1 medium onion, diced

¼ cup diced celery

¼ cup diced carrots

½ cup organic sweet corn, fresh or frozen

¼ cup minced fresh parsley

Sherried Black Bean Soup with Organic Long Grain Brown Rice

PREP: 10 minutes

COOK: 20 minutes

YIELD: 6 servings

Reserve 1 cup black beans. Puree remaining beans with water in electric blender or food processor; set aside. Cook onion, celery, and carrots in oil in Dutch oven over medium-high heat until crisp-tender. Add broth, chilies, pepper, and whole and pureed beans. Simmer uncovered 10 to 15 minutes. Remove from heat; stir in sherry. Top each serving with ½ cup rice. Garnish with green onions and tomato.

Courtesy of Lundberg Family Farms

2 (16-oz.) cans black beans, drained

1 ½ cups water

1 medium onion, chopped

1 cup sliced celery

1 cup diced carrots

1 tablespoon olive oil

2 cups chicken broth

1 (4-oz.) can diced green chilies, drained

¼ teaspoon ground black pepper

1 tablespoon dry sherry

2 **LUNDBERG® HEAT & EAT ORGANIC Long Grain Brown Rice Bowls**, heated according to package directions

½ cup sliced green onions (for garnish)

½ cup finely chopped tomato (for garnish)

"Black Gold" Black Bean Soup

PREP: 10 minutes

COOK: 20 minutes

YIELD: 6 servings

In a blender or food processor, puree 1 can of broth with 3 cups of beans. Set aside. In a large saucepan, heat oil. Add onion and carrot and cook until onion is tender, about 3 minutes. Add red pepper and garlic; cook 1 minute. Add coriander and cumin; cook 30 seconds. Add remaining broth, pureed black bean mixture, remaining drained black beans, corn, salt, and pepper. Bring to a boil, stirring occasionally. Reduce heat and simmer 10 minutes. Garnish with cilantro, if desired. Serve with tortilla chips.

Courtesy of Hain Celestial Group

2 (14.5-oz.) cans **HAIN® All Natural Vegetable** or **Chicken Broth**

5 (15-oz.) cans black beans, drained and rinsed

2 tablespoons **HAIN® Safflower** or **Canola Oil**

1 ½ cups chopped onion

½ cup chopped carrot

½ cup chopped red or green pepper

2 teaspoons minced garlic

½ teaspoon ground coriander

½ teaspoon ground cumin

1 (15.25-oz.) can **HAIN PURE FOODS® Organic Whole Kernel Golden Corn**, drained

¾ teaspoon salt

½ teaspoon ground black pepper

Fresh cilantro (for garnish, optional)

GARDEN OF EATIN'® All Natural Chili & Lime Cantina Chips or **Blue Tortilla Chips**

Tuscan Pasta and Bean Soup

PREP: 10 minutes

COOK: 20 minutes

YIELD: 6 servings

Heat oil in large saucepan over medium-high heat. Add onion; cook 2 to 3 minutes or until tender. Stir in tomatoes, broth, beans, water, basil, parsley, and pepper. Bring to boil. Add pasta; reduce heat to low. Cook, stirring occasionally, 12 to 15 minutes or until pasta is tender.

Courtesy of Del Monte Foods

2 tablespoons olive oil

1 small onion, chopped

1 (28-oz.) can **CONTADINA® Recipe Ready Crushed Tomatoes with Roasted Garlic**

2 (14.5-oz.) cans **COLLEGE INN® Chicken Broth**

1 (15.5-oz.) can kidney or pinto beans, undrained

⅓ cup water

2 teaspoons dried basil, crushed

2 tablespoons chopped fresh parsley or 2 teaspoons dried parsley, crushed

¼ teaspoon black pepper

½ cup dried small pasta shells or macaroni

Easy Creamy Broccoli Soup

PREP: 10 minutes

COOK: 15 minutes

YIELD: 4 servings

Melt **SHEDD'S SPREAD COUNTRY CROCK®** in 4-quart saucepot and cook onion, stirring occasionally, 5 minutes or until tender. Stir in broth and milk. Bring to a boil over high heat. Add broccoli. Reduce heat to low and simmer 5 minutes or until broccoli is tender. Working in batches, process soup in blender until smooth and return to saucepot. Season with pepper and heat through. Remove from heat, then stir in cheese until melted. Garnish with additional cheese, if desired.

Courtesy of Unilever

2 tablespoons **SHEDD'S SPREAD COUNTRY CROCK® Calcium plus Vitamin D**

1 small onion, chopped

1 (14 ½-oz.) can chicken broth

1 cup reduced fat (2%) milk

1 (10-oz.) package frozen broccoli florets, thawed

Ground black pepper

½ cup shredded Cheddar cheese (about 2 oz.)

Broccoli Cheese and Wild Rice Soup with Smoked Almonds

1 (10-oz.) box **BIRDS EYE®
Broccoli & Cheese Sauce**, cooked according to package directions

¾ cup cooked wild rice

¾ cup chicken broth

¼ cup jarred diced roasted red bell pepper

2 tablespoons bacon bits

⅛ teaspoon garlic powder

Freshly ground black pepper

Smoked almonds
(for garnish, optional)

PREP: 15 minutes

COOK: 15 minutes

YIELD: 2 servings

Combine cooked **BIRDS EYE® Broccoli & Cheese Sauce** with wild rice, chicken broth, roasted red bell pepper, bacon bits, and garlic powder in a medium-size saucepan. Bring to a boil; reduce heat and simmer 5 to 10 minutes. Season to taste with ground black pepper. Garnish with smoked almonds, if desired.

Courtesy of Birds Eye Foods, Inc.

Creamy Broccoli Soup

PREP: 15 minutes

COOK: 15 minutes

YIELD: 7 servings

Heat oil in a soup pot and sauté onion. Add all ingredients except parsley and pepper. Cover and simmer over a low flame for 10 minutes or until broccoli is soft. Blend ingredients in a food processor or blender until smooth and creamy. Place back in the pot. Add the parsley and white pepper. Simmer 1 to 2 minutes. Serve hot or chilled.

Courtesy of Eden Foods

2 tablespoons **EDEN Extra Virgin Olive Oil**

1 medium onion, diced

½ cup diced celery

2 medium organic potatoes, peeled and chopped

4 cups chopped broccoli

1 cup water

3 cups **EDENSOY Original, EDENSOY Extra Original**, or **EDENSOY Unsweetened**

1 teaspoon **EDEN Sea Salt**

2 teaspoons minced fresh parsley

¼ teaspoon white pepper or black pepper

Carrot Soup

PREP: 15 minutes

COOK: 15 minutes

YIELD: 6 servings

Bring carrots, water, 1 cup **EDENSOY** or **EDENBLEND**, sea salt, and potatoes to a boil in a medium soup pot. Simmer until tender. Heat oil in a skillet and sauté onions, garlic, cashews, and ginger until the onions are translucent. Combine all ingredients and puree in two separate batches, in a blender or food processor with the remaining **EDENSOY** or **EdenBlend**. Return to the soup pot and heat slowly. Do not boil. Serve and garnish with parsley.

Courtesy of Eden Foods

- 4 cups carrots, sliced
- 2 cups water or vegetable broth
- 32 oz. **EDENSOY Original, EDENSOY Unsweetened,** or **EdenBlend,** divided
- 1 teaspoon **EDEN Sea Salt**
- 3 medium organic potatoes, peeled and cubed
- 2 medium onions, chopped
- 2 cloves garlic, pressed
- ⅓ cup unsalted cashews
- 1½ teaspoons finely grated fresh ginger root
- 2 tablespoons minced fresh parsley (for garnish)

Vodka Soup with Mushrooms

- 1 (14.5-fl. oz.) can chicken or vegetable broth
- 1 (15-oz.) container **BUITONI Refrigerated Vodka Sauce**
- 1 cup half-and-half
- 2 cups (6 oz.) sliced mushrooms
- 2 tablespoons thinly sliced fresh basil leaves

PREP: 5 minutes

COOK: 10 minutes

YIELD: 4 servings

Combine broth, sauce, and half-and-half in medium saucepan. Cook over medium-high heat. When soup begins to simmer, add mushrooms; cook, stirring occasionally, for 5 minutes. Stir in basil.

VARIATION

For a lighter version, use 1 cup whole milk in place of half-and-half.

Courtesy of Nestlé USA

French Onion Soup

2 large onions, sliced

2 tablespoons butter

1 quart water

2 tablespoons **FRONTIER Broth Powder**

4 slices French bread

1 cup grated Cheddar cheese or mozzarella

PREP: 5 minutes

COOK: 25 minutes

YIELD: 4 servings

Preheat oven to 350°F. Sauté onion slices in butter until translucent. Add water and heat through. Add **FRONTIER Broth Powder** and stir well. Pour soup into individual ovenproof soup bowls. Place one slice of bread in each bowl and top with grated cheese. Place in oven until cheese melts, about 15 minutes.

Courtesy of Frontier Natural Products Co-op

Southwest Potato Corn Chowder

PREP: 10 minutes

COOK: 20 minutes

YIELD: 8 servings

Cook bacon in large saucepan until crisp, stirring frequently. Remove bacon from pan, reserving 2 tablespoons of the drippings in pan. Discard remaining drippings; drain bacon on paper towels. Add potatoes, onion, and celery to saucepan. Cook and stir 2 minutes. Stir in soup and milk; bring to boil. Reduce heat to low; simmer 8 minutes, stirring occasionally. Add remaining ingredients; cook an additional 5 minutes or until process cheese food is completely melted and potatoes are tender, stirring occasionally.

Courtesy of Kraft Foods

4 slices **OSCAR MAYER Bacon**, chopped

1 ½ lbs. potatoes, peeled and cubed (about 3 cups)

1 small onion, chopped

2 medium celery stalks, sliced

1 (10 ¾-oz.) can condensed cream of chicken soup

3 cups milk

8 oz. **HOFFMAN'S Hot Pepper Pasteurized Process Cheese Food**, cubed

1 (10-oz.) package frozen whole kernel corn, thawed

¼ teaspoon pepper

"Vegged-Out" Pumpkin & Black Bean Soup

1 tablespoon olive oil

5 green onions, white and light green parts thinly sliced, dark parts sliced and set aside for garnish

1 red bell pepper, chopped

3 cloves garlic, chopped

1 ½ teaspoons ground cumin

½ teaspoon dried thyme

2 (15-oz.) cans black beans, rinsed and drained

1 (15-oz.) can **LIBBY'S® 100% Pure Pumpkin**

1 (14.5-oz.) can no-salt-added diced tomatoes, undrained

1 (14-oz.) can vegetable broth

½ cup water

½ teaspoon salt or more to taste

⅛ teaspoon cayenne pepper or more to taste

PREP: 10 minutes

COOK: 20 minutes

YIELD: 8 servings

Heat oil in large saucepan over medium heat. Add white and light green parts of green onions, bell pepper, and garlic; cook, stirring occasionally, for 4 to 5 minutes or until soft. Stir in cumin and thyme; cook, stirring occasionally, for 1 minute. Add beans, pumpkin, tomatoes and juice, broth, and water; bring to a boil. Reduce heat to low; cook for 10 minutes. Stir in salt and cayenne pepper. Top each serving with dark green onion tops.

Courtesy of Nestlé USA

Creamy Curried Pumpkin Soup

1 tablespoon olive oil

1 small onion, finely chopped

1 (29-oz.) can pumpkin

1 (14-oz.) can chicken broth

2 cups water

3 tablespoons brown sugar

¾ teaspoon curry powder

½ teaspoon salt

4 oz. (½ of 8-oz. package) **PHILADELPHIA Cream Cheese**, cubed

PREP: 10 minutes

COOK: 20 minutes

YIELD: 7 (1-cup) servings

Heat oil in large saucepan on medium heat. Add onion; cook and stir 3 minutes or until crisp-tender. Stir in remaining ingredients except cream cheese until well blended. Bring to boil. Reduce heat to medium-low. Add cream cheese; cook until cream cheese is completely melted and mixture is well blended, beating constantly with wire whisk.

Courtesy of Kraft Foods

Asian Flavors Winter Squash Soup

PREP: 10 minutes

COOK: 20 minutes

YIELD: 6 servings

Heat peanut oil in saucepan; add shallots, ginger, and chilies. Cook over medium heat, stirring often, until shallots are tender. Add stock and squash purée. Simmer slowly for about 10 minutes. Stir in soy milk and heat through. Stir in fish sauce, lime juice, and cilantro. Add additional soy milk, if desired, for thinner consistency. Season to taste (if you've used canned stock, take care not to add too much salt). Garnish each bowl with coconut flakes.

Copyright by Terese Allen; inspired by a recipe from *Crossroads Cooking* by Elisabeth Rozin; courtesy of Organic Valley Family of Farms

2 tablespoons peanut oil

¼ cup minced shallots

1 tablespoon minced fresh ginger root

1 to 3 jalapeños or serranos, seeded and minced

2 cups homemade vegetable or chicken stock or 1 (14.5-oz.) can broth

3 cups cooked winter squash purée (pie pumpkin, butternut, etc.)

2 cups **ORGANIC VALLEY Original Soy Milk**, plus additional soy milk as desired, divided

2 teaspoons bottled Thai-style fish sauce

2 or more tablespoons fresh-squeezed lime juice

Handful of cilantro, finely chopped

Salt and pepper

Unsweetened coconut flakes

Tomato-Black Bean Barley Soup

PREP: 10 minutes

COOK: 20 minutes

YIELD: 4 servings

Cook onion and garlic in dressing in large saucepan on medium heat, 5 minutes, or until onion is tender, stirring frequently. Add all remaining ingredients except green pepper; mix well. Bring to boil. Reduce heat to medium-low; simmer 15 minutes, stirring occasionally. Remove from heat. Stir in green pepper; cover. Let stand 5 minutes.

Courtesy of Kraft Foods

1 medium yellow onion, chopped

2 cloves garlic, chopped

½ cup **KRAFT Sun-Dried Tomato Dressing**

4 cups water

1 (15-oz.) can black beans, drained

1 (14 ½-oz.) can diced tomatoes, undrained

½ cup quick-cooking barley

1 teaspoon dried basil leaves

½ teaspoon black pepper

1 medium green bell pepper, chopped

Chipotle Tomato Soup

1 cup chopped onion

2 tablespoons olive oil

2 (14 ½-oz.) cans diced tomatoes, undrained

2 medium carrots, chopped

1 (14-oz.) can low-sodium chicken broth

¼ cup **KRAFT Light Thousand Island Dressing**

1 tablespoon chopped chipotle peppers in adobo sauce

PREP: 10 minutes

COOK: 15 minutes

YIELD: 5 (1-cup) servings

Cook and stir onion in hot oil in large skillet until tender. Add tomatoes, carrots, and chicken broth; mix well. Bring to a boil on medium-high heat. Reduce heat to medium-low; simmer 15 minutes or until vegetables are tender, stirring occasionally. Transfer vegetable mixture to a blender container in small batches; cover. Blend until smooth, adding dressing and chipotles to the last batch. Serve warm or chilled.

Courtesy of Kraft Foods

Creamy Basil & Tomato Soup

PREP: 10 minutes

COOK: 10 minutes

YIELD: 6 (¾-cup) servings

Combine milk, flour, and broth in 2-quart saucepan with wire whisk. Cook over medium heat, stirring occasionally, until mixture comes to a boil, 5 to 7 minutes. Reduce heat to low. Stir in basil, tomatoes, and Parmesan. Cook, stirring constantly, until soup is slightly thickened, 5 to 7 minutes. Do not boil. Season to taste with pepper. To serve, divide mozzarella evenly among individual serving bowls. Pour soup over mozzarella. Garnish with Parmesan.

Courtesy of Land O'Lakes, Inc.

1 cup milk (do not use fat-free skim milk)

¼ cup all-purpose flour

1 (14-oz.) can vegetable broth (1 ½ cups)

¼ cup chopped fresh basil leaves

1 (14 ½-oz.) can diced tomatoes

1 tablespoon shredded Parmesan

Coarsely ground pepper

2 oz. **LAND O LAKES® Mozzarella Cheese**, shredded (½ cup)

Shredded Parmesan (for garnish)

Swiss Chard Soup with Cream Cheese "Croutons"

PREP: 15 minutes

COOK: 15 minutes

YIELD: 3 or 4 servings

Bring chicken broth to a simmer in a pot. Stir in chard and cook gently until it is wilted and tender, about 6 minutes. You may leave it as is or puree it with an immersion blender or in a food processor or blender. If you've pureed it, reheat the soup. Season to taste with salt and pepper (if you've used canned stock, you may not need to add any salt). Divide the cubed cream cheese into three or four wide, shallow soup bowls. Ladle the hot soup over the cream cheese and serve immediately.

Copyright by Terese Allen; courtesy of Organic Valley Family of Farms

4 ½ cups chicken stock

3 packed cups finely cut strips of chard leaves

Salt and pepper

4 oz. (½ of 8-oz. package) **ORGANIC VALLEY Cream Cheese**, cubed and at room temperature

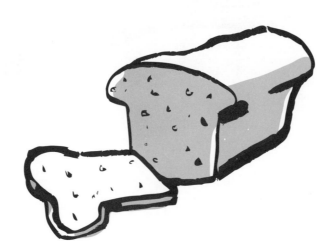

Cheddar Cheese Soup

1 medium onion, chopped (about 1 cup)

¼ cup (½ stick) margarine or butter

¼ cup flour

2 tablespoons **GREY POUPON Dijon Mustard**

¼ teaspoon ground white pepper

Dash ground nutmeg

2 (14 ½-oz.) cans chicken broth

2 cups milk

4 cups **KRAFT Shredded Cheddar Cheese**

40 **PREMIUM Saltine Crackers**

PREP: 10 minutes

COOK: 15minutes

YIELD: 8 (1-cup) servings

Cook and stir onion in margarine in large saucepan on medium-high heat until tender. Add flour, mustard, pepper, and nutmeg; stir until well blended. Gradually stir in broth. Add milk; mix well. Bring to boil; cook until thickened, stirring constantly. Remove from heat. Stir in cheese until completely melted. Serve hot with crackers.

Courtesy of Kraft Foods

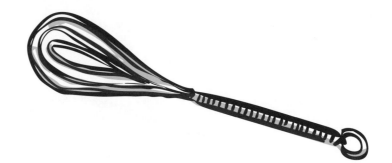

Easy Chicken Soup

PREP: 10 minutes

COOK: 20 minutes

YIELD: 9 (1-cup) servings

Cook and stir chicken and onion in hot oil in large saucepan on medium-high heat until chicken is cooked through. Add broth, water, carrots, and dressing mix. Bring to boil. Reduce heat to low; cover. Simmer 5 minutes or until carrots are tender. Stir in parsley.

Courtesy of Kraft Foods

1 lb. boneless skinless chicken breasts, cut into 1-inch chunks

¼ cup chopped onion

2 teaspoons oil

2 (14 ½-oz.) cans chicken broth

3 cups water

2 cups carrot slices

1 envelope **GOOD SEASONS Italian Dressing Mix**

2 tablespoons chopped fresh parsley

Chunky Chicken Vegetable Soup

½ lb. boneless skinless chicken breasts, cut into bite-size pieces

1 teaspoon oil

1 (14 ½-oz.) can chicken broth

1 ½ cups water

2 cups assorted cut-up vegetables (sliced carrots, broccoli florets, and chopped red peppers)

1 envelope **GOOD SEASONS Italian Dressing Mix**

½ cup instant white rice, uncooked

2 tablespoons chopped fresh parsley

PREP: 10 minutes

COOK: 20 minutes

YIELD: 5 (1-cup) servings

Cook and stir chicken in hot oil in large saucepan on medium-high heat 5 minutes or until chicken is cooked through. Add broth, water, vegetables, and dressing mix. Bring to boil. Reduce heat to low; cover. Simmer 5 minutes. Stir in rice and parsley; cover. Remove from heat. Let stand 5 minutes,

Courtesy of Kraft Foods

Quick Chicken Minestrone

PREP: 5 minutes

COOK: 15 minutes

YIELD: 8 (1-cup) servings

Mix all ingredients except Parmesan in large saucepan. Bring to boil on high heat, stirring occasionally. Reduce heat to medium; simmer 10 minutes or until chicken is cooked through and pasta is tender, stirring occasionally. Sprinkle each serving with 1 ½ teaspoons of the Parmesan.

Courtesy of Kraft Foods

2 cups water

2 cups frozen Italian-style vegetable combination

2 (14 ½-oz.) cans Italian-style diced tomatoes, undrained

6 oz. boneless skinless chicken breasts, cut into bite-size pieces

1 cup rotini pasta, uncooked

1 envelope **GOOD SEASONS Italian Dressing Mix**

¼ cup **KRAFT Grated Parmesan Cheese**

Hearty Italian Chicken Chowder

PREP: 10 minutes

COOK: 15 minutes

YIELD: 2 servings

¼ cup **KRAFT Light Zesty Italian Dressing**

½ lb. boneless skinless chicken breasts, chopped

1 (14 ¼-oz.) can stewed tomatoes, undrained

1 cup reduced-sodium chicken broth

1 medium zucchini, chopped

½ cup elbow macaroni, uncooked

1 teaspoon dried basil leaves

½ cup **KRAFT 2% Milk Shredded Mozzarella Cheese**

Heat dressing in large saucepan on medium heat. Add chicken; cook 3 minutes, stirring once. Add tomatoes, broth, zucchini, macaroni, and basil. Bring to boil on high heat. Reduce heat to medium; simmer 8 minutes or until macaroni is tender. Sprinkle with cheese.

Courtesy of Kraft Foods

Speedy Asian Chicken Soup Bowls

1 cup instant white rice, uncooked

¼ cup **KRAFT Asian Toasted Sesame Dressing**

2 teaspoons reduced-sodium soy sauce

2 cups chopped cooked chicken

2 cups frozen stir-fry vegetables

2 cups fat-free reduced-sodium chicken broth

2 cups water

PREP: 5 minutes

MICROWAVE: 10 minutes

YIELD: 4 (1 ¾-cup) servings

Combine ¼ cup of the rice, 1 tablespoon of the dressing, and ½ teaspoon of the soy sauce in each of 4 microwave-able soup bowls. Top each with ½ cup chicken and ½ cup vegetables; stir until well blended. Add ½ cup broth and ½ cup water to each bowl; cover with vented plastic wrap. Microwave at high 3 to 5 minutes or until soup is heated through. Let stand 5 minutes before serving.

Courtesy of Kraft Foods

Soup Parmesano

1 (1-lb.) package **PERDUE® Fresh Ground Chicken** (alternate: **PERDUE® Fresh Ground Turkey**

1 envelope dried Italian salad dressing mix

1 tablespoon olive oil

6 (10 ½-oz.) cans chicken broth (not condensed)

1 (9-oz.) package cheese-filled tortellini

½ cup frozen carrot slices

1 (14 ½-oz.) can diced tomatoes, drained

½ cup chopped fresh or frozen spinach

PREP: 10 minutes

COOK: 20 minutes

YIELD: 4 servings

In bowl, mix ground chicken or turkey and salad dressing until well combined. Form into small, 1-inch-diameter meatballs. In skillet, heat olive oil over medium heat. Add meatballs and brown on all sides (7 to 10 minutes). Remove meatballs from pan and drain on paper towels. Heat chicken broth in large saucepan until just boiling. Add tortellini and carrots and cook for 5 minutes. Reduce heat and add meatballs. Simmer for 10 minutes. Add tomatoes and spinach. Stir until spinach wilts slightly.

Courtesy of Perdue Farms, Inc.

Spicy Bean & Sausage Soup with Elbows

PREP: 5 minutes

COOK: 25 minutes

YIELD: 4 servings

Heat oil in large pot over medium heat. Add sausage, rosemary, garlic, and crushed red pepper. Sauté until sausage is cooked through and no longer pink, breaking up with a spoon. Add tomatoes, beans, and broth. Bring to a boil and add elbow pasta. Simmer until pasta is al dente, about 7 minutes. Serve, passing grated cheese.

Courtesy of Lundberg Family Farms

1 tablespoon olive oil

1 lb. Italian sausage, bulk (turkey or chicken sausage, optional)

4 teaspoons chopped fresh rosemary

2 to 4 garlic cloves, minced

⅛ to ¼ teaspoon crushed red pepper

1 (15-oz.) can diced tomatoes

1 (15-oz.) can cannellini beans, drained (kidney or garbanzo beans, optional)

5 cups canned low-sodium chicken broth

8 oz. (about 2 cups) **LUNDBERG® Elbow Brown Rice Pasta**

Grated Romano

Italian Sausage & Spinach Soup

Vegetable cooking spray

½ lb. sweet Italian pork sausage, cut into ¾-inch pieces

4 cups **SWANSON® Chicken Broth** (regular, **NATURAL GOODNESS™**, or **Certified Organic**)

½ teaspoon dried oregano leaves, crushed

1 medium onion, chopped (about ½ cup)

1 medium carrot, sliced (about ½ cup)

2 cups coarsely chopped fresh spinach leaves

PREP: 5 minutes

COOK: 20 minutes

YIELD: 5 servings

Spray a 4-quart saucepot with cooking spray and heat over medium-high heat. Add the sausage and cook until it's well browned. Stir in the broth, oregano, onion, and carrot and heat the mixture to a boil. Cover and reduce the heat to low. Cook for 10 minutes or until the vegetables are tender. Stir in the spinach and cook for 1 minute more.

Courtesy of Campbell Soup Company

Southwestern Pork and Bean Soup

PREP: 10 minutes

COOK: 20 minutes

YIELD: 4 servings

In deep saucepan, brown pork with onion; stir in remaining ingredients, bring to a boil, lower heat, cover, and simmer 10 to 15 minutes. Serve with warm flour tortillas and salad.

Courtesy of National Pork Board

2 boneless pork chops, diced

½ onion, chopped

1 (14½-oz.) can chicken broth

1 (15-oz.) can Mexican-style chopped tomatoes

1 (15-oz.) can pinto beans, drained and rinsed

2 teaspoons chili powder

Asian Noodle Soup

2 (3-oz.) packages pork-flavored ramen noodles, cooked according to package directions

1 (12-oz.) package **BIRDS EYE® STEAMFRESH® Specially Seasoned Asian Medley**, cooked according to package directions

6 oz. pork loin, fully cooked and cut into strips

½ cup scallions, sliced

Soy sauce or Asian chili sauce (optional)

PREP: 5 minutes

COOK: 15 minutes

YIELD: 4 servings

Combine soup, vegetables, pork, and scallions and simmer until heated through, about 10 minutes. Soup can be seasoned with soy sauce or Asian chili sauce if desired.

Courtesy of Birds Eye Foods, Inc.

Szechwan Pork Soup

PREP: 10 minutes

COOK: 15 minutes

YIELD: 4 servings

In medium saucepan, heat sesame oil. Add pork and ginger and quickly sauté. Add broth and spicy stir-fry sauce; bring to a boil and add noodles; cook for 4 to 5 minutes or until hot, stirring occasionally. Add green onions and serve.

Courtesy of Del Monte Foods

1 tablespoon sesame oil

½ lb. pork tenderloin, cut into thin ½-inch strips

1 tablespoon ginger, minced

2 (14.5-oz.) cans **COLLEGE INN® Beef Broth French Onion Style**

1 to 2 tablespoons spicy stir-fry sauce

2 ½ oz. Japanese curly noodles, broken*

4 green onions, thinly sliced diagonally

*May substitute broken linguine

Ham, Mac & Cheese Soup

4 oz. (1 ½ cups) uncooked dried small macaroni shells

2 tablespoons **LAND O LAKES® Butter**

2 tablespoons all-purpose flour

1 teaspoon Dijon-style mustard

1 (14-oz.) can chicken broth

1 ½ cups **LAND O LAKES® Fat Free Half & Half** or milk

1 (8-oz.) slice (1-inch thick) **LAND O LAKES® Deli American Cheese**, cut into 1-inch cubes

1 cup chopped ham

Salt and pepper (optional)

PREP: 10 minutes

COOK: 8 minutes

YIELD: 6 (1-cup) servings

Cook macaroni according to package directions; set aside. Melt butter in 3-quart saucepan until sizzling; stir in flour and mustard. Add broth and half-and-half. Cook over medium-high heat, stirring constantly, until mixture comes to a boil (4 to 5 minutes). Reduce heat to low; stir in cheese until melted. Stir in macaroni and ham. Cook until heated through, 4 to 5 minutes. Add salt and pepper to taste, if desired.

VARIATION

Try chopped or sliced hot dogs instead of ham.

Courtesy of Land O'Lakes, Inc.

Taco Soup

PREP: 5 minutes

COOK: 20 minutes

YIELD: 12 servings

Brown meat with onion in large saucepan; drain. Add all remaining ingredients except cheese; stir, breaking up tomatoes. Bring to boil. Reduce heat to medium-low; simmer 5 minutes, stirring occasionally. Serve topped with the cheese.

Courtesy of Kraft Foods

TACO BELL® and HOME ORIGINALS® are trademarks owned and licensed by Taco Bell Corp.

1 lb. extra-lean ground beef

1 onion, chopped

3 (15.5-oz.) cans mild chili beans, undrained

1 (14.5-oz.) can whole tomatoes, undrained

1 (14.25-oz.) can corn, undrained

1 (8-oz.) can tomato sauce

1 (1 ¼-oz.) package **TACO BELL® HOME ORIGINALS®** Taco **Seasoning Mix**

1 ½ cups water

1 ½ cups **KRAFT 2% Milk Shredded Cheddar Cheese**

Seafood Bisque

1 lb. chopped seafood (try scallops and crab)

1 tablespoon olive oil

½ cup water

2 ½ cups milk

4 tablespoons melted butter

2 tablespoons tomato paste

1 tablespoon lemon juice

1 (1.13-oz.) package **SIMPLY ORGANIC Southwest Taco Seasoning**

¼ cup diced celery stalk

PREP: 15 minutes

COOK: 15 minutes

YIELD: 5 servings

In a medium skillet, lightly sauté seafood in olive oil for 2 to 3 minutes. Set aside. In a blender, place water, milk, butter, tomato paste, lemon juice, and SIMPLY ORGANIC Southwest Taco Seasoning Mix; liquefy. Add seafood and celery; puree. Transfer to a medium saucepan and heat on medium-low heat until simmering. Serve with fresh bread slices.

Courtesy of Simply Organic

Seafood Chowder

PREP: 10 minutes

COOK: 15 minutes

YIELD: 4 servings

Heat oil in saucepan. Add onion and garlic powder and cook until tender. Add soups, milk, and dill. Heat to a boil. Add shrimp and fish. Cook 5 minutes over low heat or until done. Garnish with parsley.

Courtesy of Campbell Soup Company

1 tablespoon vegetable oil

1 large onion, chopped

¼ teaspoon garlic powder or 1 clove garlic, minced

1 (10 ¾-oz.) can **CAMPBELL'S® Condensed Cream of Celery Soup (Regular or 98% Fat Free)**

1 (10 ¾-oz.) can **CAMPBELL'S® Condensed Cream of Potato Soup**

1 ½ soup cans milk

¼ teaspoon dried dillweed, crushed

½ lb. medium fresh or thawed frozen shrimp, shelled and deveined

½ lb. fresh or thawed frozen firm white fish fillets, cut into 1-inch pieces*

Chopped fresh parsley (for garnish)

*Cod, haddock, or halibut

Chicken & White Bean Stew

1 small onion, chopped

¼ cup **KRAFT Light House Italian Dressing**

1 lb. boneless skinless chicken breasts, cut into 1-inch pieces

2 cloves garlic, minced

1 (14.5-oz.) can diced tomatoes, undrained

1 teaspoon dried basil leaves

1 (15-oz.) can no-salt-added navy beans, drained

½ cup **KRAFT 2% Milk Shredded Mozzarella Cheese**

PREP: 10 minutes

COOK: 18 minutes

YIELD: 4 (1 ½-cup) servings

Cook onion in dressing in medium saucepan on medium heat 3 minutes, stirring occasionally. Add chicken and garlic; cook 5 minutes or until chicken is no longer pink, stirring occasionally. Stir in tomatoes and basil; simmer 8 minutes or until chicken is cooked through. Add beans; stir. Cook 2 minutes or until heated through, stirring occasionally. Serve topped with the cheese.

Courtesy of Kraft Foods

Chicken Rice Gumbo

PREP: 10 minutes

COOK: 20 minutes

YIELD: 10 servings

Heat all ingredients except rice and crackers in large saucepan on medium-high heat to boil. Reduce heat to low; cover. Simmer 15 minutes. Stir in rice; simmer an additional 5 minutes or until chicken is cooked through and rice is tender. Serve with the crackers.

Courtesy of Kraft Foods

3 (14 ½-oz.) cans reduced-sodium chicken broth

1 lb. boneless skinless chicken breasts, cut into bite-size pieces

1 (15-oz.) can whole kernel corn, drained

1 (14 ½-oz.) can no-salt-added stewed tomatoes, undrained, chopped

½ teaspoon hot pepper sauce

½ cup instant white rice, uncooked

PREMIUM Saltine Crackers, any variety

Turkey and White Bean Stew

PREP: 10 minutes

COOK: 20 minutes

YIELD: 4 servings

Heat oil in large saucepan over medium-high heat. Add onion and celery; cook for 3 to 5 minutes or until just tender. Stir in garlic; cook for 30 seconds. Add half of beans to saucepan; mash with fork. Stir in remaining beans, water, wine, and bouillon. Bring to a boil; reduce heat and cook for 5 minutes. Stir in turkey and evaporated milk. Cook for 3 minutes or until heated through. Stir in parsley. Season with ground black pepper, if desired.

Courtesy of Nestlé USA

1 tablespoon olive oil

1 cup chopped onion

½ cup sliced celery

3 large cloves garlic, finely chopped

2 (15-oz.) cans cannellini or other white beans, rinsed and drained, divided

1 ½ cups water

2 tablespoons dry white wine (optional)

1 teaspoon **MAGGI Granulated Chicken Flavor Bouillon**

2 cups shredded, cooked turkey

2/3 cup **NESTLÉ® CARNATION® Evaporated Lowfat 2% Milk**

1 tablespoon chopped parsley

Freshly ground black pepper (optional)

Italian Stew

½ lb. Italian sausage

2 tablespoons vegetable oil

½ cup diced celery

½ cup diced carrots

½ cup diced tomatoes

4 cups water

1 (14-oz.) can white beans, drained

2 (0.71-oz.) packages **SIMPLY ORGANIC Apple Basil Vinaigrette Dressing Mix**

Grated Parmesan

PREP: 5 minutes

COOK: 25 minutes

YIELD: 6 servings

In a large saucepan, sauté sausage in oil. Add vegetables and sauté 2 to 3 more minutes. Add water, beans, and Apple Basil Dressing Mix. Bring to a boil, then reduce heat and simmer 15 to 20 minutes. Top with grated Parmesan.

COOK'S TIP

Substitute apple juice for one of the cups of water for extra apple flavor.

Courtesy of Simply Organic

Oyster Stew

PREP: 5 minutes

COOK: 15 minutes

YIELD: 4 servings

Combine oysters, their liquid, and butter in a saucepan over medium-low flame. Heat gently until the edges of the oysters just begin to curl, 3 to 5 minutes. Meanwhile, combine heavy cream, milk, onion, and rosemary or thyme, if desired, in another saucepan. Bring to a simmer over medium flame; cook 3 minutes. Slowly add cream mixture to oyster mixture, stirring slowly but constantly. Add a dash or two of hot pepper sauce, if desired. Season to taste. Ladle into warm bowls, sprinkle with paprika or minced parsley, and serve immediately with crackers on top.

Copyright by Terese Allen; courtesy of Organic Valley Family of Farms

1 pint freshly shucked oysters, with their liquid

2 tablespoons **ORGANIC VALLEY Butter**

1 cup **ORGANIC VALLEY Heavy Whipping Cream**

1 cup **ORGANIC VALLEY Milk** (or more if desired)

2 tablespoons grated onion

½ teaspoon minced fresh rosemary or thyme (optional)

Salt and freshly ground pepper to taste

Bottled hot pepper sauce (optional)

Paprika, minced parsley, or chopped chives

Oyster or saltine crackers

30-Minute Chili

2 tablespoons **EDEN Extra Virgin Olive Oil**

1 clove garlic, minced

1 cup diced onion

½ cup diced red bell pepper

½ cup diced green bell pepper

½ cup organic sweet corn, fresh or frozen

2 (15-oz.) cans **EDEN ORGANIC Chili Beans** (seasoned dark red kidney)

1 (15-oz.) can **EDEN ORGANIC Pinto Beans**

1 (28-oz.) can **EDEN ORGANIC Whole Tomatoes with Basil**, do not drain

1 (15-oz.) can **EDEN ORGANIC Rice & Kidney Beans**

1 (14 ½-oz.) can **EDEN ORGANIC Diced Tomatoes with Green Chilies**, do not drain Eden Foods confirm can size

PREP: 10 minutes

COOK: 20 minutes

YIELD: 8 servings

Heat oil in a medium soup pot and sauté the garlic and onion for 2 to 3 minutes. Add all remaining ingredients. Mix thoroughly, cover, and bring to a boil. Reduce the flame to medium-low and simmer for 15 minutes. Serve.

Courtesy of Eden Foods

Quick Chicken Chili

PREP: 5 minutes

COOK: 18 minutes

YIELD: 4 servings

In medium saucepan, combine all ingredients and bring to a boil over medium-high heat. Reduce heat to medium, cover, and cook, stirring occasionally, 10 minutes. Uncover and cook an additional 3 minutes. Serve with cornbread, if desired.

Courtesy of Perdue Farms, Inc.

1 (9-oz.) package **PERDUE® SHORT CUTS® Carved Chicken Breast, Southwestern Style**

1 (15 ¼-oz.) can red kidney beans, rinsed and drained

1 (14 ½-oz.) can diced tomatoes

½ cup water

1 teaspoon chili powder

Cornbread (optional)

Best-Ever Chili

½ lb. extra lean ground beef

1 teaspoon chili powder

1 (15-oz.) can no-salt-added kidney beans, drained

1 (14.5-oz.) can fire-roasted tomatoes, undrained

1 cup **TACO BELL® HOME ORIGINALS® Thick 'N Chunky Salsa**

½ cup **KRAFT 2% Milk Shredded Sharp Cheddar Cheese**

¼ cup **BREAKSTONE'S Reduced Fat or KNUDSEN Light Sour Cream**

PREP: 5 minutes

COOK: 15 minutes

YIELD: 4 (1-cup) servings

Brown meat with chili powder in large skillet on medium-high heat. Stir in beans, tomatoes and salsa. Bring to boil. Cover; simmer on medium heat 10 minutes, stirring occasionally. Serve topped with cheese and sour cream.

Courtesy of Kraft Foods

TACO BELL® and HOME ORIGINALS® are trademarks owned and licensed by Taco Bell Corp.

Champion Chicken Chili

PREP: 10 minutes

COOK: 20 minutes

YIELD: 4 servings

Brown thawed ground chicken with onions and spices over medium heat in a heavy Dutch oven or large stockpot. Add chopped veggies and beans and cook over medium heat until tender. Add tomato purée. Reduce heat and allow to simmer for 15 minutes. Remove from heat and allow to cool prior to serving. Can be made 1 to 2 days ahead of time.

SERVING SUGGESTIONS

Top chili with shredded **ORGANIC VALLEY Cheese** and sour cream, chives or scallions, avocado, roasted corn, or cilantro.

Courtesy of Organic Valley Family of Farms

2 lbs., or 2 or 3 (12-oz.) packages, **ORGANIC PRAIRIE Ground Chicken**, thawed

⅓ cup chopped sweet red onion

2 teaspoons chili powder

¾ teaspoon cumin

1 dash cinnamon

Salt and pepper (to taste)

½ cup shredded or chopped carrots

½ cup finely chopped celery

1 small red or green bell pepper, chopped

1 ½ cups chopped summer squash (zucchini, crookneck, pattypan)

1 teaspoon fresh minced jalapeño (optional)

1 large fresh tomato, chopped (optional)

1 (15-oz.) can black beans, rinsed and drained

1 (15-oz.) can tomato purée

Chili with Rotini Rice Pasta, Beans and Beef

1 lb. lean ground beef

1 large onion, chopped

3 cloves garlic, pressed

¼ to ½ teaspoon crushed red pepper

5 to 6 cups low-sodium beef broth

1 tablespoon chili powder

1 (15-oz.) can kidney or pinto beans, drained

1 (6-oz.) can tomato paste

1 (14-oz.) can diced tomatoes, undrained

1 (12-oz.) box **LUNDBERG® Rotini Brown Rice Pasta**

Salt and pepper to taste

PREP: 5 minutes

COOK: 25 minutes

YIELD: 4 servings

Sauté ground beef in large pot until no longer pink, breaking up large pieces. Drain fat. Add onion, garlic, and red pepper and cook until onion is tender. Stir in broth, chili powder, beans, tomato paste, and tomatoes; bring to boil. Mix in Rotini. Reduce heat to medium and simmer uncovered until Rotini is al dente, stirring often, about 7 minutes. Season with salt and pepper. Serve in bowls. Pass grated cheese, chopped onions, and sour cream for toppings.

Courtesy of Lundberg Family Farms

Salads & Sandwiches

Apple, Pecan, and Gorgonzola Side Salad

2 Granny Smith apples, sliced

2 tablespoons toasted **PLANTERS Chopped Pecans**

2 tablespoons **ATHENOS Crumbled Gorgonzola Cheese**

½ cup **GOOD SEASONS Italian Dressing Mix** prepared with balsamic vinegar

PREP: 10 minutes

YIELD: 4 servings

Arrange apples on four salad plates. Sprinkle with pecans and cheese. Top with dressing.

Courtesy of Kraft Foods

Apple-Cranberry Salad Toss

PREP: 15 minutes

YIELD: 8 (1 ½-cup) servings

Toss greens with fruit, nuts, and onions. Add dressing just before serving; mix lightly.

Courtesy of Kraft Foods

1 (10-oz.) package mixed salad greens

2 apples, sliced

1 cup dried cranberries

1 cup **PLANTERS Walnut Halves**, toasted

½ cup sliced green onions

½ cup **KRAFT Light Raspberry Vinaigrette Dressing**

Autumn Apple, Ham, and Goat Cheese Salad

PREP: 20 minutes

YIELD: 8 to 12 side-dish servings

Combine salad greens, apples, pomegranate seeds, walnuts, and onion in very large salad bowl. Pour vinaigrette over mixture; gently toss until lightly coated. Spoon salad mixture onto individual salad plates. Top with ham; sprinkle with goat cheese. Serve immediately.

Courtesy of National Pork Board

3 (5-oz.) packages spring mix salad greens

3 Gala apples, cored and thinly sliced

1 cup pomegranate seeds or dried cranberries

1 (7-oz.) package glazed walnuts or 1 ½ cups toasted walnut pieces

½ small red onion, halved, thinly sliced, and separated into pieces

2/3 to ¾ cup bottled Champagne or balsamic vinaigrette

6 oz. cooked boneless ham, cut into matchstick-size strips

1/3 cup goat cheese crumbles

Shaved Fennel and Apple Salad

3 fennel bulbs, cored and sliced thin

2 Cortland, Macintosh, or Granny Smith apples, peeled, cored, and sliced thin

¼ cup canola oil

¼ cup fresh lemon juice

1 cup **STONYFIELD FARM Plain Yogurt**

2 tablespoons fresh tarragon, minced

Salt and pepper to taste

PREP: 25 minutes

YIELD: 8 servings

In medium-size mixing bowl combine fennel and apples. In a small bowl combine canola oil, lemon juice, yogurt, and tarragon. Mix well. Fold into fennel and apple mixture. Add salt and pepper to taste.

Courtesy of Stonyfield Farm

Juicy Pear and Blue Cheese Salad

5 cups torn mixed salad greens

1 large pear, thinly sliced

½ cup **KRAFT Natural Blue Cheese Crumbles**

½ cup candied pecans

¼ cup dried cherries

½ cup **KRAFT Zesty Italian Dressing**

PREP: 15 minutes

YIELD: 6 (1-cup) servings

Toss all ingredients except dressing in large bowl. Add dressing just before serving; mix lightly.

Courtesy of Kraft Foods

Cranberry and Feta Salad with Dijon Vinaigrette

PREP: 15 minutes

YIELD: 4 servings

Toss greens with cranberries, cheese, and walnuts in salad bowl. Beat vinegar, honey, mustard, and pepper with wire whisk until well blended. Gradually add oil, beating until well blended. Pour over salad; toss to coat.

Courtesy of Kraft Foods

1 (10-oz.) package mixed salad greens

1 cup dried cranberries

1 (4-oz.) package **ATHENOS Traditional Crumbled Feta Cheese**

½ cup **PLANTERS Walnut Pieces**, toasted

2 tablespoons balsamic vinegar

1 tablespoon honey

1 teaspoon **GREY POUPON Dijon Mustard**

¼ teaspoon ground black pepper

¼ cup extra virgin olive oil

Berry Sensational Salad

1 (3.5-oz.) package mixed greens

¾ cup **WELCH'S® Berry Medley**

½ cup chopped pecans

½ cup Gorgonzola

3 tablespoons balsamic vinegar

1 tablespoon extra virgin olive oil

1 tablespoon **WELCH'S 100% White Grape Juice**

1 tablespoon honey

½ teaspoon salt

PREP: 10 minutes

YIELD: 4 servings

In a large bowl, toss greens, Berry Medley, pecans, and cheese. In a separate bowl, mix remaining ingredients and stir vigorously until blended. Drizzle dressing over salad, toss, and serve.

Courtesy of Welch Foods Inc., A Cooperative

Strawberry Salad

PREP: 15 minutes

YIELD: 8 servings

Toss lettuce with oranges, strawberries, and onion in large bowl. Sprinkle with Caramelized Almonds. Add Poppy Seed Dressing; mix lightly. Serve immediately.

CARAMELIZED ALMONDS: Toss 1 cup **PLANTERS Sliced Almonds** with 6 tablespoons sugar in nonstick skillet; cook on medium-high heat until sugar is caramelized, stirring frequently. Spread into single layer on greased baking sheet or sheet of wax paper; cool at least 1 hour. Break into small pieces. Store in tightly covered container at room temperature.

POPPY SEED DRESSING: Beat ½ cup sugar, 1 teaspoon salt, 1 teaspoon dry mustard, and ¼ cup wine vinegar in medium bowl with wire whisk until well blended. Add ½ cup olive oil, ½ cup canola oil, and 1 tablespoon onion juice; mix until well blended. Add 3 tablespoons **KRAFT Real Mayo Mayonnaise** and 4 ½ teaspoons poppy seed; mix well. Cover. Refrigerate until ready to serve. Makes 1 ¾ cups.

Courtesy of Kraft Foods

2 (10-oz.) packages torn romaine lettuce

2 (15-oz.) cans mandarin orange segments, drained

4 cups sliced strawberries

1 medium red onion, sliced

1 cup Caramelized Almonds (recipe below)

1 cup Poppy Seed Dressing (recipe below)

Layered Strawberry Salad

4 cups baby spinach leaves

1 (8-oz.) package **KRAFT Shredded Low-Moisture Part-Skim Mozzarella Cheese**

3 cups torn Boston lettuce

1 small red onion, thinly sliced, separated into rings

2 cups strawberries, sliced

½ cup **PLANTERS Walnut Halves**, toasted

½ cup **KRAFT Creamy Poppyseed Dressing**

PREP: 15 minutes

YIELD: 8 (1 ½-cup) servings

Place half of the spinach on serving plate. Top with half each of the cheese, Boston lettuce, onions, and strawberries. Repeat layers. Sprinkle with walnuts. Drizzle with dressing just before serving.

Courtesy of Kraft Foods

Spring Bouquet Salad

PREP: 8 minutes

COOK: 7 minutes

YIELD: 4 servings

Cook asparagus* in boiling water in large saucepan, 2 minutes or until crisp-tender. Drain and immediately plunge into ice water. Let stand 5 minutes; drain. Toss salad blend, strawberries, and asparagus in large bowl. Pour dressing over salad and toss to evenly coat. Sprinkle with almonds and serve.

*TO MICROWAVE ASPARAGUS: Place asparagus in microwave-safe dish with 1 tablespoon water. Microwave on high 3 to 5 minutes or until crisp-tender, stirring once during heating. Proceed as above, draining and placing asparagus into ice water.

Courtesy of Dole Food Company

½ lb. **DOLE® Asparagus**, cut into 1 ½-inch pieces

1 (10-oz.) package **DOLE Italian** or **Romaine Salad Blend** or other variety

1 cup halved **DOLE Strawberries** or 1 cup **DOLE Raspberries**

½ cup bottled fat-free or regular raspberry vinaigrette

¼ cup sliced almonds, toasted

Avocado Strawberry Salad

1 avocado, peeled and cut into bite-size chunks

1 large orange, peeled and cut into bite-size chunks

1 cup strawberries, sliced

⅓ cup chopped pecans

⅓ cup plain yogurt

1 tablespoon honey

⅛ teaspoon **FRONTIER** cardamom seed powder

⅛ teaspoon **FRONTIER** ground cinnamon

¼ teaspoon **FRONTIER** peppermint leaf

PREP: 15 minutes

YIELD: 4 servings

Combine avocado, orange, strawberries, and pecans in a serving bowl. In a small, separate bowl, combine remaining ingredients. Pour over salad and mix well.

Courtesy of Frontier Natural Products Co-op

SUNKIST® Grapefruit Avocado Salad

PREP: 30 minutes

YIELD: 4 servings

With sharp knife, cut ¼-inch rings horizontally around the avocados, being careful not to cut through the pit. Gently remove the rings one by one and remove the skin. Evenly divide avocado rings among four plates, stacking the rings vertically on each plate (approximately 4 rings per plate) to create a tower. Peel and segment 2 grapefruits, gently cut segments into bite-size pieces, and divide among the four plates, placing segments in the center of the avocado tower. Discard peel. Slice remaining grapefruit in half. Cut one half into 4 slices and juice the other half, reserving juice for dressing. Place a grapefruit slice next to each avocado and grapefruit tower and top with baby lettuce. For the dressing, whisk together lime juice, olive oil, reserved grapefruit juice, and a pinch of salt. Drizzle each salad with dressing, and top with grapefruit zest.

Courtesy of Sunkist Growers, Inc.

2 medium avocados

3 **SUNKIST® Grapefruits**, (Pummelo, Oroblanco, or Melogold)

3 cups baby lettuce mix

Juice of 1 **SUNKIST® Lime**

¼ cup olive oil

Salt, to taste

Zest of 1 grapefruit

Baby Spinach, Avocado, and Grapefruit Salad with Raspberry Yogurt Vinaigrette

PREP: 20 minutes

YIELD: 6 servings

Arrange baby spinach, avocado, and grapefruit on six separate plates or one large serving platter. In a small bowl whisk together vinegar, oil, honey, and salt. Slowly whisk yogurt into mixture. Drizzle dressing over salad and garnish with pecans.

Courtesy of Stonyfield Farm

6 cups baby spinach

2 avocados, pitted, peeled and cut into 6 wedges each

2 grapefruits, peeled and sectioned

3 tablespoons raspberry vinegar

3 tablespoons olive oil

2 teaspoons honey

¼ teaspoon salt

1 cup **STONYFIELD FARM Plain Yogurt**

¼ cup pecans (optional)

Papaya and Avocado Salad

1 (6-oz.) package spinach leaves

1 papaya, peeled, sliced

1 avocado, sliced

1 small red onion, thinly sliced

1 nectarine, thinly sliced

½ cup prepared **GOOD SEASONS Italian Dressing Mix for Fat Free Dressing**

PREP: 15 minutes

YIELD: 4 servings

Cover platter with spinach. Top with papaya, avocado, onion, and nectarine. Toss with dressing just before serving.

Courtesy of Kraft Foods

Blackberry Salad with Avocado And Pecans

1 (6-oz.) package **DOLE Spring Mix** or other variety

3 stalks **DOLE Celery**, thinly sliced

1 ½ cups pecans, toasted

1 (16-oz.) package **DOLE® Fresh Frozen Blackberries**, defrosted and drained

1 ripe **DOLE Avocado**, pitted, peeled, and cubed

⅓ cup prepared raspberry vinaigrette

3 oz. feta, crumbled

PREP: 15 minutes

YIELD: 7 servings

Combine greens, celery, and pecans in salad bowl. Add blackberries, avocado, and dressing just before serving. Toss to mix. Sprinkle with crumbled feta.

Courtesy of Dole Food Company

Orange-Asparagus Salad with Raspberry Vinaigrette

PREP: 15 minutes

COOK: 6 minutes

YIELD: 6 servings

Steam asparagus for 4 to 6 minutes or until crisp-tender. Rinse in cool water; drain well and set aside. Toss together salad blend, asparagus, onion, and mandarin oranges in large serving bowl. Pour dressing over salad; toss to evenly coat. Serve immediately.

Courtesy of Dole Food Company

1 lb. **DOLE® Fresh Asparagus**, trimmed and cut into 1-inch pieces

1 (5- to 12-oz.) package **DOLE Spring Mix** or **European Salad Blends** or any variety

½ cup thinly sliced **DOLE Red Onion**

1 (15-oz.) can **DOLE Mandarin Oranges**, drained

½ cup bottled raspberry dressing

Tomato & Orange Salad with Feta

PREP: 15 minutes

YIELD: 8 servings

Arrange tomatoes, oranges, and cheese alternately on serving platter. Sprinkle with basil. Mix remaining ingredients; drizzle over salad.

Courtesy of Kraft Foods

4 large tomatoes, cut into ¼-inch-thick slices

4 seedless oranges, peeled, cut into ¼-inch-thick slices

1 (8-oz.) package **ATHENOS Traditional Feta Cheese**, cut into ⅛-inch-thick slices

⅔ cup lightly packed small fresh basil leaves

¼ cup olive oil

1 tablespoon balsamic vinegar

¼ teaspoon salt

¼ teaspoon pepper

Fruit & Feta Salad

1 (10-oz.) bag mixed salad greens

1 (11-oz.) can mandarin orange segments, drained

½ cup thinly sliced red onion

1 cup **PLANTERS Walnut Pieces**, toasted

1 (4-oz.) package **ATHENOS Traditional Crumbled Feta Cheese**

¾ cup **KRAFT Light Raspberry Vinaigrette Dressing**

PREP: 20 minutes

YIELD: 6 servings

Toss greens, oranges, onion, walnuts, and feta in large bowl. Add dressing; mix lightly.

Courtesy of Kraft Foods

Asian Mandarin Salad

1 (6-oz.) package **DOLE®**
Tender Garden or **7 Lettuces**
Salad

1 (11- or 15-oz.) can **DOLE**
Mandarin Oranges, drained

½ cup sesame ginger
dressing

⅓ cup wonton strips

PREP: 15 minutes

YIELD: 6 servings

Toss together salad and mandarin oranges in large serving
bowl. Pour dressing over salad; toss to evenly coat. Sprinkle
with wonton strips.

Courtesy of Dole Food Company

Mixed Green Salad with Black Grapes and Farmers Cheese

PREP: 10 minutes

YIELD: 4 servings

Wash and tear lettuce into bite-size pieces. Layer in
serving bowl. Add grapes and cheese to lettuce. Whisk
together oil, grape juice, and lemon juice. Season with
salt and pepper. Pour dressing over salad and toss at
the table.

Courtesy of Welch Foods Inc., A Cooperative

8 cups mixed salad greens

½ cup black grapes, seedless,
cut in half

6 oz. farmer cheese, cubed, or
⅔ cup cottage cheese, large curd

4 tablespoons olive oil

2 tablespoons **WELCH'S White**
Grape Juice

2 tablespoons lemon juice

Salt and pepper to taste

Watermelon Salad

2 cups seedless watermelon, cubed

2 vine-ripened red and 2 vine-ripened yellow tomatoes, deseeded and cut into wedges

½ English cucumber, sliced into half-moons

10 basil leaves

3 cloves garlic, minced

2 tablespoons lemon juice

½ cup **STONYFIELD FARM Plain Yogurt**

3 tablespoons chopped mint

½ red onion, sliced

½ cup crumbled feta

Salt and pepper to taste

PREP: 25 minutes

YIELD: 6 servings

Mix together watermelon, tomatoes, cucumbers, and basil. Place watermelon mixture into serving dish or divide among 6 salad plates. Fold together garlic, lemon juice, yogurt, and mint. Drizzle dressing over watermelon salad and garnish with red onion, feta, and salt and pepper.

Courtesy of Stonyfield Farm

Grilled Fruit Salad

PREP: 15 minutes

COOK: 6 minutes

YIELD: 6 servings

Preheat greased grill to medium-high heat. Combine sour cream, drink mix, and ground red pepper until well blended; cover. Refrigerate until ready to use. Grill fruit 6 minutes or until lightly browned on both sides, turning over after 3 minutes. Arrange fruit on platter. Serve immediately with the sour cream mixture. Or cover and refrigerate the fruit platter and sour cream mixture separately until ready to serve. Spoon sour cream mixture over fruit just before serving.

Courtesy of Kraft Foods

½ cup **BREAKSTONE'S Reduced Fat** or **KNUDSEN Light Sour Cream**

1 tablespoon **KOOL-AID Orange Flavor Sugar-Sweetened Soft Drink Mix**

¼ teaspoon ground red pepper

1 medium pineapple, peeled, cored, and cut into wedges

1 medium mango, peeled, pitted, and cut into wedges

1 medium papaya, peeled, seeded, and cut into wedges

2 medium bananas, diagonally sliced

King of the Jungle Spinach Salad

PREP: 10 minutes

YIELD: 4 servings

Place spinach leaves in large salad bowl. Drain tropical fruit salad, reserving 1 tablespoon syrup. Add fruit to spinach with raisins, peanuts, and sliced onions. Stir together yogurt, sour cream, and reserved syrup in small bowl or cup. Spoon mixture over salad and toss to evenly coat. Serve immediately.

Courtesy of Dole Food Company

4 cups packed fresh spinach leaves, torn

1 (15.25-oz.) can **DOLE® Tropical Fruit Salad**

½ cup **DOLE Seedless** or **Golden Raisins**

½ cup roasted peanut halves

⅓ cup sliced green onions

¼ cup lowfat peach, lemon, orange, or lime-flavored yogurt

2 tablespoons sour cream

Spinach Salad with Warm Balsamic Walnut Dressing

1 (10-oz.) package spinach, washed and drained

1 cup sliced fresh mushrooms

1 (4-oz.) package **ATHENOS Traditional Crumbled Feta Cheese**

½ medium red onion, sliced

8 slices **OSCAR MAYER Center Cut Bacon**

½ cup coarsely chopped **PLANTERS Walnuts**

¼ cup balsamic vinegar

¼ cup olive oil

½ teaspoon salt

¼ teaspoon pepper

2 hard-cooked eggs, quartered

PREP: 15 minutes

COOK: 15 minutes

YIELD: 6 (2-cup) servings

Toss spinach with mushrooms, cheese, and onion in large bowl; set aside. Cook bacon in large skillet on medium heat to desired crispness, turning frequently. Remove bacon from skillet; reserve 2 tablespoons of the drippings in skillet. Place bacon on paper towels to drain. Add walnuts to reserved drippings in skillet. Cook 1 to 2 minutes or until lightly toasted, stirring occasionally. Stir in vinegar, oil, salt, and pepper. Cook 30 seconds or until heated through. Pour hot dressing over salad; toss to coat. Top with eggs. Crumble bacon; sprinkle over salad.

Courtesy of Kraft Foods

Spinach-Avocado Salad with Lime Vinaigrette

¼ cup lime juice

1 clove garlic, minced

2 teaspoons honey

½ teaspoon **FRONTIER** mustard

¼ teaspoon **FRONTIER** oregano

¼ cup each extra virgin olive oil and vegetable oil

10 oz. fresh spinach leaves

2 ripe avocados, cut in cubes

2 Roma tomatoes, sliced

PREP: 14 minutes

YIELD: 4 servings

Combine the lime juice, garlic, honey, mustard, and oregano in blender. Blend briefly. With blender running, gradually drizzle in the oils through the opening in the lid. Place the spinach in a large bowl; top with avocado pieces and tomato. Add dressing and toss gently to combine. Serve immediately.

Courtesy of Frontier Natural Products Co-op

BLT Salad

PREP: 20 minutes

YIELD: 4 servings

Coarsely crumble bacon and set aside. In large bowl, toss together romaine, tomatoes, and mushrooms. Whisk together olive oil, vinegar, sugar, and seasonings; toss with salad mixture and divide evenly among four dinner plates. Top each salad with some bacon and sliced green onion.

Courtesy of National Pork Board

12 slices crisply cooked bacon

4 cups shredded romaine

16 dried tomato halves: drained if packed in oil, rehydrated if dried

8 oz. fresh mushrooms, thinly sliced

4 tablespoons olive oil

3 tablespoons red wine vinegar

⅛ teaspoon sugar

Salt and pepper, to taste

¼ cup sliced green onions

Chopped Asparagus & Bacon Salad

PREP: 20 minutes

YIELD: 4 servings

FOR THE DRESSING: In a small mixing bowl, add the garlic, anchovy, parsley, lemon juice, salt, and pepper. While whisking, add the olive oil in a slow steady stream.

FOR THE SALAD: Mix together the Romano and hot water in a big bowl until the cheese has melted. Whisk in the dressing and season with pepper to your taste. Add the asparagus and scallions and toss until well coated. Arrange the lettuce leaves on individual plates or a large platter. Spoon the asparagus onto the leaves, then scatter bacon and mint over the asparagus.

Courtesy of Applegate Farms, an Organic & Natural Meat Company

DRESSING:

1 small garlic clove, peeled and minced

1 anchovy filet, chopped, or a small dollop of anchovy paste

A handful of parsley leaves, finely chopped

Juice of half a lemon, or more if you like

Salt and freshly ground pepper

¼ cup extra-virgin olive oil

Freshly ground black pepper

SALAD:

¼ cup finely grated Romano

¼ cup hot water

Freshly ground black pepper

2 bunches pencil-thin fresh asparagus, trimmed and finely chopped

4 young scallions, trimmed and finely chopped

4 to 8 large butter lettuce leaves

8 slices cooked **APPLEGATE FARMS Bacon**, finely chopped

A handful of fresh mint leaves, finely chopped

Ranch-Bacon Chopped Salad

6 cups torn lettuce

1 large tomato, chopped

1 medium zucchini, chopped

1 cup frozen corn, thawed

¼ cup **OSCAR MAYER Real Bacon Bits**

½ cup **KRAFT Ranch Dressing with Bacon**

PREP: 15 minutes

YIELD: 4 (1 ½-cup) servings

Toss lettuce with tomato, zucchini, corn, and bacon bits in large salad bowl. Add dressing just before serving; mix lightly.

Courtesy of Kraft Foods

BBQ Potato, Bacon & Corn Salad

PREP: 25 minutes

YIELD: 12 (½-cup) servings

Mix dressing, barbecue sauce, and mustard in large bowl. Add all remaining ingredients except for the bacon; mix lightly. Sprinkle top of salad with bacon. Serve immediately or refrigerate until ready to serve.

Courtesy of Kraft Foods

⅓ cup **KRAFT Ranch Dressing**

⅓ cup **KRAFT Original Barbecue Sauce**

2 tablespoons **GREY POUPON Dijon Mustard**

3 lbs. small red potatoes, cooked, quartered

1 (11-oz.) can whole kernel corn, drained

½ cup sliced celery

½ cup chopped red peppers

½ cup chopped red onions

8 slices **OSCAR MAYER Bacon**, crisply cooked, crumbled

Grilled Corn Salad

¾ cup **KRAFT Zesty Italian Dressing**, divided

¼ cup yellow mustard

4 medium ears corn on the cob, husks and silk removed

2 cups cut trimmed fresh green beans (about ½ lb.), cooked

1 medium (1-lb.) jicama, peeled, cut into ½-inch cubes

2 medium tomatoes, cored, cut into wedges

½ cup chopped fresh basil

PREP: 10 minutes

COOK: 20 minutes

YIELD: 6 (½-cup) servings

Place ¼ cup of the dressing and mustard in large resealable plastic bag. Add corn; close bag and shake gently until corn is evenly coated with the dressing mixture. Remove corn from bag, reserving dressing mixture. Place corn on rack of grill over low heat. Grill 15 to 20 minutes or until corn is tender, turning and brushing occasionally with the reserved dressing mixture. Remove corn from grill; cool. Cut off the kernels; place in medium bowl. Add beans, jicama, tomatoes, basil, and remaining ½ cup dressing; toss to coat. Serve immediately or cover and refrigerate until ready to serve.

Courtesy of Kraft Foods

Green Bean and Tomato Salad

PREP: 10 minutes

COOK: 8 minutes

YIELD: 4 to 6 servings

Heat oil in a pan set over medium heat. Add onion, celery, green pepper, basil, and hot pepper sauce. Cook for 5 minutes. Stir in sugar and cider vinegar. Add ketchup and toss to combine. Taste and adjust salt and pepper as necessary. Cool completely. Arrange beans in a serving dish. Spoon the ketchup mixture over beans. Sprinkle with almonds, if using.

Courtesy of H.J. Heinz Company, L.P.

1 teaspoon vegetable oil

¼ cup each finely chopped onion, celery, and green pepper

1 teaspoon dried basil leaves

Dash of hot pepper sauce

½ teaspoon granulated sugar

1 teaspoon **HEINZ® Apple Cider Vinegar**

⅓ cup **HEINZ® Tomato Ketchup**

Salt and pepper to taste

1 lb. cooked, chilled green beans

2 tablespoons toasted, slivered almonds (optional)

Minted Cucumber Salad

1 teaspoon **FRONTIER** dried mint

½ teaspoon **FRONTIER** garlic powder

1 cup yogurt

1 large cucumber, peeled and sliced thin

Lettuce leaves

4 red radishes, chopped

PREP: 10 minutes

YIELD: 2 servings

Mix mint and garlic powder into yogurt. Distribute cucumber slices on crisp leaves of lettuce and pour yogurt on top. Garnish with chopped radishes. Serve cold.

Courtesy of Frontier Natural Products Co-op

Slice-and-Serve Fennel Salad with Parmesan and Parsley

PREP: 15 minutes

YIELD: 4 servings

Cut fennel bulbs in half lengthwise. Cut out cores. Use a sharp knife or mandoline to slice bulbs as thinly as possible. Scatter slices evenly over the entire surface of an oversized plate. Sprinkle on the lemon juice, pepper, and parsley. Sprinkle Parmesan evenly over all. Garnish with fennel fronds. Serve dish right after it is assembled.

COOK'S TIP

If California-grown Meyer lemons are available to you, use one in this salad to add a really bright flavor.

Copyright by Terese Allen; courtesy of Organic Valley Family of Farms

2 medium fennel bulbs, stalks removed

Juice of ½ lemon

Freshly ground black pepper to taste

3 to 4 tablespoons chopped flat leaf parsley

⅓ cup **ORGANIC VALLEY Shredded Parmesan**

A few fennel fronds

Midsummer Artichoke Salad

3 cups torn lettuce

2 (6-oz.) jars marinated artichoke hearts, reserve marinade

1 (8-oz.) package (2 cups) fresh mushrooms, halved

4 oz. (1 cup) **Land O' Lakes® Mozzarella Cheese**, cut into ½-cubes

2 tablespoons freshly grated Parmesan

¼ teaspoon course ground pepper

PREP: 15 minutes

YIELD: 8 servings

Toss together all ingredients in large bowl except reserved marinade. Refrigerate until serving time. Before serving, add reserved marinade; toss to coat.

Courtesy of Land O Lakes, Inc.

Tomato, Prosciutto, & Fresh Mozzarella Salad

1 (5-oz.) package **DOLE® Organic Spring Mix with Herbs** or **Baby Lettuces**

1 cup yellow and red pear or cherry tomatoes, halved

1 ½ oz. prosciutto, chopped, or 5 strips bacon, cooked, drained, and crumbled

4 oz. fresh mozzarella, drained and torn into bits, or regular mozzarella cut into julienne strips

1 cup sliced **DOLE Red Onion**

1 cup croutons

¼ cup prepared balsamic vinaigrette dressing

PREP: 20 minutes

YIELD: 4 servings

Combine salad blend, tomatoes, prosciutto, cheese, onion, and croutons in large bowl. Pour vinaigrette over salad; toss to evenly coat.

Courtesy of Dole Food Company

Tuscan Tomato Salad

3 tablespoons olive oil, divided

3 thick slices bread (Italian, French, or sourdough)

½ teaspoon **FRONTIER** oregano leaf

½ teaspoon **FRONTIER** basil leaf

¼ teaspoon **FRONTIER** thyme leaf

¼ teaspoon **FRONTIER** sage leaf

¼ teaspoon **FRONTIER** garlic granules

1 teaspoon red wine vinegar

3 large tomatoes, chopped

½ cup cubed mozzarella

¼ cup sliced black olives

Freshly ground black pepper

PREP: 15 minutes

YIELD: 4 servings

Brush 2 tablespoons olive oil on the bread. Sprinkle with the oregano, basil, thyme, sage, and garlic. Place on baking sheet and broil until browned. Cool, then break bread apart into bite-size pieces. In a small bowl, whisk together remaining oil and vinegar. In serving bowl combine tomatoes, mozzarella, olives, and bread. Toss with oil and vinegar. Sprinkle with pepper.

Courtesy of Frontier Natural Products Co-op

Greek Vegetable Salad

3 large tomatoes, chopped

1 medium cucumber, sliced

½ cup kalamata olives

½ small red onion, thinly sliced

½ cup **KRAFT Greek Vinaigrette Dressing**

1 (4-oz.) package **ATHENOS Traditional Crumbled Feta Cheese**

PREP: 15 minutes

YIELD: 4 servings

Mix vegetables in large bowl. Add dressing and feta; toss lightly. Serve immediately or refrigerate until ready to serve.

Courtesy of Kraft Foods

Southwest Caesar Salad

PREP: 20 minutes

YIELD: 6 servings

Place mayonnaise, lime juice, onions, ground red pepper, and salt in food processor or blender container; cover. Process until well blended. Gradually add oil through feed tube at top, processing until well blended after each addition. Toss lettuce with the croutons, corn, bell peppers, cilantro, and cheese in large bowl. Add mayonnaise mixture; toss to evenly coat. Serve immediately.

Courtesy of Kraft Foods

2 tablespoons **KRAFT Real Mayo Mayonnaise**

2 tablespoons fresh lime juice

2 tablespoons chopped green onions

¼ teaspoon ground red pepper (cayenne)

⅛ teaspoon salt

¼ cup olive oil

1 head romaine, washed, shredded (about 6 cups)

1 cup croutons

1 cup frozen whole kernel corn, thawed

½ red bell pepper, cut into thin strips

½ cup chopped cilantro

⅓ cup **KRAFT Grated Parmesan Cheese**

String Cheese "Slaw"

1 (6-oz.) package **ORGANIC VALLEY "Stringles" String Cheese**

1 ½ cups carrot matchsticks (or shredded carrot)

3 tablespoons chopped cilantro or parsley

4 teaspoons fresh lemon juice

2 teaspoons olive oil

Freshly ground black pepper

PREP: 15 minutes

CHILL: ½ to 1 hour

YIELD: 6 servings

Pull threads of cheese off each string cheese stick (not too thin). Toss with carrots, cilantro or parsley, lemon juice, and olive oil. Add pepper to taste. Serve immediately, or chill salad in the refrigerator, tossing occasionally, ½ to 1 hour.

COOK'S TIP

This slaw makes an unusual and fun side dish to sandwiches or burgers. Or it may be added to tacos or burritos, or piled into pita bread with sliced tomatoes. For color, add slivered red peppers to the salad; for heat, add minced jalapeños.

Copyright by Terese Allen; courtesy of Organic Valley Family of Farms

Fusilli Fanfare

PREP: 5 minutes

CHILL: 20 minutes

YIELD: 8 servings

Combine broccoli, beans, and pasta in a serving bowl. Combine remaining ingredients in a blender and process until well mixed. Pour over pasta and mix. Chill mix again and serve.

Courtesy of Frontier Natural Products Co-op

2 cups broccoli florets, steamed until just tender

2 cups cooked cannellini beans, drained

1 lb. fusilli pasta, cooked al dente and drained

2 teaspoons **FRONTIER** mustard powder

1 tablespoon **FRONTIER** tarragon

1 tablespoon **FRONTIER** basil

2 teaspoons **FRONTIER** thyme

2 tablespoons **FRONTIER** oregano

½ teaspoon **FRONTIER** garlic powder

½ cup olive oil

½ cup lemon juice

½ cup wine vinegar

Kamut Spiral Salad with Broccoli and Peanuts

12 oz. **EDEN ORGANIC Kamut Spirals**

2 lbs. broccoli (about 2 heads)

3 tablespoons **EDEN Toasted Sesame Oil**, divided

½ teaspoon red pepper flakes

1 ¼ cups water, divided

⅓ cup **EDEN ORGANIC Brown Rice Vinegar**

¼ cup organic creamy peanut butter

2 tablespoons **EDEN Shoyu Soy Sauce**

1 cup scallions, thinly sliced

½ cup organic dry-roasted, unsalted peanuts, coarsely chopped

PREP: 10 minutes

COOK: 20 minutes

YIELD: 6 servings

Cook pasta according to package directions. Drain, rinse, and set aside. Meanwhile trim the stem end of the broccoli stalks. Thinly slice broccoli stems. Separate florets into bite-size pieces. Heat 1 tablespoon oil in a large skillet over medium heat. Add pepper flakes, broccoli, and ¾ cup water. Cover and cook 5 to 7 minutes until tender but still bright green. Uncover and cook until liquid has evaporated, about 2 minutes. Whisk together remaining oil and water, vinegar, peanut butter, and soy sauce in a medium bowl until smooth. Add pasta, broccoli, scallions, and peanuts. Toss. Serve immediately or refrigerate and serve chilled.

Courtesy of Eden Foods

Quick Sun-Dried Tomato Pasta Salad

PREP: 15 minutes

YIELD: 6 servings

Cook pasta according to package directions; drain. Rinse with cold water; drain well. Place in large bowl. Add vegetables, olives, and dressing; toss to coat. Serve immediately or cover and refrigerate until ready to serve.

Courtesy of Kraft Foods

1 (9-oz.) package refrigerated cheese tortellini

1 cup broccoli florets

⅔ cup chopped or sliced green peppers

⅔ cup thinly sliced carrots

1 (2 ¼-oz.) can pitted ripe olives, drained

¾ cup **KRAFT Sun-Dried Tomato Dressing**

Mediterranean Pasta Salad

PREP: 10 minutes

COOK: 10 minutes

YIELD: 6 servings

Cook pasta as package directs, rinse, and drain. Add olives, tomatoes, onion, parsley, or celery leaves. Mix. Prepare dressing by combining all ingredients. Mix dressing with pasta.

COOK'S TIP

For a hot salad, do not rinse pasta under cold water; simply drain after cooking. Proceed as above.

Courtesy of Eden Foods

PASTA SALAD

12 oz. **EDEN ORGANIC Flax Rice Spirals** or any **EDEN ORGANIC Spiral Pasta**

12 whole pitted jumbo black olives

1 (14 ½-oz.) can **EDEN ORGANIC Diced Tomatoes**, drained

⅓ cup finely chopped red onion

¼ cup minced fresh parsley or minced celery leaves

DRESSING

¼ cup **EDEN Extra Virgin Olive Oil**

¼ cup **EDEN Red Wine Vinegar**

2 cloves garlic, minced

1 tablespoon dried oregano or 2 tablespoons finely minced fresh oregano

1 teaspoon **EDEN Shoyu Soy Sauce**, or to taste

Southwestern Portobello Pasta Salad

PREP: 10 minutes

COOK: 15 minutes

YIELD: 4 to 6 servings

Cook mushrooms over medium heat in medium skillet sprayed with vegetable cooking spray, until very tender, 5 to 8 minutes. Stir in taco seasoning; mix well. Set aside to cool slightly. Stir together pasta, mushrooms, bell peppers, black beans, and green onions in large bowl. Stir together salsa, sour cream, and mayonnaise in small bowl. Pour dressing over pasta mixture; toss to evenly coat.

Courtesy of Dole Food Company

2 large (8-oz.) **DOLE® Portobello Mushrooms**, cut into ½-inch pieces

1 tablespoon mild taco seasoning

1 (8-oz.) package small pasta shells, cooked and drained

1 **DOLE Red Bell Pepper**, diced

1 **DOLE Yellow** or **Orange Bell Pepper**, diced

1 (15-oz.) can black beans, drained and rinsed

½ cup **DOLE Green Onions**, diced

¼ cup salsa (or to taste)

¼ cup light sour cream

2 tablespoons light mayonnaise

Crunchy Asian Salad

1 envelope **GOOD SEASONS Italian Dressing Mix**

½ cup sugar

2 tablespoons soy sauce

2 (3-oz.) packages ramen noodle soup mix

2 (16-oz.) packages coleslaw blend

4 green onions, sliced

½ cup **PLANTERS Dry Roasted Sunflower Kernels**

½ cup **PLANTERS Sliced Almonds**, toasted

PREP: 15 minutes

YIELD: 12 (1-cup) servings

Prepare dressing mix in small bowl as directed on envelope. Stir in sugar and soy sauce. Break apart noodles and place in large bowl; discard seasoning packet or reserve for another use. Add coleslaw blend, onions, sunflower kernels, and almonds to noodles; mix lightly. Add dressing; toss to coat. Serve immediately.

Courtesy of Kraft Foods

Curried Asian Salad

PREP: 20 minutes

COOK: 10 minutes

YIELD: 6 servings

Boil pasta in large saucepan for 7 to 8 minutes (pasta won't be fully cooked). Add sliced vegetables and continue cooking until vegetables and pasta are fully cooked. In a medium bowl, stir vinegar, soy sauce, water, and oil with **SIMPLY ORGANIC Red Pepper Curry Vinaigrette Dressing Mix** package ingredients. When pasta and vegetables are fully cooked, drain pasta and toss with liquid mixture. Serve warm.

Courtesy of Simply Organic

8 oz. dry capellini or 8 oz. other thin noodle

½ cup sliced shiitake or other mushroom

½ cup thinly sliced red bell pepper

¼ cup rice vinegar

3 tablespoons soy sauce

½ cup water

1 tablespoon vegetable oil

1 package **SIMPLY ORGANIC Red Pepper Curry Vinaigrette Dressing Mix**

Calico Couscous Salad

½ cup fat-free Caesar salad dressing

⅓ cup sliced green onions

⅓ cup chopped green bell pepper

⅓ cup chopped yellow bell pepper

1 tomato, finely chopped

2 oz. (½ cup) **LAND O LAKES® Mozzarella Cheese**, cut into ¼-inch cubes

1 tablespoon chopped fresh basil leaves

2 cups cooked Mediterranean (not quick-cooking) couscous, cooled

PREP: 15 minutes

YIELD: 6 servings

Combine all ingredients except couscous in large bowl; toss gently. Gently stir in couscous. Cover; refrigerate until serving time.

COOK'S TIP

Mediterranean couscous is larger with a more uniform round shape than traditional couscous. The cooking time is longer so follow package directions.

Courtesy of Land O'Lakes, Inc.

Whole Wheat Couscous Salad

1 cup water

1 teaspoon **MAGGI Granulated Chicken Flavor Bouillon**

¾ cup whole wheat couscous

2 tablespoons fresh lemon juice

1 tablespoon extra virgin olive oil

½ cup halved cherry or pear tomatoes

¼ cup sliced and quartered cucumber

¼ cup diced green bell pepper

1 tablespoon chopped fresh parsley and/or sliced green onion

¼ teaspoon ground black pepper

PREP: 10 minutes

COOK: 10 minutes

YIELD: 6 servings

Combine water and bouillon in small saucepan. Bring to a boil; remove from heat. Stir in couscous. Cover; let stand for 5 minutes. Fluff with fork. Transfer couscous to medium bowl; stir in lemon juice and oil. Add tomatoes, cucumber, bell pepper, parsley, and black pepper; toss lightly. Serve immediately or refrigerate.

Courtesy of Nestlé USA

Summer Citrus & Minted Couscous

PREP: 15 minutes

COOK: 10 minutes

YIELD: 4 servings

Place the orange juice and salt in a medium saucepan and bring to a boil. Stir in the couscous, bring to a boil, cover, and turn off the flame. Allow the couscous to sit and steam for about 5 minutes with the cover on. Place the garbanzo beans, pine nuts, apricots, blueberries or cranberries, cucumber, and scallions in a mixing bowl. Combine the vinegar, oil, lemon juice, ¼ cup orange juice, and mint in a jar. Cover and shake to mix. Fluff the couscous to cool and place in the mixing bowl with the garbanzo beans and vegetables. Pour the dressing over and toss to evenly mix. Place in a serving bowl.

Courtesy of Eden Foods

1 ½ cups freshly squeezed orange juice

1 pinch **EDEN Sea Salt**

1 ½ cups organic couscous

½ cup **EDEN ORGANIC Garbanzo Beans**, drained

¼ cup pine nuts, lightly dry-pan roasted

¼ cup Turkish apricots, coarsely chopped

½ cup organic currants, **EDEN ORGANIC Dried Wild Blueberries**, or **EDEN ORGANIC Dried Cranberries**

1 small cucumber, seeded, quartered, and sliced

½ cup finely chopped scallions

2 tablespoons **EDEN Red Wine Vinegar**

2 tablespoons **EDEN Extra Virgin Olive Oil**

¼ cup freshly squeezed lemon juice

¼ cup freshly squeezed orange juice

¼ cup finely chopped fresh mint leaves

Confetti Sweet Brown Rice Salad

3 cups cooked **LUNDBERG® Organic Sweet Brown Rice**, chilled

2 celery stalks, cut into ¼-inch dice

2 tomatoes, seeded and cut into ¼-inch dice

½ carrot, cut into ¼-inch dice

½ red onion, chopped finely

½ red bell pepper, cut into ¼-inch dice

½ green bell pepper, cut into ¼-inch dice

½ yellow bell pepper, cut into ¼-inch dice

½ cup sliced almonds, toasted

½ to ¾ cup raisins

6 tablespoons balsamic vinegar

2 to 3 tablespoons olive oil

1 teaspoon minced garlic

Salt and pepper

PREP: 25 minutes

YIELD: 6 servings

In a large bowl combine cooked Sweet Brown Rice, vegetables, almonds, and raisins. In a bowl whisk together vinegar, oil, garlic, and salt and pepper to taste. Pour dressing over salad and toss well to combine.

Courtesy of Lundberg Family Farms

Organic Short Grain Brown Rice Salad with Garbanzo Beans & Peppers

PREP: 20 minutes

YIELD: 6 servings

Combine chilled cooked rice with garbanzo beans, raisins, green onions, and bell peppers. Toss to blend. Whisk together Dijon Vinaigrette and pour over rice and garbanzo mixture, then toss well. Stir in the basil, parsley, and almonds.

Courtesy of Lundberg Family Farms

SALAD

3 cups cooked **LUNDBERG® Organic Short Grain Brown Rice**, chilled

¾ cup canned garbanzo beans, rinsed and drained

⅓ cup golden raisins

¼ cup sliced green onions

1 large bell pepper, chopped (may mix red and green peppers)

¼ cup chopped fresh basil

¼ cup chopped fresh parsley

4 tablespoons slivered almonds

DIJON VINAIGRETTE

⅓ cup extra virgin olive oil

¼ cup white wine vinegar

1 tablespoon honey

1 tablespoon Dijon mustard

½ teaspoon salt

¼ teaspoon pepper

Chicken Summer Salad with Organic Long Grain Brown Rice

1 **LUNDBERG® HEAT & EAT ORGANIC Long Grain Brown Rice Bowl**, unheated

1 boneless, skinless chicken breast, cooked and cut into 1-inch cubes

⅓ cup julienned sun-dried tomatoes, drained

1 tablespoon chopped kalamata olives

2 tablespoons vinaigrette dressing

1 tablespoon fresh parsley

Lettuce greens

PREP: 15 minutes

YIELD: 2 servings

In a large bowl, combine rice, chicken, sun-dried tomatoes, olives, vinaigrette, and parsley. Toss well. Place lettuce greens on two plates. Divide rice and chicken mixture equally on the greens and serve.

Courtesy of Lundberg Family Farms

Chicken Couscous Salad

⅓ cup **LEA & PERRINS® Worcestershire Sauce**

1 teaspoon **WYLER'S® Chicken Flavored Granules**

1 (10- to 12-oz.) box couscous

4 cups diced fresh vegetables, such as zucchini, peppers, and tomatoes

¼ cup diced dried apricots

¼ cup chopped green onions

4 cooked boneless chicken breast, cut in strips

PREP: 25 minutes

YIELD: 4 servings

In a large bowl, combine Worcestershire Sauce, granules, and 1 cup of boiling water, stirring until dissolved. Add couscous and mix well. Stir in vegetables, apricots, and green onions. Cover tightly and let stand for 15 minutes. Stir in chicken and serve warm, or cover and chill until ready to serve.

COOK'S TIP

Since apricots stick to the knife, making them difficult to dice, use kitchen shears. It's an easier and safer way to cut them.

SERVING SUGGESTIONS

Couscous is a granular semolina that varies from country to country. Moroccans include saffron, Algerians like to add tomatoes, and Tunisians spice theirs up. Couscous may be served with milk, as porridge, or with vegetables, as in this salad recipe.

Courtesy of H.J. Heinz Company, L.P.

Balsamic Chicken Salad

PREP: 10 minutes

YIELD: 4 servings

In bowl, combine chicken, peppers, and cheese. Drizzle with dressing and toss until evenly coated. Serve over salad greens.

Courtesy of Perdue Farms, Inc.

1 (12-oz.) package **PERDUE® SHORT CUTS® Carved Chicken Breast, Original Roasted**

1 (7-oz.) jar roasted red peppers, drained and coarsely chopped

4 oz. mozzarella, cubed

¼ cup bottled balsamic vinaigrette

8 cups salad greens

Citrus-Spinach Salad with Chicken and Smoked Almonds

1 (10-oz.) package baby spinach leaves (about 8 cups)

¾ lb. boneless skinless chicken breast, cooked, cut into strips

2 medium clementines, peeled, sectioned

¼ cup thinly sliced red onion, separated into rings

½ cup **KRAFT FREE Honey Dijon Dressing**

½ cup **PLANTERS Smoked Almonds**, coarsely chopped

PREP: 20 minutes

YIELD: 4 (2 ½-cup) servings

Toss spinach with chicken, clementines, and onion in large salad bowl. Add dressing; mix lightly. Sprinkle with almonds.

Courtesy of Kraft Foods

Chicken Salad with Greens and Grape Vinaigrette

PREP: 20 minutes

YIELD: 4 servings, 1 ½ cups vinaigrette

FOR THE GRAPE VINAIGRETTE: Mix all the ingredients in a jar or bowl. Store in refrigerator.

FOR THE SALAD: Place salad greens and dill on serving platter. Top with chicken and almonds. Dress with grape vinaigrette. Serve.

COOK'S TIPS

- If fresh tomatoes taste too tart, sprinkle a tablespoon of grape juice over them to sweeten them up.

- Use this grape vinaigrette to pan cook fish or chicken.

Courtesy of Welch Foods Inc., A Cooperative

GRAPE VINAIGRETTE

1 orange, peeled and chopped

¼ cup chopped red onion

¼ cup chopped fresh parsley

½ cup **WELCH'S WHITE GRAPE JUICE**

¼ cup **WELCH'S PURPLE GRAPE JUICE**

¼ cup lemon juice

¼ cup olive oil

Salt to taste

Fresh ground black pepper to taste

SALAD

8 cups mixed salad greens

2 or 3 sprigs dill

1 cup of cooked chicken breast, cut in chunks

1 tablespoon sliced or slivered almonds

Mandarin Orange Chicken Salad

PREP: 20 minutes

YIELD: 4 servings

Combine salad blend, chicken, mandarin oranges, pea pods, green onions, and almonds in large bowl. Pour dressing over salad; toss to evenly coat. Sprinkle noodles over salad; serve.

Courtesy of Dole Food Company

1 (12-oz.) package **DOLE® American Salad Blend** or any variety

3 boneless, skinless chicken breasts, cooked, shredded, or chopped (9 oz.)

1 (11- or 15-oz.) can **DOLE Mandarin Oranges**, drained

½ cup pea pods or bean sprouts (optional)

¼ cup chopped **DOLE Green Onions**

¼ cup slivered almonds, toasted

½ cup oriental or oriental chicken salad dressing

½ cup chow mein noodles or fried wonton strips

Black Bean and Mango Chicken Salad

½ lb. boneless skinless chicken breasts, grilled, cut up

1 (16-oz.) can black beans, drained, rinsed

1 (10-oz.) package frozen corn, thawed

1 cup chopped ripe mango

½ cup chopped red pepper

⅓ cup chopped red onion

⅓ cup chopped cilantro

¼ cup lime juice

1 envelope **GOOD SEASONS Italian Dressing Mix**

PREP: 20 minutes

YIELD: 4 servings

Toss all ingredients in large bowl. Refrigerate. Serve with baked tortilla chips, if desired.

Courtesy of Kraft Foods

Warm Chicken Salad with Tangerine, Tarragon & Arugula

CHICKEN

12 oz. chicken breasts, boneless and skinless

2 tablespoons fresh tarragon leaves

¼ cup **TROPICANA Pure Premium Tangerine Orange Juice**

½ teaspoon minced garlic

¼ teaspoon kosher salt

½ teaspoon freshly ground black pepper

1 teaspoon olive oil

1 cup **TROPICANA Pure Premium Tangerine Orange Juice**

1 small red onion, peeled and thinly sliced in rings

SAUCE

¾ cup **TROPICANA Pure Premium Tangerine Orange Juice**

2 tablespoons red wine vinegar

1 teaspoon olive oil

1 teaspoon Dijon mustard

½ teaspoon chopped garlic

¼ teaspoon salt

¼ teaspoon black pepper

1 tablespoon fresh tarragon leaves

6 cups arugula, washed and dried

1 (11-oz.) can mandarin orange slices, drained (1 cup)

1 tablespoon fresh tarragon leaves

PREP: 15 minutes

COOK: 10 minutes

YIELD: 4 servings

FOR THE CHICKEN: Place chicken breasts in a large bowl. Season the chicken with tarragon, ¼ cup **TROPICANA Pure Premium Tangerine Orange Juice**, garlic, salt, and pepper. Warm olive oil in large sauté pan; add chicken breast and sauté over medium heat for 3 to 4 minutes. Turn chicken breast over; add 1 cup Tangerine Orange Juice, simmering for 4 to 5 minutes until cooked through.

FOR THE SAUCE: In a medium bowl whisk together Tangerine Orange Juice, red wine vinegar, olive oil, Dijon mustard, garlic, salt, pepper, and tarragon. Arrange arugula on the plates along with a warm chicken breast, onions, and mandarin orange slices. Drizzle with salad dressing sauce. Garnish each chicken breast with remaining tarragon leaves.

Courtesy of Tropicana Products, Inc.

Warm Chicken Salad

1 (14 ½ oz.) can **DEL MONTE® Diced Tomatoes with Garlic & Onion**, drained

¼ cup olive oil

3 tablespoons balsamic vinegar

1 small clove garlic, minced

4 skinless, boneless chicken breast halves

Salt and pepper (optional)

6 cups washed salad greens

½ cup red cabbage, shredded

½ cup diced cucumber

½ cup sliced mushrooms

1 (14 ½ oz.) can **DEL MONTE® FreshCut® Cut Green Beans**

PREP: 10 minutes

COOK: 10 minutes

YIELD: 4 servings

For dressing, combine tomatoes, oil, vinegar, and garlic. Season chicken with salt and pepper, if desired. Grill or broil chicken. Slice chicken diagonally and arrange on bed of salad greens with cabbage, cucumber, mushrooms, and beans. Top with tomato dressing.

Courtesy of Del Monte Foods

Warm Chicken Taco Salad

PREP: 15 minutes

COOK: 10 minutes

YIELD: 4 servings

Cook chicken in 2 tablespoons of the dressing in large skillet on medium-high heat 5 minutes, stirring occasionally. Reduce heat to medium. Stir in remaining dressing, the tomato, and seasoning mix. Cook and stir 5 minutes or until chicken is cooked through. Place chips on large serving platter; top with layers of lettuce, chicken mixture, cheese, olives, and onions.

Courtesy of Kraft Foods

TACO BELL® and HOME ORIGINALS® are trademarks owned and licensed by Taco Bell Corp.

4 small boneless skinless chicken breast halves (1 lb.), cut into thin strips

⅓ cup **MIRACLE WHIP Dressing**, divided

1 cup chopped tomato

1 (1 ¼-oz.) package **TACO BELL® HOME ORIGINALS® Taco Seasoning Mix**

4 cups tortilla chips

4 cups shredded lettuce

1 cup **KRAFT Shredded Sharp Cheddar Cheese**

¼ cup sliced pitted ripe olives

¼ cup green onion slices

Cobb Pasta Salad

PREP: 20 minutes

YIELD: 8 servings

FOR THE DRESSING: In a medium bowl combine Parmesan, yogurt, avocado, lime juice, apple cider vinegar, olive oil, and garlic. Refrigerate 30 minutes until ready to serve.

FOR THE SALAD: Cook penne according to package directions. In a large pot bring 3 to 4 cups of water to a boil. Add the fresh corn and cook 4 to 8 minutes. Scrape the kernels from the cob. If using frozen corn, cook according to package directions. On a platter arrange baby greens. Toss penne with half of the yogurt dressing. Place pasta on salad greens. Arrange turkey, avocado slices, corn, eggs, and crumbled bacon over pasta. Top with remaining dressing.

Courtesy of Stonyfield Farm

DRESSING

1 cup shredded Parmesan

½ cup **STONYFIELD FARM Plain Yogurt**

½ ripe avocado, peeled

2 tablespoons lime juice

1 teaspoon apple cider vinegar

1 teaspoon extra virgin olive oil

1 clove garlic, minced

SALAD

3 cups cooked penne pasta

2 ears fresh corn or 1 cup frozen corn

2 cups baby greens

½ lb. smoked turkey deli slices, rolled

2 avocados, sliced

2 hard-cooked eggs, cut into wedges

6 slices of bacon, cooked, drained, and crumbled

Harvest Salad to Go

½ cup Granny Smith apple wedges

2 tablespoons **KRAFT Light Ranch Dressing**

¼ cup seedless red grapes

4 slices **OSCAR MAYER Deli Fresh Shaved Oven Roasted Turkey Breast**, cut into strips

2 cups torn mixed salad greens

¼ cup **KRAFT 2% Milk Colby & Monterey Jack Cheese Crumbles**

1 ½ teaspoons **OSCAR MAYER Real Bacon Bits**

PREP: 5 minutes

YIELD: 1 serving

Place apples in resealable container. Add dressing; toss to coat. Top with layers of remaining ingredients; seal container. Toss salad just before serving.

Courtesy of Kraft Foods

Grilled Steak Salad with Creamy Avocado Dressing

PREP: 15 minutes

COOK: 14 minutes

YIELD: 4 servings

Preheat grill to medium-high heat. Sprinkle steak with chili powder. Grill 5 to 7 minutes on each side or until medium doneness (160°F). Remove from grill; cover loosely with foil. Let stand 5 minutes. Meanwhile, toss greens with tomatoes, onions, and olives; place on serving platter. Place dressing and avocado in blender; cover. Blend until smooth. Cut steak across the grain into thin slices; place over salad. Drizzle with dressing mixture. Serve with the crackers.

Courtesy of Kraft Foods

1 lb. boneless beef sirloin steak

Dash of chili powder

8 cups torn mixed salad greens

1 cup cherry tomatoes, halved

¼ cup sliced red onions

¼ cup sliced black olives

¼ cup **KRAFT Light House Italian Dressing**

½ of a medium ripe avocado, peeled, pitted

20 **PREMIUM Saltine Crackers**

Summer Pork and Vegetable Garden Salad

3 boneless pork chops, cut into ½-inch cubes

2 tablespoons low-sodium soy sauce

1 tablespoon water

10 small red new potatoes, quartered

½ lb. fresh green beans, trimmed and cut into ½-inch lengths

1 medium summer squash or zucchini, thinly sliced

8 cherry tomatoes, halved

¾ cup fat-free Italian dressing

2 teaspoons vegetable oil

6 cups shredded iceberg lettuce

PREP: 10 minutes

COOK: 20 minutes

YIELD: 4 servings

In medium self-sealing bag combine pork cubes, soy sauce, and water; seal bag and set aside. Cover potatoes with water in saucepan; bring to boil and simmer for 12 to 15 minutes until potatoes are just tender, adding green beans to simmering water during last 5 to 7 minutes. Drain; place in large bowl with squash and tomatoes. Pour dressing over vegetables; toss lightly. Drain pork cubes, discarding marinade. In large skillet heat oil over medium-high heat; stir-fry pork for 4 to 5 minutes or until nicely browned. Remove from heat. Arrange shredded lettuce on individual plates. Spoon vegetable mixture over lettuce and top with pork cubes.

Courtesy of National Pork Board

Classic Romaine with Country Ham, Apple, and Sour Cream Dressing

½ cup light sour cream

1 tablespoon apple cider vinegar

1 tablespoon maple syrup

2 teaspoons Dijon-style mustard

2 tablespoons vegetable oil

Salt and black pepper

1 (10-oz.) package **DOLE® Classic Romaine Salad Blend**

2 **DOLE Red Apples**, cored and cut into cubes

½ cup pecans, toasted, coarsely chopped

8 oz. boneless ham, thinly cut into 1-inch long strips (about 2 cups)

PREP: 20 minutes

YIELD: 4 to 6 servings

Mix sour cream, vinegar, maple syrup, and mustard in small bowl. Whisk in oil and season with salt and pepper. Combine salad blend, apples, pecans, and ham in medium bowl. Add dressing; gently toss to evenly coat.

Courtesy of Dole Food Company

Little Lettuces with Hard-Cooked Eggs & Ham

PREP: 15 minutes

COOK: 10 minutes

YIELD: 4 servings

FOR THE SALAD: Wash the lettuce in a large bowl or a sink full of cold water, lifting the leaves out of the water, leaving any dirt to settle on the bottom of the bowl or sink. Shake off any water from the leaves or use a salad spinner, wrap the leaves in paper towels, then store in plastic bags in the refrigerator. Greens can be prepped several days ahead of use.

FOR THE EGGS: Mix together the mayonnaise and mustard in a small bowl. Thickly spread the cut side of the eggs with the mayonnaise and season with pepper to your taste. (Here's a tip: Put 8 dabs of mayonnaise on a dinner plate. Set the eggs on top of the "dabs" to hold them steady and keep them upright.) Pile the chopped ham on top of each egg and garnish generously with chives. Set aside while you make the dressing.

FOR THE SALAD DRESSING: Puree the garlic and anchovy together in a mortar and pestle or a food processor. (Tip: You can also simply use a heavy knife to chop and mash the anchovy, garlic and parsley together on a cutting board. Add a little kosher salt to add "grit," which will help the chopping process. Then transfer to a small bowl and continue.) Add the lemon juice and oil, whisking everything together until emulsified. Season to your taste with salt and pepper. Stir in the chopped parsley.

TO ASSEMBLE THE SALAD: Put the lettuce in a large bowl, add the dressing, and toss together until the leaves are well coated. Arrange the dressed lettuce on individual plates or a large platter and add the eggs.

Courtesy of Applegate Farms, an Organic & Natural Meat Company

SALAD GREENS

4 handfuls young spring lettuces, like arugula, Lola Rosa, or any other little leaves you find in the market

EGGS

2 tablespoons mayonnaise

2 teaspoons Dijon mustard

4 hard-cooked eggs, peeled and halved

Freshly ground black pepper

1 (4-oz.) package **APPLEGATE FARMS Ham**, finely chopped

¼ cup finely chopped fresh chives

SALAD DRESSING

1 small garlic clove, peeled and minced

1 anchovy filet or a small dollop of anchovy paste

Juice of half a lemon, or more if you like

¼ cup extra-virgin olive oil

Salt and freshly ground black pepper

A handful of parsley leaves, finely chopped

Surfing Shrimp Salad

2 lbs. cooked medium-size shrimp

2 stalks **DOLE® Celery**, chopped

½ small **DOLE Red Onion**, finely chopped

1 large **DOLE Red Apple**, cored and chopped

½ cup chopped fresh **DOLE Tropical Gold® Pineapple**

½ cup **DOLE Golden Raisins**

½ cup sliced almonds

Pepper to taste

½ teaspoon poppy seed

½ teaspoon curry powder

1 cup light mayonnaise

PREP: 15 minutes

YIELD: 10 servings

Combine shrimp, celery, onion, apple, pineapple, raisins, almonds, pepper, poppy seed, curry powder, and mayonnaise in large bowl. Mix together, tossing to coat. Garnish with additional almonds, if desired.

COOK'S TIP

Very pretty when served in half of a scooped out pineapple shell!

Courtesy of Dole Food Company

Light Caesar with Smoked Salmon Pita Pizza Triangles

PREP: 15 minutes

COOK: 10 minutes

YIELD: 3 servings

Preheat oven to 400°F. Lightly brush one side of pita breads with oil. Sprinkle onion on each pita bread. Bake for 5 to 7 minutes or until pita crisps around edges. Top each pita with salmon slices; sprinkle with dill. Return to oven until the salmon is warmed through, about 2 minutes. Cut pita pizzas into quarters. Combine salad and croutons in large bowl. Add prepared dressing, and toss to coat. Divide salad between 3 plates and arrange 4 pizza triangles over salad.

Courtesy of Dole Food Company

3 (6-inch) pita breads

2 teaspoons olive oil

½ cup thinly sliced red onion

4 oz. sliced smoked salmon, divided into 3 portions

2 tablespoons chopped fresh dill

1 (12-oz.) package **DOLE® Light Caesar Salad Kit**

Salmon & Cheddar Farfalle Salad

PASTA

3 ½ oz. (2 cups) uncooked dried farfalle (bow tie pasta)

SALAD DRESSING

6 tablespoons red wine vinegar

2 tablespoons chopped fresh basil leaves

1 tablespoon water

1 teaspoon sugar

⅛ teaspoon coarsely ground pepper

SALAD

2 cups fresh spinach leaves

6 cherry tomatoes, cut in half (½ cup)

½ cucumber, scored, sliced ¼-inch thick (1 cup)

4 (¾-oz.) slices **LAND O LAKES® Deli Cheddar Cheese**, cut into 2 x ¼-inch strips

1 (4.5-oz.) package smoked salmon, torn into bite-size pieces

PREP: 20 minutes

COOK: 10 minutes

YIELD: 6 (1 ½-cup) servings

Cook pasta according to package directions. Rinse with cold water. Drain. Set aside. Combine all dressing ingredients in small bowl; mix well. Combine cooked pasta with salad ingredients in large bowl. Drizzle salad dressing over salad; toss gently.

Courtesy of Land O'Lakes, Inc.

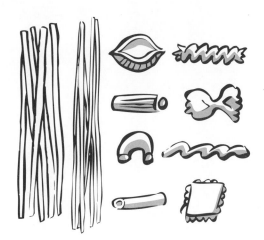

Asian Salmon Salad

PREP: 15 minutes

YIELD: 4 servings

Stir the ketchup with teriyaki sauce, lime juice, sesame oil, and brown sugar until well blended. Reserve. Place the salad greens in a large bowl. Separate the salmon into large chunks. Add salmon to the bowl along with the carrot, cucumber, cilantro leaves, and radish. Toss gently with enough dressing to coat the ingredients. Add more dressing to taste. Sprinkle with sesame seeds just before serving.

Courtesy of H.J. Heinz Company, L.P.

¼ cup **HEINZ® Tomato Ketchup**

3 tablespoons teriyaki sauce

2 tablespoons lime juice

2 tablespoons sesame oil

2 tablespoons brown sugar

8 cups lightly packed mesclun (salad greens)

2 (7-oz.) cans salmon, skin and bones removed

1 cup thinly sliced carrot

1 cup thinly sliced cucumber

¼ cup lightly packed cilantro leaves

¼ cup sliced radish

1 teaspoon toasted sesame seeds

Asian Sesame Salad with Seared Tuna

2 (4-oz.) tuna steaks

2 teaspoons olive oil

½ teaspoon cracked black pepper (optional)

2 cups baby spinach leaves

1 cup shredded green cabbage

1 cup shredded red cabbage

1 cup shredded carrots

¼ cup sliced green onions

¼ cup **KRAFT GOOD SEASONS Asian Sesame with Ginger Dressing**

¼ cup **PLANTERS COCKTAIL Peanuts**

PREP: 15 minutes

COOK: 8 minutes

YIELD: 2 servings

Preheat grill to medium heat. Brush tuna steaks with olive oil; season with pepper, if desired. Grill tuna 3 to 4 minutes on each side for medium-rare doneness. Remove from grill; cover to keep warm. Place spinach in large bowl. Add cabbages, carrots, and onions; mix lightly. Add dressing; toss to coat. Place on serving platter. Cut tuna into slices; place on top of salad. Sprinkle with the peanuts.

Courtesy of Kraft Foods

Tossed Italian Salad with Tuna

2 cups sliced plum tomatoes

1 (14-oz.) can artichoke hearts, drained, coarsely chopped

1 (12-oz.) can white tuna in water, drained, flaked

1 (10-oz.) package salad greens

½ lb. fresh green beans, cooked, drained, and halved (2 cups)

1 cup **KRAFT 2% Milk Shredded Mozzarella Cheese**

½ cup **KRAFT Roasted Red Pepper Italian with Parmesan Dressing**

PREP: 15 minutes

YIELD: 4 servings

Toss all ingredients except dressing in large bowl. Add dressing just before serving; mix lightly.

Courtesy of Kraft Foods

Vegetarian Melts

4 slices **NATURE'S OWN 100% Whole Wheat Bread**

⅓ cup mayonnaise

2 tablespoons prepared pesto sauce

1 avocado, sliced

1 (7-oz.) jar roasted red peppers, drained, cut into ½-inch strips

⅓ cup thinly sliced red onion

1 cup sliced mushrooms

½ cup shredded Monterey Jack

Alfalfa sprouts (optional)

PREP: 13 minutes

COOK: 7 minutes

YIELD: 4 servings

Lightly toast one side of the bread slices under broiler. Meanwhile, combine mayonnaise and pesto in small bowl. Spread 1 tablespoon pesto mixture on untoasted side of each bread slice, making sure to spread it slightly over edges of bread. (There will be some pesto mixture left over.) Broil 1 to 2 minutes or until golden. Layer avocado, red pepper, onion, and mushrooms over pesto side of bread slices, dividing evenly. Brush remaining pesto mixture over the tops of the sandwiches. Broil for 2 minutes. Sprinkle 2 tablespoons cheese over top of each sandwich. Return to broiler for 3 minutes or until cheese is melted and golden. If desired, top sandwiches with sprouts before serving.

Courtesy of Flowers Foods

Portobello Cheddar Melts

PREP: 14 minutes

COOK: 16 minutes

YIELD: 4 servings

Heat 1 tablespoon oil in 12-inch nonstick skillet over medium-high heat. Add onion and thyme; cook 7 minutes, stirring often. Add vinegar; continue cooking 3 minutes or until onion is tender and lightly browned. Season with salt, as desired. Remove from skillet. Spread cut sides of bagels evenly with butter; place buttered sides down in same skillet. Cook over medium heat 3 minutes or until toasted. Meanwhile preheat broiler. Brush mushrooms on both sides with remaining 1 tablespoon oil; season with salt and pepper. Arrange, bottom sides up, on foil-lined baking sheet. Broil 3 minutes; turn and broil 2 minutes. Top each mushroom with 1 slice cheese; broil 1 minute or until cheese melts. Divide half of onions evenly over toasted bagel halves. Top each with tomato slice; season with salt and pepper. Place mushroom and remaining onions over tomato. Serve with desired condiments.

Courtesy of Flowers Foods

2 tablespoons olive oil, divided

1 large Vidalia or other sweet onion, thinly sliced (about 3 ½ cups)

½ teaspoon dried thyme

1 tablespoon red wine vinegar

Salt

2 **NATURE'S OWN Everything Bagels**, split

2 tablespoons butter, softened

4 large (4- to 5-inch-diameter) portobello mushrooms, stems removed

Pepper

4 slices Cheddar cheese

4 large slices tomato

Pacific Rim Wraps with Creamy Citrus Ginger Dressing

PREP: 20 minutes

YIELD: 6 servings

FOR THE DRESSING: Place evaporated milk, lemon juice, oil, sugar, ginger, salt, and black pepper in small jar or resealable container; cover with lid. Shake well until blended. Makes 1 cup.

FOR THE SALAD: Combine salad greens, chicken, carrots, sugar snap peas, dried cranberries, and almonds, if using, in large bowl. Add ⅔ cup dressing; toss until evenly coated. Place 1 cup salad mixture on each tortilla. Roll up tightly. Cut in half and serve along with remaining dressing, if desired. Or wrap each in wax paper, foil, or plastic wrap and refrigerate to eat later.

COOK'S TIPS

• Dressing can be made a day ahead and refrigerated. Shake well before using.

• Use precooked grilled chicken strips to save time.

• Look for prepackaged matchstick carrots in your local store's produce section.

Courtesy of Nestlé USA

DRESSING

⅔ cup (5 fl. oz. can) **NESTLÉ® CARNATION® Evaporated Milk**

5 tablespoons lemon juice

¼ cup vegetable oil

3 tablespoons granulated sugar

2 teaspoons ground ginger

1 teaspoon salt

¼ teaspoon ground black pepper

SALAD

1 (6.5-oz.) package or 4 cups washed salad greens

3 cups shredded cooked chicken (2 or 3 boneless, skinless chicken breast halves)

1 cup matchstick or shredded carrots

1 cup fresh sugar snap pea pods, cut in half

½ cup sweetened dried cranberries

¼ cup toasted slivered almonds (optional)

6 (8-inch) flour tortillas

Asian Chicken Sandwiches

¼ cup peanut butter

2 tablespoons chopped green onions

1 tablespoon reduced sodium soy sauce

1 teaspoon sesame oil

4 slices **NATURE'S OWN Honey Wheat Bread**

¼ cup shredded carrots

½ cup thinly sliced English hothouse cucumber (16 slices)

¼ cup cilantro leaves or to taste

1 cup shredded cooked chicken breast

PREP: 25 minutes

YIELD: 2 servings

Combine peanut butter, green onions, soy sauce, and sesame oil in small bowl. Spread evenly over bread slices. Layer 2 bread slices evenly with carrots, half of the cucumber, cilantro, chicken, and remaining cucumber. Top with remaining bread slices, peanut butter side down.

COOK'S TIP

Save time by purchasing a rotisserie chicken from the supermarket.

Courtesy of Flowers Foods

Chicken, Grape & Pecan Salad Sandwiches

PREP: 25 minutes

YIELD: 6 servings

Combine mayonnaise, lemon juice, tarragon, salt, and pepper in large bowl. Add chicken, grapes, celery, onion, and pecans; mix lightly to coat. Line each of 6 muffin halves with spinach leaves. Top evenly with chicken salad. Close sandwiches.

Courtesy of Flowers Foods

⅔ cup light mayonnaise

1 tablespoon lemon juice

1 teaspoon dried tarragon

⅛ teaspoon salt

⅛ teaspoon pepper

1 ½ cups diced cooked chicken breast

¾ cup seedless red grapes, cut in half

½ cup thinly sliced celery

⅓ cup thinly sliced red onion

⅓ cup chopped pecans

6 **NATURE'S OWN 100 Calorie Multigrain English Muffins**, split, toasted

Fresh baby spinach leaves

Spicy Chicken Chipotle Sandwiches

⅓ cup mayonnaise

1 canned chipotle pepper, minced

8 chicken tenders (about 1 lb.)

¼ teaspoon salt

¼ teaspoon chili powder

¼ teaspoon ground black pepper

1 tablespoon vegetable oil

4 **COBBLESTONE MILL Potato Hot Dog Rolls**, toasted

Baby spinach leaves

½ small red onion, thinly sliced (optional)

4 slices crisp-cooked bacon

Plum tomato slices

PREP: 14 minutes

COOK: 10 minutes

YIELD: 4 servings

For chipotle mayonnaise, combine mayonnaise and chipotle pepper in small bowl. Set aside. Place chicken tenders on large plate. Combine salt, chili powder, and black pepper in small bowl. Sprinkle mixture onto both sides of chicken tenders. Heat oil in large skillet over medium-high heat. Add chicken; cook about 8 minutes, turning once, until chicken is cooked through. Spread toasted rolls with chipotle mayonnaise. Arrange spinach on each roll bottom. Top with onion slices, if desired. Arrange 2 chicken tenders on each roll. Top with one slice bacon and tomato slices. Close sandwiches.

Courtesy of Flowers Food

Chipotle Turkey Sandwiches

PREP: 15 minutes

YIELD: 2 servings

Combine mayonnaise and peppers in small bowl. Spread evenly over bread slices. Layer 2 bread slices evenly with turkey, tomato, avocado, and cheese. Top with remaining bread slices, mayonnaise side down.

COOK'S TIP

Freeze leftover chipotle peppers in single layer on waxed-paper-lined baking sheet. Transfer frozen peppers to plastic freezer bag and store in freezer. Remove single peppers as needed.

Courtesy of Flowers Foods

⅓ cup light mayonnaise

2 teaspoons minced chipotle peppers in adobo sauce, or to taste

4 slices **NATURE'S OWN All Natural 12-Grain Bread**

6 oz. deli-sliced smoked turkey

4 thin tomato slices

1 small avocado, sliced

2 (1-oz.) slices Co-Jack cheese

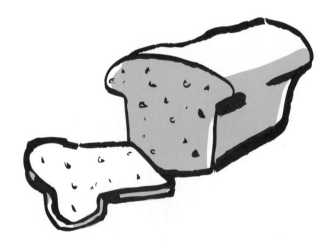

Mediterranean Turkey Rolls

1 tablespoon fresh lemon juice

1 clove garlic, crushed

½ teaspoon dried basil leaves

⅛ teaspoon salt

⅛ teaspoon black pepper

1 tablespoon extra virgin olive oil

6 oz. oven-roasted turkey breast, cut into 2 x ¼-inch strips

⅓ cup thinly sliced seeded English hothouse cucumber

⅓ cup thinly sliced red onion

¼ cup chopped roasted red pepper

Shredded lettuce

4 **NATURE'S OWN 100% Whole Wheat Hot Dog Rolls,** toasted

¼ cup crumbled feta

PREP: 25 minutes

YIELD: 4 servings

Combine lemon juice, garlic, basil, salt, and black pepper in medium bowl. Whisk oil in gradually. Add turkey, cucumber, onion, and red pepper to bowl; toss gently to coat with vinaigrette. Divide lettuce and turkey mixture evenly among toasted rolls. Top with cheese.

Courtesy of Flowers Foods

Turkey Caesar Salad Sandwiches

PREP: 20 minutes

COOK: 2 minutes

YIELD: 4 servings

Preheat broiler. Combine mayonnaise and dressing in medium bowl. Add lettuce, turkey, and red pepper; toss to coat with dressing mixture. Set aside. Brush cut sides of rolls lightly with oil; sprinkle evenly with garlic powder and cheese. Place in single layer on baking sheet. Broil 2 minutes or until toasted. Divide chicken salad evenly among roll bottoms. Close sandwiches.

Courtesy of Flowers Foods

3 tablespoons mayonnaise

3 tablespoons creamy Caesar dressing

1 ½ cups shredded romaine

1 ½ cups cubed oven-roasted turkey breast

⅓ cup chopped roasted red pepper

4 **COBBLESTONE MILL Sandwich Rolls**

1 tablespoon olive oil

½ teaspoon garlic powder

¼ cup grated Parmesan

Roast Beef, Caramelized Onion & Goat Cheese Panini

1 tablespoon olive oil

1 large Vidalia or other sweet onion, thinly sliced (about 4 cups)

1 ½ teaspoons dried Italian seasoning

1 tablespoon balsamic vinegar

Salt

4 oz. chèvre (goat cheese), softened

4 oz. light cream cheese, softened

8 slices **COBBLESTONE MILL New York Style Jewish Rye Bread**

¾ lb. deli-sliced roast beef

Olive oil

PREP: 20 minutes

COOK: 3 minutes

YIELD: 4 servings

Heat 1 tablespoon oil in large nonstick skillet over medium-high heat. Add onion and Italian seasoning; cook 10 minutes, stirring often. Add vinegar; continue cooking 2 to 5 minutes or until onion is tender and lightly browned. Season with salt, as desired. Meanwhile combine cheeses in small bowl. Spread one side of each bread slice evenly with 2 tablespoons cheese mixture. Layer each of 4 bread slices with ¼ of caramelized onions and roast beef. Top with remaining bread slice, cheese side down; press sandwich together slightly. Brush outside of sandwiches lightly with oil. Preheat panini grill according to manufacturer's instructions. Cook sandwiches 3 minutes or until browned and cheese melts.

COOK'S TIP

Onions may be cooked up to one day in advance. Refrigerate, covered, until ready to use. Reheat gently in microwave oven until slightly warm before assembling sandwiches.

Courtesy of Flowers Foods

Grilled Italian Sausage Sandwiches with Peppers & Onions

PREP: 10 minutes

COOK: 20 minutes

YIELD: 6 servings

Preheat grill to medium heat. Grill sausages, covered, 15 minutes or until cooked through (180°F), turning often. Meanwhile, heat oil in 12-inch skillet over medium-high heat. Add onion, bell peppers, and Italian seasoning; cook 10 minutes or until vegetables are tender, stirring often. Stir in garlic; cook 2 minutes. Remove from heat; stir in barbecue sauce and salt. Keep warm until ready to serve. Serve sausages in buns; top evenly with onions and peppers.

Courtesy of Flowers Foods

6 Italian sausage links (about 1 ½ lbs.)

1 tablespoon vegetable oil

1 large onion, cut in half, sliced ⅛-inch thick

1 large green bell pepper, cut into ¼ -inch strips

1 large red bell pepper, cut into ¼-inch strips

1 ½ teaspoons Italian seasoning

3 cloves garlic, minced

2 tablespoons barbecue sauce

Salt to taste

6 **NATURE'S OWN 100% Whole Wheat Hot Dog Rolls**

Smoked Ham, Pear & Cheddar Panini

¼ cup spicy brown mustard

8 slices **NATURE'S OWN Grains & Granola Specialty Bread**

8 slices sharp white Cheddar cheese

2 cups packed baby arugula

1 ripe Bartlett pear, cut into 20 thin slices

½ lb. deli-sliced smoked ham

Olive oil

PREP: 20 minutes

COOK: 6 minutes

YIELD: 4 servings

Spread mustard evenly over one side of each bread slice. Top 4 bread slices with 1 slice cheese each and half the arugula. Layer pear and ham slices over arugula. Top with remaining arugula, cheese, and bread slices; press sandwiches together slightly. Brush outside of sandwiches lightly with oil. Preheat panini grill according to manufacturer's instructions. Cook sandwiches 3 minutes or until browned and cheese melts.

SKILLET COOKING: Place sandwiches in large skillet over low heat. Cook, covered, 3 to 5 minutes per side or until browned and cheese melts, pressing down with spatula to slightly compress.

Courtesy of Flowers Foods

Shrimp, Cucumber & Radish Sandwiches

⅓ cup light mayonnaise

⅓ cup light sour cream

2 tablespoons finely chopped red onion

1 tablespoon lemon juice

¼ teaspoon dried dillweed

⅛ teaspoon salt

⅛ teaspoon pepper

8 slices **NATURE'S OWN Dark Multigrain Specialty Bread**

2 cups packed mixed baby greens

½ cup thinly sliced English hothouse cucumber

4 large radishes, thinly sliced

¾ lb. large cooked shelled shrimp, cut lengthwise in half

PREP: 25 minutes

YIELD: 4 servings

Combine mayonnaise, sour cream, red onion, lemon juice, dillweed, salt, and pepper in small bowl. Spread evenly over one side of each bread slice. Layer greens, cucumber, radishes, and shrimp evenly over 4 bread slices. Top with remaining bread slices, spread side down.

Courtesy of Flowers Foods

Salmon Caesar Salad Sandwiches

PREP: 10 minutes

COOK: 14 minutes

YIELD: 4 servings

Preheat broiler. Place salmon fillets skin side down on broiler pan. Season with salt and pepper. Broil 10 to 12 minutes or until fish turns opaque and is cooked through. Separate salmon into chunks with fork; cool slightly. Discard skin. Meanwhile brush cut sides of bagels lightly with oil; sprinkle evenly with garlic powder and cheese. Place in single layer on baking sheet. Broil about 2 minutes or until toasted. Combine mayonnaise and dressing in large bowl. Add salmon and lettuce; fold gently to combine. Divide salmon mixture evenly among bagel bottoms. Close sandwiches.

Courtesy of Flowers Foods

2 (6- to 7-oz.) salmon fillets

Salt

Pepper

4 **NATURE'S OWN 100% Whole Wheat Bagels**, split

2 tablespoons olive oil

½ teaspoon garlic powder

¼ cup grated Parmesan

¼ cup light mayonnaise

¼ cup creamy Caesar dressing

2 cups shredded romaine

Favorite Fishwiches

PREP: 14 minutes

COOK: 6 minutes

YIELD: 4 servings

Combine tartar sauce ingredients in small bowl; set aside. Brush both sides of fish fillets with 1 tablespoon oil; sprinkle with seasoning blend. Heat remaining 1 tablespoon oil in 12-inch nonstick skillet over medium heat until hot. Add fillets; cook about 3 minutes per side or until fish turns opaque. (If necessary, cook fish in 2 batches using half the oil with each batch.) Layer lettuce, tomato, and fillets on 4 bread slices. Top with tartar sauce. Close sandwiches.

Courtesy of Flowers Foods

OLD BAY® is a trademark of McCormick & Company, Inc.

TARTAR SAUCE

½ cup reduced-fat mayonnaise

2 tablespoons drained sweet pickle relish

1 tablespoon finely chopped onion

2 teaspoons lemon juice

SANDWICH

4 (4- to 5-oz.) tilapia fillets

2 tablespoons vegetable oil

1 tablespoon crab boil seasoning blend (such as **OLD BAY®** brand)

4 lettuce leaves

4 tomato slices

8 slices **NATURE'S OWN All Natural 100% Whole Wheat Bread**, toasted

Tuna, Artichoke, and Manchego Panini

1 (12-oz.) jar quartered marinated artichoke hearts

2 (6-oz.) cans tuna, drained

½ cup reduced-fat mayonnaise

⅓ cup sliced kalamata olives

8 slices **NATURE'S OWN 100% Whole Wheat Organic Bread**

8 oz. Manchego, shredded

3 plum tomatoes, sliced

Olive oil

PREP: 20 minutes

COOK: 3 minutes

YIELD: 4 servings

Drain artichokes, reserving 1 tablespoon marinade. Cut each artichoke quarter crosswise in half. Combine artichokes, tuna, mayonnaise, olives, and reserved marinade in medium bowl. Top each of 4 bread slices with ¼ cup cheese. Spread ¼ of tuna mixture evenly over cheese. Top each with tomato slices, another ¼ cup cheese, and bread slice; press sandwich together slightly. Brush outside of sandwiches lightly with oil. Preheat panini grill according to manufacturer's instructions. Cook sandwiches 3 minutes or until browned and cheese melts.

SKILLET COOKING: Place sandwiches in large skillet over low heat. Cook, covered, 3 to 5 minutes per side or until browned and cheese melts, pressing down with spatula to slightly compress.

Courtesy of Flowers Foods

Main Dishes

Nacho Pizza

1 cup **CONTADINA® Original Pizza Sauce**

¾ cup refried beans

12-inch prepared pizza crust

1 cup (4 oz.) shredded mozzarella

½ cup (2 oz.) shredded Cheddar cheese

¼ cup sliced ripe olives, drained

1 tablespoon diced green chilies

Tortilla chips (optional)

Fresh chopped cilantro (optional)

PREP: 10 minutes

COOK: 12 minutes

YIELD: 4 servings

Preheat oven according to pizza crust directions. Combine pizza sauce and beans in small saucepan. Cook, stirring constantly, over low heat for 1 to 2 minutes or until smooth. Spread sauce mixture over crust to within 1 inch of the edge; top with mozzarella, Cheddar cheese, olives, and chilies. Bake according to pizza crust package directions or until crust is crisp and cheese is melted. Garnish with tortilla chips and cilantro.

Courtesy of Del Monte Foods

Anytime Quesadilla

PREP: 10 minutes

COOK: 5 minutes

YIELD: 2 servings

Melt 1 tablespoon **SHEDD'S SPREAD COUNTRY CROCK® Plus Calcium Spread** in 12-inch skillet and cook 1 tortilla over medium heat until bottom is crispy, about 2 minutes. Spread tortilla with salsa, then sprinkle with cheese and olives; top with remaining tortilla. Spread tortilla with remaining 1 tablespoon Spread. Turn tortilla and cook until bottom is crispy and cheese is melted, about 2 minutes. Cut into wedges and serve immediately.

VARIATION

For a heartier meal, add ¼ cup cooked chicken.

Courtesy of Unilever

2 tablespoons **SHEDD'S SPREAD COUNTRY CROCK® Calcium plus Vitamin D**

2 (10-inch) burrito-size flour tortillas

⅓ cup prepared salsa

½ cup (2 oz.) reduced-fat shredded Cheddar cheese

2 tablespoons sliced pitted ripe olives (optional)

Fast & Easy Long Grain Brown Rice & Black Bean Burritos

PREP: 20 minutes

COOK: 10 minutes

YIELD: 6 servings

Empty **LUNDBERG® Heat & Eat Rice Bowls** into a large bowl and separate the rice grains. Heat olive oil in a large skillet over medium-high heat. Add onion, garlic, chili powder, and cumin. Sauté 5 minutes until onion is tender. Stir in rice, beans, and corn and heat until warmed through. Remove from heat. To assemble, spoon ½ cup rice and bean mixture down the center of a warmed tortilla. Garnish with Cheddar cheese, green onions, salsa, and a tablespoon of yogurt. Roll up tortilla and top with additional salsa.

Courtesy of Lundberg Family Farms

2 **LUNDBERG® Heat & Eat Organic Long Grain Brown Rice Bowls**

1 tablespoon olive oil

½ medium onion, finely chopped

2 cloves garlic, pressed

1 ½ teaspoons chili powder

½ teaspoon ground cumin

1 (15-oz.) can black beans, rinsed and drained

1 (8.75-oz.) can whole kernel corn, drained, or 1 cup frozen corn, thawed

6 (8-inch) whole wheat flour tortillas, warmed

6 oz. (¾ cup) shredded Cheddar cheese (for garnish)

2 or 3 green onions, sliced (for garnish)

Salsa (for garnish)

Plain yogurt (for garnish)

The Woodward Veggyburger

⅓ cup sunflower seeds

⅓ cup cashews

⅓ cup raw walnuts

⅓ cut raw almonds

1 cup chopped onion

2 tablespoons minced garlic

2 tablespoons **NEWMAN'S OWN® ORGANICS Olive Oil**, divided

2 teaspoons dried basil or 3 tablespoons fresh basil, minced

2 cups cooked short grain brown rice

¼ cup tamari or soy sauce

⅔ cup tahini (sesame seed paste)

Pita bread or burger buns

Ketchup, mustard, or relish

What do you do when your husband was a hamburger devotee and you are inclined toward vegetarianism? Well, if you're Joanne Woodward, you turn to your oldest daughter Nell, and together invent the Veggyburger. It looks like a Newmanburger, but contains no meat and can nestle in a bun, just as appealingly as a ground chuck special.

PREP: 12 minutes

CHILL: 1 hour

COOK: 18 minutes

YIELD: 6 to 8 servings

Lightly toast sunflower seeds and nuts in frying pan until browned and fragrant. Cool nuts and grind in blender or electric spice grinder. Sauté onion and garlic in 1 table-spoon olive oil until lightly browned. Using large mixing bowl, add basil, rice, and ground nuts, and combine with tamari and tahini. Refrigerate for 1 hour and shape into patties. Brown in a nonstick pan with the remaining table-spoon of olive oil over medium heat, 3 to 5 minutes on each side depending on patty size. Serve in pita bread or on burger buns. Top with your favorite condiments or my father's favorite, a ripe summer tomato.

Courtesy of Nell Newman, Co-Founder and President, Newman's Own Organics

Cheese Ravioli with Pumpkin Sage Sauce

½ cup dry white wine

¼ cup chopped shallots

1 (10-oz.) container **BUITONI Refrigerated Alfredo Sauce**

½ cup **LIBBY'S® 100% Pure Pumpkin**

1 tablespoon chopped fresh sage or 1 teaspoon ground sage

2 (9-oz.) packages **BUITONI Refrigerated Four Cheese Ravioli**

2 tablespoons chopped green onion

Freshly ground black pepper

PREP: 10 minutes

COOK: 15 minutes

YIELD: 4 servings

Cook wine and shallots in medium saucepan over medium heat, stirring occasionally, until reduced to about 1 tablespoon. Stir in sauce, pumpkin, and sage. Cook, stirring occasionally, until heated through. Prepare pasta according to package directions; drain, reserving ¼ cup cooking water. Stir reserved water into sauce; toss with pasta. Sprinkle with green onion. Season with ground black pepper.

Courtesy of Nestlé USA

Whole Wheat Cheese Ravioli, Marinara Sauce and Fresh Asparagus

PREP: 10 minutes

COOK: 10 minutes

YIELD: 3 servings

Heat sauce according to package directions. Stir in basil, if using. Prepare pasta according to package directions. During last 3 minutes of cooking time, add asparagus and bell pepper and cook until vegetables are crisp-tender; drain. Add sauce to pasta and vegetables; gently toss. Serve immediately with cheese.

Courtesy of Flowers Foods

1 (15-oz.) container **BUITONI Refrigerated Marinara Sauce**

1 tablespoon finely chopped fresh basil (optional)

1 (9-oz.) package **BUITONI Refrigerated Whole Wheat Four Cheese Ravioli**

1 lb. fresh asparagus, cut into 1-inch pieces (about 2 cups)

½ cup sliced red bell pepper

BUITONI Refrigerated Freshly Shredded Parmesan Cheese (optional)

Fettuccine with Vegetables

16 oz. fettuccine

6 cups broccoli florets

3 cups sliced carrots

2 cups julienned red peppers

1 cup sliced red onion

1 teaspoon **FRONTIER** oregano

1 teaspoon **FRONTIER** black pepper (medium grind)

1 teaspoon olive oil

4 tablespoons Parmesan

½ teaspoon **FRONTIER** chives

PREP: 10 minutes

COOK: 20 minutes

YIELD: 12 servings

Bring 5 quarts of water to a boil. Add the pasta and cook for 5 minutes. Add broccoli and carrots and cook for 5 more minutes. Remove from heat and drain. Coat a large skillet with a nonstick spray. Add peppers and onion; sauté for 5 minutes. Add oregano and black pepper; cook for 2 minutes. Toss the pasta and vegetables together with the olive oil and top with cheese and chives.

Courtesy of Frontier Natural Products Co-op

Garden Pasta Primavera

PREP: 15 minutes

COOK: 15 minutes

YIELD: 4 servings

Heat oil in a large skillet set over medium-high heat. Add garlic and mixed vegetables and cook, stirring often, for 5 minutes. Stir in green onions, chili sauce, and broth. Bring to a boil. Reduce heat and simmer for 5 minutes or until thickened slightly. Cook the pasta according to package directions. Toss the vegetable mixture, Parmesan, basil, salt, and pepper with the hot pasta. Adjust seasonings to taste.

Courtesy of H.J. Heinz Company, L.P.

1 tablespoon vegetable oil

1 clove garlic, minced

4 cups chopped mixed vegetables, such as celery, carrots, broccoli, cauliflower, mushrooms

¼ cup sliced green onions

1 cup **HEINZ® Chili Sauce**

½ cup vegetable or chicken broth

12 oz. dry spaghetti

¼ cup grated Parmesan

2 tablespoons chopped fresh basil

½ teaspoon salt

½ teaspoon pepper

Parsley Garlic Ribbons with Garbanzo Beans, Olives, and Artichokes

4 (8-oz.) boxes **EDEN ORGANIC Parsley Garlic Ribbons**

¼ cup **EDEN Extra Virgin Olive Oil**

¼ teaspoon red pepper flakes, or to taste

1 cup diced onion

6 cloves garlic, diced

1 cup water-packed artichoke hearts, quartered

1 medium yellow bell pepper, chopped

2 cups vegetable stock

1 cup whole pitted black olives

1 (15-oz.) can **EDEN ORGANIC Garbanzo Beans**, drained

1 (28-oz.) can **EDEN ORGANIC Whole Tomatoes with Basil**, undrained, chopped

½ teaspoon **EDEN Sea Salt**

⅛ teaspoon freshly ground black pepper, or to taste

1 tablespoon minced fresh parsley (for garnish)

PREP: 15 minutes

COOK: 15 minutes

YIELD: 8 servings

Cook pasta according to directions until al dente. While the pasta is cooking, place olive oil, red pepper flakes, and onion in a large skillet. Sauté on medium until golden. Add garlic, artichokes, and yellow pepper. Sauté until golden. Add broth, olives, garbanzo beans, and tomatoes. Simmer 5 minutes. Place drained pasta in a large bowl, pour sauce over and toss. Season to taste with pepper and salt. Garnish with parsley and serve.

Courtesy of Eden Foods

Golden Chicken Nuggets

PREP: 10 minutes

COOK: 15 minutes

YIELD: 6 servings

Preheat oven to 425°F. In small bowl, combine **LIPTON® RECIPE SECRETS® Golden Onion Soup Mix** and bread crumbs. Dip chicken in bread crumb mixture until evenly coated. On lightly greased baking sheet, arrange chicken; drizzle with Spread. Bake, turning once, for 15 minutes or until chicken is thoroughly cooked.

VARIATIONS

Also terrific with **LIPTON® RECIPE SECRETS®** Onion Soup Mix, **LIPTON® RECIPE SECRETS®** Onion Mushroom Soup Mix or **LIPTON® RECIPE SECRETS®** Savory Herb with Garlic Soup Mix.

Courtesy of Unilever

1 envelope **LIPTON® RECIPE SECRETS® Golden Onion Soup Mix**

½ cup plain dry bread crumbs

1 ½ lbs. boneless, skinless chicken breasts, cut into 2-inch pieces

2 tablespoons **I CAN'T BELIEVE IT'S NOT BUTTER!® Spread**, melted

Chicks in a Blanket

1 (16-oz.) tube extra-large refrigerated biscuits

4 slices American cheese, each cut in half

1 (12-oz.) package **PERDUE® Baked Breaded Chicken Breast Tenderloins**

Dipping sauces (optional)

PREP: 10 minutes

COOK: 18 minutes

YIELD: 6 servings

Preheat oven to 375°F. Remove dough from tube and separate into 8 pieces. Place biscuits several inches apart on lightly greased baking sheet. Flatten each biscuit with palm of hand. Place one strip of cheese and one chicken tender in center of each biscuit. Wrap dough partially around tender to enclose, leaving top of tender showing. Press edges of dough firmly together to seal. Bake for 15 to 18 minutes or until golden brown. Let stand 1 minute before serving. Serve with favorite dipping sauces, if desired.

Courtesy of Perdue Farms, Inc.

Honey-Spice Drumsticks

¾ cup **HEINZ® Tomato Ketchup**

½ cup honey

1 teaspoon finely grated orange zest

¼ cup orange juice

2 teaspoons **HEINZ® Worcestershire Sauce**

2 tablespoons chopped fresh rosemary

2 cloves garlic, minced

2 teaspoons ground cumin

2 teaspoons pepper

8 chicken drumsticks, trimmed

MARINATE: 30 minutes

PREP: 10 minutes

COOK: 20 minutes

YIELD: 4 servings

Preheat barbecue to medium-high and lightly grease the grate. Stir ketchup with honey, orange zest, orange juice, Worcestershire sauce, rosemary, garlic, cumin, and pepper. Divide in half. Toss one half with the drumsticks and marinate for 30 minutes. Reserve remaining sauce mixture. Discard the marinade and grill the chicken, turning occasionally, for 15 minutes. Brush chicken all over with reserved sauce and grill for 5 minutes more or until no longer pink near the bone.

Courtesy of H.J. Heinz Company, L.P.

Baked Thighs with Port and Fresh Mushroom Sauce

COOK: 30 minutes

YIELD: 4 servings

Preheat oven to 350°F. Arrange thighs skin side up in an 8 x 8-inch baking pan. Bake 30 minutes, or until a thermometer inserted into the thickest part of the thigh measures 180°F. About 10 minutes before thighs are done cooking, prepare noodles according to package directions. Meanwhile, simmer Port in a large skillet over medium heat about 5 minutes. Add mushrooms and simmer, stirring occasionally, for 5 minutes. In a small bowl, combine 3 tablespoons chicken broth and cornstarch and stir until cornstarch is dissolved. Pour remaining broth into pan and bring back to simmer. Slowly pour in cornstarch mixture, bring to a boil, and continue boiling, stirring frequently, until sauce thickens, about 1 minute. Serve chicken and sauce over hot cooked noodles.

Courtesy of Perdue Farms, Inc.

6 **PERDUE® Fresh Chicken Thighs**

8 oz. wide egg noodles

1 cup Port wine

1 (8-oz.) package presliced fresh mushrooms, cleaned

1 (14 ½-oz.) can chicken broth, divided

1 tablespoon cornstarch

Brown Sugar Chicken Thighs

PREP: 14 minutes

COOK: 14 minutes

YIELD: 6 servings

½ cup brown sugar, loosely packed

¼ cup dry mustard

½ teaspoon salt

1 teaspoon ground pepper

1 (about 1 ½-lb.) package **PERDUE® FIT & EASY® Boneless, Skinless Chicken Thigh Filets**

Orange slices and chives (for garnish, optional)

In large resealable plastic bag, add brown sugar, mustard, salt, and pepper. Shake to mix well. Place thighs in bag and shake well. Let sit for 2 minutes and shake again. Grill thighs directly over medium high heat for 20 to 30 minutes, turning occasionally. Remove from heat when juices run clear and a meat thermometer inserted sideways into thickest part of thigh reads 180°F. Garnish with orange slices and chives, if desired.

Courtesy of Perdue Farms, Inc.

Lemon Garlic Chicken

4 boneless, skinless chicken breast halves (about 1 ¼ lbs.)

¼ cup all-purpose flour

2 tablespoons **I CAN'T BELIEVE IT'S NOT BUTTER!® Spread**

1 envelope **LIPTON® RECIPE SECRETS® Savory Herb with Garlic Soup Mix**

1 ¾ cups water

2 tablespoons lemon juice

Hot cooked rice (optional)

PREP: 5 minutes

COOK: 15 minutes

YIELD: 4 servings

Dip chicken in flour, shaking off excess. In 12-inch nonstick skillet, melt Spread over medium-high heat and brown chicken 4 minutes, turning once. Stir in **LIPTON® RECIPE SECRETS® Savory Herb with Garlic Soup Mix** blended with water and lemon juice. Reduce heat to low, cover, and simmer 5 minutes or until sauce is slightly thickened and chicken is thoroughly cooked. Serve with hot cooked rice, if desired.

Courtesy of Unilever

Pan-Grilled Sausage with Apples and Onions

PREP: 5 minutes

COOK: 20 minutes

YIELD: 2 servings

Preheat oven to 250°F. Melt 1 tablespoon of the butter in a large skillet over medium heat. Add sausages and cook until browned, turning occasionally, about 5 minutes. Remove sausages from skillet and transfer to a heatproof dish. Cover with foil and place in oven to keep warm. Add onion and apple to pan; cook until onion and apple are tender and brown, stirring often, about 5 minutes. Add apple cider and chicken broth; increase heat to high and stir until liquid is reduced and thickened slightly, 2 to 3 minutes. Stir in lemon juice. Season to taste with salt and pepper. Remove sausages from oven and transfer to serving platter. Remove pan from heat. Whisk sage and remaining 2 tablespoons butter into cider mixture. Drizzle over sausage and serve.

Courtesy of Applegate Farms, an Organic & Natural Meat Company

3 tablespoons butter, divided

4 **APPLEGATE FARMS Chicken & Apple Sausages**

1 small onion, minced

1 Granny Smith apple peeled, sliced

½ cup apple cider

½ cup chicken broth

1 ½ teaspoons fresh lemon juice

Salt and pepper

1 tablespoon fresh chopped sage

Chicken Breasts with Blue Cheese Butter

CHICKEN

2 tablespoons **LAND O LAKES®
Butter**, softened

¼ teaspoon garlic powder

6 (5-oz.) boneless skinless chicken
breast halves

Blue Cheese Butter (recipe below)

BLUE CHEESE BUTTER

2 tablespoons **LAND O LAKES®
Butter**, softened

2 tablespoons crumbled blue cheese

2 green onions, sliced

1 tablespoon chopped fresh basil
leaves or 1 teaspoon dried basil leaves

PREP: 10 minutes

COOK: 13 minutes

YIELD: 6 servings

Heat gas grill on medium or charcoal grill until coals
are ash white. Stir together butter and garlic powder.
Place chicken breasts onto grill; brush with butter
mixture. Grill, turning and brushing occasionally with
butter mixture, until chicken is no longer pink, 10 to 13
minutes. Meanwhile, combine all Blue Cheese Butter
ingredients in small bowl; mix well. To serve, top each
grilled chicken breast with about 2 teaspoons blue
cheese butter.

Courtesy of Land O'Lakes, Inc.

Coconut Curry Chicken with Grilled Pineapple

¾ cup unsweetened coconut milk

¼ cup brown sugar, firmly packed

1 tablespoon curry powder

1 teaspoon grated lemon zest

½ teaspoon salt

1 (about 1-lb.) package **PERDUE® FIT & EASY® Boneless, Skinless Chicken Breasts**

1 pineapple, peeled, cored, and cut into 1-inch-thick rings

PREP: 7minutes

COOK: 18 minutes

YIELD: 4 servings

Preheat grill or broiler. In small saucepan, over medium heat, cook coconut milk, brown sugar, curry powder, lemon zest, and salt 2 minutes or until brown sugar is dissolved; remove from heat. Pour 1/4 cup of the coconut basting sauce into a small bowl and reserve for the pineapple. Grill or broil chicken, turning occasionally and basting frequently with coconut sauce, 15 minutes or until meat thermometer inserted in center registers 170°F. Do not baste during the last 5 minutes of grilling. Grill or broil pineapple wedges, and with a different basting brush, baste pineapple with reserved coconut sauce, 5 minutes or until just warm. Serve chicken with pineapple.

Courtesy of Perdue Farms, Inc.

Pineapple Teriyaki Chicken Kabobs

MARINATE: 30 minutes

PREP: 15 minutes

GRILL: 15 minutes

YIELD: 7 servings

Combine pineapple juice, teriyaki marinade, and mustard. Set aside ¼ cup for grilling. Pour remaining marinade into resealable plastic bag; add chicken pieces, bell peppers, and zucchini. Refrigerate and marinate for 30 minutes. Remove chicken and vegetables from plastic bag and discard marinade. Thread bell peppers, pineapple chunks, chicken, and zucchini on skewers. Brush with reserved marinade. Grill or broil 10 to 15 minutes, turning and brushing occasionally with teriyaki marinade or until chicken is no longer pink. Discard any remaining marinade.

Courtesy of Dole Food Company

LAWRY'S® is a trademark of McCormick & Company, Inc.

1 (20-oz.) can **DOLE® Pineapple Chunks**, drained, 2 tablespoons juice reserved

¾ cup **LAWRY'S® Teriyaki Marinade with Pineapple Juice**

1 teaspoon Dijon-style mustard

4 boneless, skinless chicken breasts, cut into 1-inch pieces (1 ½ to 1 ¾ lbs.)

2 red or green bell peppers, cut into 1 ½-inch pieces

1 zucchini, cut into ½-inch-thick slices

12 (12-inch-long) wooden skewers, soaked in water

Chicken Sticks with Pineapple-Peanut Sauce

8 or 9 metal skewers

3 boneless, skinless chicken breasts

1 (8-oz.) can **DOLE® Crushed Pineapple**

⅓ cup creamy peanut butter

3 tablespoons brown sugar, packed

1 tablespoon lime juice

1 ½ teaspoons curry powder

½ teaspoon ground ginger

PREP: 20 minutes

COOK: 10 minutes

YIELD: 4 servings

Cut chicken into strips ½-inch wide and 3 to 4 inches long. Thread two to three strips of meat onto each skewer. Arrange skewers on broiler pan sprayed with vegetable cooking spray. Drain pineapple, reserving ¼ cup juice. Combine crushed pineapple, reserved juice, peanut butter, brown sugar, lime juice, curry powder, and ginger in blender or food processor container. Cover; blend until smooth. Reserve ¾ cup sauce for dipping; set aside. Brush part of the remaining pineapple sauce over chicken. Broil chicken 4 inches from heat, turning once and brushing with sauce, for about 10 minutes or until meat is no longer pink. Discard any remaining sauce used during grilling. Serve chicken with reserved pineapple sauce for dipping.

Courtesy of Dole Food Company

Country Lemon Chicken

PREP: 10 minutes

COOK: 20 minutes

YIELD: 4 servings

Combine flour, thyme, salt and pepper. Dip chicken in flour mixture. Combine any remaining flour mixture with broth; set aside. In 12-inch nonstick skillet, melt 2 tablespoons **SHEDD'S SPREAD COUNTRY CROCK®️ Spread** over medium-high heat and brown chicken. Remove chicken and set aside. In same skillet, melt remaining 2 tablespoons Spread over medium-high heat and cook onion, stirring occasionally, until golden, about 3 minutes. Stir in garlic and cook 1 minute. Stir in lemon juice and cook 1 minute. Add reserved broth mixture and bring to a boil. Return chicken and any chicken juices to skillet and simmer uncovered until chicken is thoroughly cooked, about 5 minutes. Sprinkle with parsley, if desired.

Courtesy of Unilever

2 tablespoons all-purpose flour

¼ teaspoon crushed dried thyme leaves (optional)

½ teaspoon salt

⅛ teaspoon ground black pepper

4 boneless, skinless chicken breast halves (about 1 ¼ lbs.)

1 cup chicken broth

4 tablespoons **SHEDD'S SPREAD COUNTRY CROCK®️ Spread**

1 small onion, chopped

1 clove garlic, finely chopped

2 to 3 tablespoons lemon juice

1 tablespoon chopped parsley (optional)

Lemon Chicken with Asparagus

Cooking spray

4 **PERDUE® PERFECT PORTIONS® Boneless, Skinless Chicken Breasts, All Natural** (about 1.5 lbs.)

Salt

½ lb. fresh asparagus, washed and stems trimmed

¼ cup (4 tablespoons) unsalted butter

1 tablespoon Dijon-style mustard

3 tablespoons lemon juice

2 tablespoons half-and-half

Thin lemon slices (for garnish)

PREP: 25 minutes

COOK: 25 minutes

YIELD: 4 servings

Preheat oven to 375°F. Spray a baking sheet with cooking spray. Place breasts on baking sheet and bake 15 minutes or until juices run clear and a thermometer inserted into the center of a breast reads 170°F. In a large skillet, bring about ½ inch of water to a boil. Season the water with salt and add the asparagus. Cook the asparagus for about 3 minutes or until bright green and tender. Remove asparagus and water from skillet and reduce heat to low. Melt butter in skillet over low heat and add mustard, lemon juice, and half-and-half while stirring with a whisk for about 2 minutes. Season with salt to taste. Place asparagus and a baked chicken breast on each plate, drizzle chicken with lemon-butter sauce, and garnish with thin slices of lemon.

Courtesy of Perdue Farms, Inc.

Lemon-Garlic Scallopini

PREP: 5 minutes

COOK: 10 minutes

YIELD: 4 servings

In a shallow dish, stir together flour and garlic salt. Press the chicken into the flour mixture, coating both sides completely. Coat a large, nonstick skillet with olive oil and set it over high heat. Add chicken and brown on each side approximately 45 seconds. Remove chicken and set it aside. Add lemon juice and chicken broth to skillet and let boil 30 seconds. Return chicken to pan and push it into sauce. Cover and simmer over low heat 3 minutes until meat thermometer inserted in center registers 170°F. To serve, set chicken on plates and pour sauce on top.

Courtesy of Perdue Farms, Inc.

3 tablespoons all-purpose flour

2 teaspoons garlic salt

1 (about 1-lb.) package **PERDUE® FIT & EASY® Boneless, Skinless Chicken Breasts, Thin-Sliced**, or **PERDUE® FIT & EASY® Boneless, Skinless Turkey Breast Cutlets, Thin-Sliced** (about 1-lb.)

2 tablespoons olive oil

¼ cup lemon juice

½ cup 99% fat-free chicken broth

Honey Orange Glazed Chicken

PREP: 5 minutes

COOK: 15 minutes

YIELD: 6 servings

Warm olive oil in a large skillet over medium-high heat. Add chicken and brown for 1 to 2 minutes on each side. Stir in orange juice, brown sugar, honey, and vinegar. Reduce heat to medium and simmer until sauce has thickened lightly, 6 to 8 minutes or until meat thermometer inserted in center registers 170°F. To serve, set chicken on plates and spoon sauce on top.

Courtesy of Perdue Farms, Inc.

2 tablespoons olive oil

1 (1.5-lb.) package **PERDUE® PERFECT PORTIONS® Boneless, Skinless Chicken Breasts, All Natural**

1 cup orange juice

2 tablespoons brown sugar

2 tablespoons honey

1 tablespoon cider vinegar or white wine vinegar

Tasty Chicken

4 boneless chicken breasts

¼ cup flour

Salt

Pepper

3 tablespoons butter

½ cup **WELCH'S White Grape Juice**

½ cup chicken broth

½ teaspoon dried tarragon

¼ cup half-and-half

Lemon juice

PREP: 10 minutes

COOK: 20 minutes

YIELD: 4 servings

Coat chicken with mixture of flour, salt, and pepper. Melt butter in skillet. Add chicken; cook over medium-high heat until browned on both sides and cooked to desired doneness. Remove to warm plate. Deglaze pan with grape juice and broth, loosening browned particles. Stir in tarragon and half-and-half. Cook just until slightly thickened. Season with salt and pepper; add lemon juice to taste. Spoon sauce over chicken to serve.

Courtesy of Welch Foods Inc., A Cooperative

Gingered Pear Chicken Dijon

PREP: 5 minutes

COOK: 20 minutes

YIELD: 4 servings

1 (15.25-oz.) can **DEL MONTE® Lite Sliced Pears**

4 medium boneless, skinless chicken breasts (about 1 lb.)

Salt and pepper (optional)

1 tablespoon olive oil

4 green onions, thinly sliced

2 tablespoons molasses

½ teaspoon ground ginger

1 tablespoon Dijon mustard

Additional sliced green onions (for garnish)

Drain pears, reserving syrup; set aside. Season chicken breasts with salt and pepper, if desired. Heat oil in large nonstick skillet over medium-high heat. Add chicken and cook 9 to 10 minutes, turning once, until no longer pink in the center or until temperature on an instant-read thermometer reads 160°F. Remove to a platter. Add reserved pear liquid, sliced green onions, molasses, ginger, and mustard to skillet and bring to a boil, scraping up browned bits from pan. Reduce heat; cook 2 minutes. Stir in pears and heat through. Spoon sauce and pears over chicken. Garnish with green onions, if desired.

Courtesy of Del Monte Foods

Baked Dijon Chicken

Nonstick cooking spray

¼ cup **NESTLÉ® CARNATION® Evaporated Fat Free Milk**

3 to 4 tablespoons Dijon mustard

¼ cup plain, dry bread crumbs

¼ cup (.75 oz.) **BUITONI Refrigerated Freshly Shredded Parmesan Cheese**

4 boneless, skinless chicken breast halves (about 1 ¼ lbs.)

PREP: 10 minutes

COOK: 20 minutes

YIELD: 4 servings

Preheat oven to 475°F. Spray 13 x 9-inch baking dish with nonstick cooking spray. Combine evaporated milk and mustard in shallow bowl. Combine bread crumbs and cheese in separate shallow bowl. Dip chicken into milk mixture, coating both sides, then into bread-crumb mixture. Place in prepared dish. Bake for 15 to 20 minutes or until chicken is golden brown and no longer pink in center.

Courtesy of Nestlé USA

Dijon Chicken Tenders

1 (1.10-lb.) package **PERDUE®** **Baked Breaded Chicken Breast Tenderloins**

¼ cup Dijon-style mustard

¼ cup dry white wine

1 teaspoon Tabasco sauce

2 tablespoons chopped fresh basil or 1 teaspoon dried basil

½ teaspoon salt

PREP: 5 minutes

COOK: 11 minutes

YIELD: 4 servings

Preheat oven to 400°F. Place the tenders in a shallow baking dish. Mix together the mustard, wine, Tabasco sauce, basil, and salt. Pour the mixture over the tenders and turn the tenders to coat both sides. Bake tenders in the oven for 9 to 11 minutes. Serve hot.

Courtesy of Perdue Farms, Inc.

Chicken with Apple-Dijon Sauce

PREP: 10 minutes

COOK: 20 minutes

YIELD: 4 servings

Combine flour, thyme, marjoram, and bouillon in shallow dish. Coat chicken with flour mixture; shake off excess. Heat 2 teaspoons of the oil in large, nonstick skillet over medium-high heat. Add chicken; cook on each side for 7 minutes or until no longer pink in center. Transfer to platter and keep warm. Heat remaining 1 teaspoon oil in same skillet. Add shallot and garlic; cook, stirring frequently, for 1 minute. Add **JUICY JUICE®** and mustard. Bring to a boil; cook, scraping up any brown bits, for 3 to 4 minutes or until liquid is reduced by half. Add chicken to skillet along with any juices accumulated on platter; stir to coat chicken with sauce.

Courtesy of Nestlé USA

2 tablespoons all-purpose flour

½ teaspoon crushed dried thyme

½ teaspoon crushed dried marjoram

½ teaspoon **MAGGI Instant Chicken Flavor Bouillon**

4 boneless, skinless chicken breast halves (about 1 ¼ lbs.)

3 teaspoons extra virgin olive oil, divided

1 large shallot, chopped

1 clove garlic, finely chopped

1 cup **Apple NESTLÉ® JUICY JUICE® All Natural 100% Juice**

2 tablespoons Dijon mustard

Chicken Breast with Ginger and Basil

1 lb. boneless, skinless chicken breast

Salt, divided (optional)

2 tablespoons flour

1 teaspoon butter (optional)

2 tablespoons extra virgin olive oil

½ cup **WELCH'S White Grape Juice**

2 tablespoons lemon juice

1 cup diced tomatoes, plus more for garnish

1 teaspoon finely minced fresh ginger

2 to 3 tablespoons chopped basil

4 cups lettuce or baby spinach

2 tablespoons minced parsley

Salt

PREP: 10 minutes

COOK: 20 minutes

YIELD: 4 servings

Sprinkle chicken breast with salt, if desired. Dust chicken with flour, shaking off excess. In large skillet, heat butter and oil. Brown chicken 3 to 4 minutes per side. Add grape juice and lemon juice; cook for 5 to 6 minutes. Remove chicken and keep warm. In same skillet cook tomatoes for 2 minutes, stirring gently. Add ginger and basil, add salt if desired, and cook for 1 minute. Add chicken back to the skillet to meld flavors, 2 to 3 minutes. Serve over lettuce or baby spinach garnished with tomato pieces and minced parsley.

Courtesy of Welch Foods Inc., A Cooperative

Cilantro Cream Sauce over Chicken

PREP: 10 minutes

COOK: 15 minutes

YIELD: 6 to 8 servings

Place cilantro, evaporated milk, water, and bouillon in blender; cover. Blend until smooth. Melt butter in medium saucepan over medium heat. Remove from heat. Stir in flour, stirring constantly until smooth. Stir in cilantro mixture. Cook over medium-low heat, stirring constantly, until mixture comes to a boil and thickens slightly. Season to taste with pepper. Pour sauce over chicken breasts.

Courtesy of Nestlé USA

6 to 8 boneless, skinless chicken breast halves, cooked and kept warm

2 cups loosely packed fresh cilantro

1 (12-fl. oz.) can **NESTLÉ® CARNATION® Evaporated Milk**

1 cup water

2 teaspoons **MAGGI Instant Chicken Flavor Bouillon**

3 tablespoons butter or margarine

3 tablespoons all-purpose flour

Ground black pepper to taste

PACE® Texas Two-Step Chicken

4 skinless, boneless chicken breast halves

1 ½ cups **PACE® Picante Sauce** or **Chunky Salsa**

3 tablespoons light brown sugar, packed

1 tablespoon Dijon-style mustard

3 cups hot cooked regular long grain white rice

PREP: 10 minutes

COOK: 20 minutes

YIELD: 4 servings

Preheat oven to 400°F. Place the chicken into a 2-quart shallow baking dish. Stir the picante sauce, brown sugar, and mustard in a small bowl. Pour the picante sauce mixture over the chicken. Bake for 20 minutes or until the chicken is cooked through. Serve with the rice.

Courtesy of Campbell Soup Company

Chicken with Tomato-Artichoke Sauce

PREP: 10 minutes

COOK: 12 minutes

YIELD: 4 servings

Brown chicken in hot oil in large skillet over medium heat about 2 minutes per side. Add tomato sauce, artichokes, and rosemary. Bring to boil; reduce heat. Simmer, covered, 10 to 12 minutes or until chicken is done. Remove chicken and artichokes with slotted spoon to serving platter. Bring sauce to boil; reduce heat. Simmer, uncovered, until desired consistency. Spoon over chicken. Sprinkle with olives and garnish with fresh rosemary, if desired.

Courtesy of Del Monte Foods

4 skinless, boneless chicken breast halves (about 1 ¼ lbs.)

1 tablespoon olive oil

1 (15-oz.) can **CONTADINA® Italian Style Tomato Sauce**

1 (14-oz.) can artichoke hearts, drained

1 ½ teaspoons chopped fresh rosemary or ½ teaspoon crushed dried rosemary

¼ cup halved pitted ripe olives (optional)

Fresh rosemary (for garnish, optional)

Chicken with Artichokes & Sun-Dried Tomato

PREP: 15 minutes

COOK: 15 minutes

YIELD: 4 servings

Season chicken with salt and ground black pepper, if desired. In 12-inch nonstick skillet, melt 2 tablespoons **I CAN'T BELIEVE IT'S NOT BUTTER!® Mediterranean Blend spread** over medium-high heat and cook chicken, turning once, 6 minutes or until thoroughly cooked. Remove to serving platter and keep warm. In same skillet, melt remaining tablespoon of spread over medium heat and cook garlic, stirring occasionally, 30 seconds. Add artichoke hearts and tomatoes and cook, stirring occasionally, 1 minute. Stir in broth and bring to a boil. Reduce heat and simmer 5 minutes or until sauce is slightly thickened. Stir in cheese. Spoon over chicken. Garnish with chopped fresh parsley and grated Parmesan, if desired.

Courtesy of Unilever

4 boneless, skinless chicken breast halves (about 1 ¼ lbs.)

Salt (optional)

Freshly ground black pepper (optional)

3 tablespoons **I CAN'T BELIEVE IT'S NOT BUTTER!® Mediterranean Blend spread**, divided

1 clove garlic, finely chopped

1 (14-oz.) can artichoke hearts, drained and chopped

2 tablespoons chopped sun-dried tomatoes

1 cup fat-free reduced sodium chicken broth

2 tablespoons grated Parmesan, plus more for garnish (optional)

Chopped fresh parsley (for garnish)

Chicken Sauté Mediterranean

PREP: 5 minutes

COOK: 25 minutes

YIELD: 5 servings

Sprinkle breast halves with salt and pepper; press herbs into chicken. In large nonstick skillet over medium-high heat, heat oil; add chicken and brown 2 minutes on each side. Add garlic and sun-dried tomatoes; sauté 1 minute. Stir in canned tomatoes, with their liquid, and beans. Reduce heat to medium-low; cover partially and simmer 15 to 20 minutes until meat thermometer inserted in center of chicken breast registers 170°F. Serve chicken breasts warm over the tomatoes and beans mixture.

Courtesy of Perdue Farms, Inc.

1 (32-oz.) package **PERDUE® FIT & EASY® Boneless, Skinless Chicken Breasts**

Salt and ground pepper to taste

1 ½ teaspoons Italian herb seasoning

2 teaspoons olive oil

1 clove garlic, minced

1 ½ tablespoons chopped sun-dried tomatoes

1 (14.5-oz.) can diced tomatoes, undrained

1 (16-oz.) can Great Northern or cannellini beans, drained and rinsed

Chicken Carbonara

PREP: 5 minutes

COOK: 20 minutes

YIELD: 4 servings

1 tablespoon olive oil

4 boneless, skinless chicken breast halves (about 1 ¼ lbs.)

1 small onion, chopped

1 slice bacon or pancetta, chopped

1 cup frozen green peas, thawed

⅓ cup dry white wine or chicken broth

1 (15-oz.) jar **BERTOLLI® Creamy Alfredo Sauce**

Cracked black pepper (optional)

Heat olive oil in 12-inch nonstick skillet over medium-high heat and brown chicken. Remove chicken and set aside. Cook onion, bacon, and peas in same skillet, stirring occasionally, 6 minutes or until bacon is cooked and onion is tender. Add wine and cook 1 minute. Stir in sauce. Bring to a boil over high heat. Reduce heat to low, then return chicken to skillet. Simmer, covered, 5 minutes or until chicken is thoroughly cooked. Sprinkle with cracked black pepper, if desired.

Courtesy of Unilever

Skillet Chicken Parmesan

¼ cup grated Parmesan, divided

1 ½ cups **PREGO® Traditional Italian Sauce** or **PREGO® Organic Tomato & Basil Italian Sauce**

1 tablespoon olive oil

4 to 6 skinless, boneless chicken breasts (about 1 ½ lbs.)

1 ½ cups (6 oz.) shredded part-skim mozzarella

COOK: 30 minutes

YIELD: 6 servings

Stir 3 tablespoons Parmesan into pasta sauce. Heat oil in large skillet over medium-high heat. Add chicken and cook for about 10 minutes or until browned. Pour sauce mixture over chicken, turning to coat with sauce. Cover and cook over medium heat for 10 minutes or until chicken is no longer pink. Top with mozzarella and remaining Parmesan. Let stand for 5 minutes or until cheese is melted.

Courtesy of Campbell Soup Company

Pesto Pan-Fried Chicken

PREP: 15 minutes

COOK: 15 minutes

YIELD: 4 servings

Preheat oven to 300°F. Place chicken breasts between sheets of plastic wrap and pound to an even thickness of about ¼ inch. Coat chicken with pesto, dip in flour, dip in egg mixture, and, lastly, dip in seasoned bread crumbs combined with Parmesan. In a large nonstick or well-seasoned skillet, over medium heat, heat 2 tablespoons oil. Add chicken and cook about 2 minutes on each side until coating is golden brown and chicken is cooked through. Remove to a baking sheet lined with paper towels and keep warm in oven until all chicken is cooked. Add more oil to the skillet as needed during frying. Garnish with lemon slices and basil, if desired.

Courtesy of Perdue Farms, Inc.

1 (about 1-lb.) package **PERDUE® FIT & EASY® Boneless, Skinless Chicken Breasts**

⅓ cup prepared pesto sauce

½ cup flour

1 egg, beaten with 1 tablespoon water

⅔ cup Italian seasoned bread crumbs

¼ cup shredded or grated Parmesan

3 tablespoons olive oil, divided

Lemon slices (for garnish, optional)

Fresh basil sprigs (for garnish, optional)

Zesty Skillet Chicken

3 skinless, boneless chicken breast halves, cut into cubes (about 1 lb.)

1 cup chopped onion

1 clove garlic, finely chopped

1 tablespoon oil

Salt and pepper (optional)

1 (14 ½-oz.) can **DEL MONTE® Diced Tomatoes with Zesty Mild Green Chilies**

1 (8 ¾-oz.) can **DEL MONTE Whole Kernel Golden Sweet Corn**, drained

1 cup (4 oz.) shredded Monterey Jack or Pepper Jack cheese

Chopped fresh cilantro (for garnish, optional)

PREP: 10 minutes

COOK: 15 minutes

YIELD: 4 servings

Cook chicken, onion, and garlic in oil over medium-high heat, 5 minutes or until chicken is no longer pink. Season with salt and pepper, if desired. Add tomatoes and corn; simmer 5 minutes or until liquid is gone. Sprinkle with cheese; heat until melted. Garnish with cilantro, if desired.

Courtesy of Del Monte Foods

Quick & Easy Chicken, Broccoli & Brown Rice

PREP: 5 minutes

COOK: 20 minutes

YIELD: 4 servings

Heat the oil in a 10-inch skillet over medium-high heat. Add the chicken and cook for 10 minutes or until well browned on both sides. Remove the chicken from the skillet. Stir the soup, water, paprika, and black pepper in the skillet and heat to a boil. Stir the rice and broccoli in the skillet. Reduce the heat to low. Return the chicken to the skillet. Sprinkle the chicken with additional paprika and black pepper. Cover and cook for 5 minutes or until the chicken is cooked through and the rice is tender.

Courtesy of Campbell Soup Company

1 tablespoon vegetable oil

4 skinless, boneless chicken breast halves

1 (10 ¾-oz.) can **CAMPBELL'S® Condensed Cream of Chicken Soup (Regular, 98% Fat Free**, or **Healthy Request®**)

1 ½ cups water

¼ teaspoon paprika

¼ teaspoon ground black pepper

1 ½ cups uncooked instant brown rice, preferably whole grain

2 cups fresh or frozen broccoli florets

Broccoli Chicken Potato Parmesan

2 tablespoons vegetable oil

1 lb. small red potatoes, sliced ¼-inch thick

1 (10 ¾-oz.) can **CAMPBELL'S® Condensed Broccoli Cheese Soup (Regular or 98% Fat Free)**

½ cup milk

¼ teaspoon garlic powder

2 cups fresh or frozen broccoli florets

1 (10-oz.) package refrigerated cooked chicken breast strips

¼ cup grated Parmesan

PREP: 10 minutes

COOK: 15 minutes

YIELD: 4 servings

Heat the oil in a 10-inch skillet over medium heat. Add the potatoes. Cover and cook for 10 minutes, stirring occasionally. Stir the soup, milk, garlic powder, broccoli, and chicken into the skillet. Sprinkle with the cheese. Heat to a boil. Reduce the heat to low. Cover and cook for 5 minutes or until the potatoes are fork-tender.

Courtesy of Campbell Soup Company

Sweet 'n' Sour Chicken Stir-Fry

3 tablespoons ketchup

1 tablespoon vinegar

1 tablespoon soy sauce

2 boneless, skinless chicken breasts, cut into 1-inch cubes

1 tablespoon vegetable oil

8 ozs. frozen stir-fry vegetables or other frozen vegetable combination (such as broccoli, red pepper, mushrooms and onions)

1 (20-oz.) can **DOLE®
Pineapple Chunks**, drained

Hot cooked rice

PREP: 5 minutes

COOK: 15 minutes

YIELD: 4 servings

Combine ketchup, vinegar, and soy sauce in small bowl; set aside. Cook and stir chicken in large skillet or wok in hot oil over medium-high heat until chicken is browned. Stir in vegetables; cover. Reduce heat to low; cook 2 to 3 minutes or until vegetables are crisp-tender, stirring occasionally. Stir in pineapple chunks and reserved sauce; cook and stir until pineapple is heated through. Serve over hot cooked rice.

VARIATION

Fresh stir-fry vegetable combination can be used in place of frozen vegetables. When adding fresh vegetables, add 2 tablespoons of juice from canned pineapple and increase cooking time to 4 minutes or until vegetables are crisp-tender.

Courtesy of Dole Food Company

Chicken, Broccoli & Pineapple Stir-Fry

PREP: 20 minutes

COOK: 10 minutes

YIELD: 4 servings

Heat oil in nonstick wok or large skillet. Add chicken; stir-fry 5 minutes. Remove to bowl. Add onion, ginger, and garlic to same pan; stir-fry 2 minutes. Combine broth, soy sauce, cornstarch, anise seed, and cinnamon; add to same pan. Add broccoli and bell pepper. Cover and cook 2 to 3 minutes or until broccoli is crisp-tender. Stir in pineapple and chicken. Heat through.

Courtesy of Dole Food Company

2 teaspoons olive or canola oil

½ lb. boneless, skinless chicken breasts, cut in strips

1 medium **DOLE® Onion**, thinly sliced

1 tablespoon finely chopped fresh ginger root

2 cloves garlic, finely chopped

1 cup low-sodium chicken broth

¼ cup light soy sauce or liquid aminos (soy substitute)

1 tablespoon cornstarch

½ teaspoon crushed anise seed

¼ teaspoon ground cinnamon

2 cups **DOLE Broccoli**, cut into florets

1 **DOLE Red Bell Pepper**, cut into chunks

2 cups fresh **DOLE Tropical Gold® Pineapple**, cut into chunks

Chicken Teriyaki Stir-Fry

1 (10-oz.) package **BIRDS EYE® STEAMFRESH® Long Grain White Rice**, prepared according to package directions

1 (12-oz.) package **BIRDS EYE® STEAMFRESH® Broccoli, Carrots, Sugar Snap Peas and Water Chestnuts**, prepared according to package directions

1 teaspoon minced garlic

8 oz. refrigerated fully-cooked grilled chicken breast strips, cut into bite-size pieces

¾ cup teriyaki sauce

PREP: 5 minutes

COOK: 20 minutes

YIELD: 2 servings

In a large skillet over medium heat, toss together prepared rice, vegetables, garlic, chicken, and teriyaki sauce. Cook 5 to 10 minutes or until heated through.

VARIATION

BIRDS EYE® STEAMFRESH® Whole Grain Brown Rice can be substituted for the **BIRDS EYE® STEAMFRESH® Long Grain White Rice**.

Courtesy of Birds Eye Foods, Inc.

Mix-and-Match Stir-Fry

1 cup **HEINZ®** Tomato Ketchup

½ cup **HEINZ™** Tomato Juice

2 tablespoons soy sauce

2 teaspoons **HEINZ® Worcestershire Sauce**

1 teaspoon horseradish

1 teaspoon minced fresh ginger

2 tablespoons vegetable oil

1 onion, sliced

1 lb. chicken, pork, or beef strips or shelled shrimp, uncooked

4 cups mixed chopped vegetables such as broccoli, asparagus, bok choy, sweet peppers, or snow peas

Lemon or lime wedges (optional)

PREP: 15 minutes

COOK: 15 minutes

YIELD: 4 servings

Stir ketchup with tomato juice, soy sauce, Worcestershire sauce, horseradish, and minced ginger. Reserve. Heat the oil in a deep skillet or wok set over medium-high heat. Add onion and stir-fry for 3 minutes. Add meat or shrimp and continue to stir-fry for 3 minutes. Add vegetables and stir-fry 2 minutes longer. Make a well in the center of the pan and pour in reserved chili mixture. Bring to a boil. Reduce heat and simmer for 3 to 5 minutes or until meat is cooked through and sauce is thickened. Garnish with lemon or lime wedges, if desired.

Courtesy of H.J. Heinz Company, L.P.

Spicy Cashew Chicken

PREP: 15 minutes

COOK: 14 minutes

YIELD: 4 servings

Heat oil in 12-inch nonstick skillet over medium-high heat and cook red pepper flakes 30 seconds. Add red pepper and cook, stirring occasionally, 2 minutes. Add chicken and cook, stirring occasionally, 2 minutes or until golden. Stir in **KNORR® Rice Sides™ Chicken** and water. Bring to a boil over high heat. Reduce heat to low and simmer, covered, 7 minutes or until rice is tender and chicken is thoroughly cooked. Stir in cashews and peas until heated through.

Courtesy of Unilever

1 tablespoon vegetable oil

¼ teaspoon crushed red pepper flakes

1 medium red bell pepper, thinly sliced

1 lb. boneless, skinless chicken breast halves, cut into thin strips

1 package **KNORR® Rice Sides™ Chicken**

1 ¾ cups water

1 cup chopped unsalted cashews

½ cup frozen green peas, thawed

Chicken Curry in a Hurry

PREP: 10 minutes

COOK: 15 to 20 minutes

YIELD: 4 servings

Heat half the oil in a large skillet set over medium-high heat. Add chicken and brown for about 5 minutes. Transfer to a bowl and set aside. Add the remaining oil (if needed) and sauté onion and green pepper for 5 minutes. Stir in the garlic, curry paste, tomato paste, salt, and pepper. Cook for 2 to 3 minutes. Stir in reserved chicken, tomato juice, chili sauce, lemon juice, lemon zest, and cranberries, if using. Bring to a boil; reduce heat to medium-low and simmer for 5 minutes or until sauce is slightly thickened and chicken is fully cooked.

Courtesy of H.J. Heinz Company, L.P.

2 tablespoons vegetable oil

1 lb. skinless, boneless chicken breasts, cut into bite-size chunks

2 onions, thinly sliced

1 green pepper, thinly sliced

2 cloves garlic, minced

2 teaspoons mild Indian curry paste or powder

2 teaspoons **HEINZ™ Tomato Paste**

½ teaspoon each salt and pepper

1 cup **HEINZ™ Tomato Juice**

½ cup **HEINZ® Chili Sauce**

1 tablespoon fresh lemon or lime juice

1 teaspoon finely grated lemon or lime zest

¼ cup dried cranberries or raisins (optional)

Cheddar Chicken Pasta & Vegetable Skillet Dinner

1 lb. boneless, skinless chicken breasts, cut into thin strips

Salt and pepper (optional)

2 tablespoons **I CAN'T BELIEVE IT'S NOT BUTTER!® Spread**

1 small tomato, chopped

1 clove garlic, finely chopped

1 ¾ cups water

½ cup milk

1 package **KNORR® Sides Plus™ Veggies—Cheddar Cheese Pasta with Broccoli & Carrots**

PREP: 10 minutes

COOK: 20 minutes

YIELD: 4 servings

Season chicken with salt and pepper, if desired. Melt Spread in 12-inch nonstick skillet over medium-high heat and cook chicken, stirring occasionally, 5 minutes or until chicken is thoroughly cooked. Remove chicken and set aside. Stir tomato into same skillet and cook, stirring occasionally, 3 minutes. Stir in garlic and cook 30 seconds. Stir in water and milk. Bring to a boil over high heat. Stir in **KNORR® Sides Plus™ Veggies—Cheddar Cheese Pasta with Broccoli & Carrots** and continue boiling over medium heat, stirring occasionally, 9 minutes or until pasta is tender. Stir in chicken; heat through.

Courtesy of Unilever

Angel Hair Pasta with Broccoli, Cauliflower & Carrots

PREP: 10 minutes

COOK: 15 minutes

YIELD: 4 servings

In a skillet, cook onion and garlic in oil over medium heat for 2 to 3 minutes or until onion is soft and transparent. Add chicken and cook for 2 to 3 minutes. Add tomatoes, balsamic vinegar, and frozen vegetables; cover and cook for 7 to 9 minutes or until vegetables are tender. Toss with angel-hair pasta and heat through. Serve garnished with Parmesan.

Courtesy of Birds Eye Foods, Inc.

½ cup chopped onion

½ teaspoon minced garlic

1 teaspoon olive oil

1 lb. grilled chicken, cut into strips

1 (14.5-oz.) can Italian-style tomatoes with juice

2 tablespoons balsamic vinegar

1 (16-oz.) package **BIRDS EYE® Broccoli Florets, Cauliflower and Carrots**

4 oz. angel-hair pasta, cooked according to package directions

3 tablespoons shredded Parmesan (for garnish)

Chicken Caesar Pasta

8 oz. dry rotini pasta, cooked according to package directions and drained

2 cups diced cooked chicken

1 (16-oz.) package bag **BIRDS EYE® Broccoli Florets, Cauliflower and Carrots**, cooked according to package directions and drained

1 cup Caesar salad dressing

¾ cup chicken broth

Grated Parmesan

Caesar-flavored croutons (for garnish)

PREP: 10 minutes

COOK: 15 minutes

YIELD: 6 servings

Combine cooked rotini, chicken, vegetables, salad dressing, and chicken broth in a large pan and cook over medium-high heat until heated through. Sprinkle with grated Parmesan and croutons before serving.

Courtesy of Birds Eye Foods, Inc.

Chicken Scampi

COOK: 20 minutes

YIELD: 4 servings

Heat the butter in a 10-inch skillet over medium-high heat. Add the chicken and cook for 10 minutes or until well browned on both sides. Remove the chicken and set aside. Stir in the soup, water, lemon juice, and garlic. Heat to a boil. Return the chicken to the skillet and reduce the heat to low. Cover and cook for 5 minutes or until chicken is cooked through. Serve the chicken with the pasta.

Courtesy of Campbell Soup Company

2 tablespoons butter

4 to 6 skinless, boneless chicken breasts (about 1 ½ lbs.)

1 (10 ¾-oz.) can **CAMPBELL'S® Condensed Cream of Chicken Soup (Regular or 98% Fat Free)**

¼ cup water

2 teaspoons lemon juice

2 cloves garlic, minced, *or* ½ teaspoon garlic powder

Hot cooked pasta

Chicken & Broccoli Alfredo

3 tablespoons **I CAN'T BELIEVE IT'S NOT BUTTER!® Spread**, divided

1 lb. boneless, skinless chicken breasts, cut into cubes

½ cup finely chopped red bell pepper

2 cups fresh or thawed frozen broccoli florets

1 ¾ cups water

½ cup milk

1 package **KNORR® Pasta Sides™— Alfredo**

PREP: 10 minutes

COOK: 20 minutes

YIELD: 4 servings

Melt 1 tablespoon Spread in 12-inch nonstick skillet over medium-high heat and cook chicken, stirring frequently, 5 minutes or until chicken is thoroughly cooked. Remove chicken and set aside. Melt additional 2 tablespoons Spread in same skillet over medium heat and cook red pepper 1 minute or until tender. Stir in broccoli, water, and milk. Bring to a boil over high heat. Stir in **KNORR® Pasta Sides™—Alfredo**. Return to a boil, then cook over medium heat, stirring occasionally, 8 minutes or until pasta is tender. Return chicken to skillet; heat through.

Courtesy of Unilever

CAMPBELL'S® Chicken & Broccoli Alfredo

PREP: 10 minutes

COOK: 20 minutes

YIELD: 4 servings

Prepare the linguine according to the package directions in a 3-quart saucepan. Add the broccoli during the last 4 minutes of the cooking time. Drain the linguine and broccoli well in a colander. Heat the butter in a 10-inch skillet over medium-high heat. Add the chicken and cook until well browned, stirring often. Stir the soup, milk, cheese, black pepper, and linguine mixture in the skillet. Cook until the mixture is hot and bubbling. Serve with additional Parmesan.

SERVING SUGGESTION

Serve with a mixed green salad topped with orange sections, walnut pieces, and raspberry vinaigrette. For dessert serve almond biscotti.

Courtesy of Campbell Soup Company

8 oz. (½ of a 16-oz. package) linguine

1 cup fresh or frozen broccoli florets

2 tablespoons butter

1 lb. skinless, boneless chicken breasts, cut into cubes

1 (10 ¾-oz.) can **CAMPBELL'S® Condensed Cream of Mushroom Soup (Regular, 98% Fat Free, or 25% Less Sodium)**

½ cup milk

½ cup grated Parmesan

¼ teaspoon ground black pepper

Chicken Mozzarella

PREP: 5 minutes

COOK: 25 minutes

YIELD: 4 servings

Cook pasta according to package directions; drain. Meanwhile, season chicken with garlic powder, salt, and pepper, as desired. Heat oil in large skillet over medium-high heat. Brown chicken, about 4 minutes on each side. Add undrained tomatoes, mushrooms, and rosemary. Bring to a boil; reduce heat and simmer, uncovered, 5 to 10 minutes or until sauce is thickened and chicken is no longer pink (chicken should reach 160°F on an instant-read thermometer). Sprinkle with cheese. Cover and let stand 2 minutes. Serve over pasta and garnish with fresh rosemary, if desired.

VARIATIONS

Try other **Del Monte® Tomatoes** such as **Diced Tomatoes with Basil, Garlic & Oregano**.

Courtesy of Del Monte Foods

6 oz. bow tie or penne pasta

4 skinless, boneless chicken breast halves

½ teaspoon garlic powder

Salt and pepper as preferred

1 tablespoon olive oil

1 (14.5-oz.) can **DEL MONTE® Diced Tomatoes with Garlic & Onion**

½ cup fresh sliced mushrooms

½ teaspoon crushed dried rosemary or basil

1 cup (4 oz.) shredded mozzarella

Fresh rosemary (for garnish, optional)

Cheese Tortellini with Tomatoes and Chicken

2 cups cheese tortellini

2 tablespoons olive oil

4 **PERDUE® PERFECT PORTIONS® Boneless, Skinless Chicken Breasts, Roasted Garlic with White Wine**

1 lb. fresh tomatoes, coarsely chopped

½ tablespoon Italian seasoning

2 tablespoons chopped fresh basil

2 tablespoons grated Parmesan (for garnish, optional)

COOK: 20 minutes

YIELD: 4 servings

Cook tortellini according to package directions; drain and set aside. Meanwhile, heat oil in large nonstick skillet over medium-high heat. Add chicken breasts; sauté 2 minutes per side. Reduce heat to medium-low. Stir in tomatoes and seasoning. Cover; cook 6 to 8 minutes or until juices run clear and a thermometer inserted into center of chicken breast registers 170°F. Remove chicken breasts from skillet and place one chicken breast on each of four plates. Add tortellini and basil to tomatoes in skillet and toss until blended; divide evenly among the four plates. Sprinkle with Parmesan, if desired.

Courtesy of Perdue Farms, Inc.

Pesto Chicken Flatbread Pizzas

2 (3.5-oz.) Tuscan-style flatbreads

¼ cup **BUITONI Refrigerated Reduced Fat Pesto with Basil**

⅔ cup sautéed or cooked chicken breast strips

2 tablespoons shredded mozzarella

¼ cup (.75 oz.) **BUITONI Refrigerated Freshly Shredded Parmesan Cheese**

PREP: 10 minutes

COOK: 10 minutes

YIELD: 4 servings

Preheat oven to 375°F. Place flatbreads on baking sheet. Spread pesto evenly over each flatbread to within ½ inch of edge. Top each evenly with chicken, mozzarella, and Parmesan. Bake for 8 to 10 minutes or until flatbread is crisp and cheese is melted.

COOK'S TIP

Refer to your flatbread packaging to determine recommended bake temperature and time as each brand varies.

VARIATION

Try substituting regular **BUITONI Refrigerated Pesto with Basil**.

Courtesy of Nestlé USA

Barbecued Chicken Pizza

PREP: 5 minutes

COOK: 20 minutes

YIELD: 4 servings

Heat oven to 425°F. Place pizza crust onto ungreased baking sheet; spread evenly with barbecue sauce. Sprinkle with ½ cup cheese; sprinkle with chicken. Melt butter in 10-inch skillet until sizzling; add mushrooms and bell pepper. Cook over medium-high heat until vegetables are softened, 5 to 6 minutes; sprinkle over chicken. Sprinkle with remaining cheese. Bake for 10 to 12 minutes or until cheese is melted. Sprinkle with onion.

Courtesy of Land O'Lakes, Inc.

1 (14-oz.) prepared Italian pizza crust

½ cup hickory-smoked barbecue sauce

4 oz. (1 cup) **LAND O LAKES® Mozzarella Cheese**, shredded

1 cup cooked cubed chicken

1 tablespoon **LAND O LAKES® Butter**

1 cup sliced mushrooms

1 cup thinly sliced red bell pepper

1 tablespoon sliced green onion tops

Easy Chicken Pot Pie

PREP: 5 minutes

COOK: 20 minutes

YIELD: 4 servings

Preheat oven to 450°F. Cut chicken into bite-size pieces. In a large pot, mix chicken, vegetables, soup, and milk. Heat through. Pour into an 8-inch-square casserole dish coated with nonstick spray. Place biscuits on top of chicken mixture in a single layer starting in the center (biscuits will not reach all the way to the edge). Bake for 8 to 10 minutes or until biscuits are browned.

Courtesy of Perdue Farms, Inc

1 package **PERDUE® SHORT CUTS® Carved Chicken Breast, Grilled Italian Style**

1 (9- or 10-oz.) box frozen mixed vegetables

1 (10 ¾-oz.) can cream of potato soup

½ cup milk

1 (10-count) package refrigerated buttermilk biscuits

Quick Chicken Pot Pie

1 (12-oz.) package **BIRDS EYE® STEAMFRESH® Mixed Vegetables**, cooked according to package directions

1 (4-oz.) can mushrooms, drained

2 cups cooked chicken, diced

1 (10.75-oz.) can cream of chicken soup

¾ cup milk

2 tablespoons dry sherry

Fresh ground pepper to taste

4 prepared biscuits, split

PREP: 10 minutes

COOK: 15 minutes

YIELD: 4 servings

In a large saucepan over medium heat, combine mixed vegetables, mushrooms, chicken, soup, milk, and dry sherry. Cook until mixture is heated through, about 10 minutes. Season with fresh ground pepper. Place one split biscuit on each serving plate. Evenly divide chicken mixture on top of biscuits.

Courtesy of Birds Eye Foods, Inc.

Chicken Pot Pie

1 lb. cooked and diced chicken

2 cups mixed soup vegetables

¾ cup water

1 package **SIMPLY ORGANIC Roasted Chicken Gravy Mix**

1 (10- to 12-count) package biscuit dough, prepared according to directions

PREP: 10 minutes

COOK: 20 minutes

YIELD: 6 servings

Preheat oven to 400°F. In a 2- to 3-quart casserole dish, combine chicken, vegetables, water, and **SIMPLY ORGANIC Roasted Chicken Gravy Mix**. Knead biscuit dough, flatten slightly, and lay on mixture in casserole dish. Bake 15 to 20 minutes until biscuits are golden.

VARIATIONS

Add bell peppers, onions, and tomatoes to make Fajita Chicken Pot Pie. You may also make individual servings by using oven-safe single dishes and topping each dish with dough. Try mashed potatoes as an alternative for the crust.

Courtesy of Simply Organic

Busy Night Meatball Stroganoff

COOK: 20 minutes

YIELD: 4 servings

Mix gravy and sour cream in large saucepan. Add meatballs and mushrooms; stir gently. Cook on low heat for 15 to 20 minutes, stirring occasionally. Meanwhile, cook egg noodles according to package directions; drain. Serve stroganoff over the noodles.

Courtesy of Perdue Farms, Inc.

1 (12-oz.) jar beef gravy

½ cup sour cream

1 (12-oz.) package **PERDUE® Turkey Meatballs, Italian Style**

1 (2.5-oz.) jar sliced mushrooms, drained

8 oz. egg noodles

All-American Turkey Cheeseburgers

PREP: 10 minutes

COOK: 10 minutes

YIELD: 4 servings

If grilling, grease grill. Preheat grill or broiler. In medium bowl, mix turkey, bread crumbs, Worcestershire sauce, salt, and pepper; shape into four patties. Grill or broil for about 10 minutes, flipping halfway through cooking time. Burgers are done when a meat thermometer inserted in center reaches 165°F or juices run clear and burgers bounce back to the touch. About 1 minute before burgers are done, top with cheese. Serve on roll and top with assorted condiments, if desired.

Courtesy of Perdue Farms, Inc.

1 (1 lb.) package **PERDUE® Fresh Lean Ground Turkey**

2 tablespoons bread crumbs

2 teaspoons Worcestershire sauce

1 teaspoon salt

½ teaspoon ground pepper

4 slices American cheese

4 hamburger rolls

Lettuce, tomato slices, pickle chips, and onion slices (optional)

Southwest Turkey Burgers

1 lb. ground turkey breast

⅓ cup salsa

¼ cup chopped green onions

1 teaspoon dried oregano leaves

½ teaspoon ground cumin

¼ teaspoon salt

1 small ripe avocado, mashed

1 tablespoon reduced-fat sour cream

1 tablespoon chopped fresh cilantro

1 tablespoon lime juice

4 lettuce leaves

4 **NATURE'S OWN 100% Whole Wheat Sandwich Rolls**

4 tomato slices

PREP: 20 minutes

COOK: 10 minutes

YIELD: 4 servings

Preheat broiler. Combine turkey, salsa, green onions, oregano, cumin, and salt in large bowl. Shape into four ½-inch-thick patties. Spray rack of broiler pan with nonstick cooking spray; place patties on rack. Broil 4 inches from heat source, 4 to 5 minutes per side or until burgers are cooked through. Meanwhile, combine avocado, sour cream, cilantro, and lime juice in medium bowl. Season with salt; set aside. Place lettuce leaf on each roll bottom. Top with burger, tomato slice, and avocado mixture. Close sandwiches.

Courtesy of Flowers Foods

Chesapeake Bay Burgers

1 (1 lb.) package **PERDUE® Fresh Lean Ground Turkey**

½ cup finely chopped onion

¼ cup finely crushed saltine crackers (about 5 crackers)

2 teaspoons **OLD BAY® Seasoning**

8 mini rolls

Cocktail or tartar sauce (optional)

PREP: 10 minutes

COOK: 10 minutes

YIELD: 4 servings

If grilling, grease grill. Preheat grill or broiler. In medium bowl, combine turkey, onion, crackers, and **OLD BAY® Seasoning** until blended. Shape into 8 mini burgers. Grill or broil, turning occasionally, 10 minutes or until meat thermometer inserted in center registers 165°F. Serve burgers on rolls, with cocktail or tartar sauce, if desired.

OLD BAY® is a trademark of McCormick & Company, Inc.

Courtesy of Perdue Farms, Inc.

Pan-Seared Beef with Shallot Vinaigrette

PREP: 10 minutes

COOK: 20 minutes

YIELD: 4 servings

Melt 1 tablespoon Spread in 12-inch nonstick skillet over medium-high heat and cook steak, turning once, until desired doneness. Remove steak and thinly slice. Melt remaining Spread in same skillet and cook shallots, stirring occasionally, 4 minutes. Add wine and broth. Bring to a boil over high heat. Reduce heat to low and simmer, stirring occasionally, 5 minutes. Arrange sliced steak on serving platter, then drizzle with vinaigrette. Sprinkle with freshly ground black pepper, if desired.

Courtesy of Unilever

2 tablespoons **I CAN'T BELIEVE IT'S NOT BUTTER!® Light Spread**

1 lb. lean top sirloin steak, trimmed

2 large shallots or 1 small onion, chopped (about 1 cup)

½ cup dry red wine

½ cup fat-free reduced-sodium beef broth

Freshly ground black pepper (optional)

Sirloin Steak with Red Onion Relish

PREP: 10 minutes

COOK: 20 minutes

YIELD: 6 servings

Cut steak into six equal portions. Rub both sides evenly with pepper. Heat 1 teaspoon of the oil in large nonstick skillet on medium heat. Add steak; cook 5 minutes on each side for medium doneness (160°F). Remove from skillet; cover to keep warm. Add remaining 1 teaspoon oil to drippings in skillet. Add onion; cook and stir 5 to 7 minutes or until crisp-tender. Add steak sauce and sage; cook an additional 2 minutes, stirring occasionally. Slice steak. Serve relish over the steak slices.

Courtesy of Kraft Foods

1 ½ lbs. boneless beef sirloin steak, ¾ -inch thick

¼ teaspoon coarsely ground black pepper

2 teaspoons oil, divided

1 large red onion, thinly sliced, separated into rings

¼ cup **A.1. ORIGINAL STEAK SAUCE**

½ teaspoon crushed dried sage leaves

Shortcut Stroganoff

1 tablespoon vegetable oil

1 lb. boneless beef sirloin steak, cut into ½-inch strips

1 (10 ¾-oz.) can **CAMPBELL'S® Condensed Cream of Mushroom Soup (Regular, 98% Fat Free or 25% Less Sodium)**

1 (10 ½-oz.) can **CAMPBELL'S® Condensed Beef Broth**

1 cup water

2 teaspoons Worcestershire sauce

3 cups uncooked corkscrew-shape pasta

½ cup sour cream

PREP: 5 minutes

COOK: 25 minutes

YIELD: 4 servings

Heat oil in skillet. Add beef and cook until browned and juices evaporate, stirring often. Add soup, broth, water, Worcestershire sauce, and pasta. Heat to a boil. Cook over medium heat 15 minutes or until pasta is done, stirring often. Add sour cream. Heat through.

SERVING SUGGESTION

Serve with steamed peas, baby carrots, and tomato wedges. For dessert serve sliced fresh pineapple.

Courtesy of Campbell Soup Company

Three-Step Stroganoff

1 tablespoon vegetable oil

1 lb. beef tenderloin tips

1 ½ cups thinly sliced onion

1 ½ cups thinly sliced green pepper

2 cloves garlic, minced

1 teaspoon dried thyme leaves

1 teaspoon black pepper

1 cup **HEINZ® Tomato Ketchup**

1 cup beef broth

1 tablespoon **HEINZ® Worcestershire Sauce**

½ cup sour cream

¼ cup chopped fresh parsley

Black pepper

Hot buttered egg noodles

PREP: 10 minutes

COOK: 20 minutes

YIELD: 6 servings

Heat the vegetable oil in a nonstick stir-fry pan or deep skillet set over high heat. Add the beef, onion, green pepper, garlic, thyme, and pepper. Stir-fry for 3 minutes or until meat and vegetables start to brown. Stir in the ketchup, broth, and Worcestershire sauce. Bring the mixture to a boil. Reduce the heat to medium. Simmer, uncovered, for 3 minutes. Stir in the sour cream and parsley and remove pan from the heat. Season with pepper to taste. Serve over hot buttered egg noodles.

Courtesy of H.J. Heinz Company, L.P.

Busy Night Meatball Stroganoff

PREP: 15 minutes

COOK: 15 minutes

YIELD: 4 servings

Slice beef into very thin strips. Mix cornstarch, broth, and soy sauce until smooth. Set aside. Heat oil in skillet. Add beef and stir-fry until browned and juices evaporate. Push beef to one side of skillet. Add vegetables and garlic powder and stir-fry until crisp-tender. Stir cornstarch mixture and add. Cook and stir until mixture boils and thickens. Serve over rice.

Courtesy of Campbell Soup Company

1 lb. boneless beef sirloin steak or beef top round steak, ¾-inch thick, frozen for 1 hour (for easier slicing)

2 tablespoons cornstarch

1 (10 ½-oz.) can **CAMPBELL'S® Condensed Beef Broth**

2 tablespoons soy sauce

2 tablespoons vegetable oil

3 cups cut-up vegetables, such as broccoli florets, sliced carrots, green or red pepper strips

¼ teaspoon garlic powder *or* 1 clove garlic, minced

Hot cooked rice

Weeknight Beef & Broccoli Stir-Fry

½ cup **HEINZ® Chili Sauce**

¼ cup water

2 tablespoons soy sauce

1 tablespoon cornstarch

½ teaspoon ground ginger

½ teaspoon red pepper flakes

2 tablespoons vegetable oil

1 lb. boneless sirloin steak, thinly sliced

1 ½ cups broccoli florets

1 small onion, thinly sliced

1 small red pepper, thinly sliced

1 can sliced water chestnuts

12 oz. cooked Asian-style or other noodles

PREP: 15 minutes

COOK: 15 minutes

YIELD: 4 servings

Blend chili sauce with water, soy sauce, cornstarch, ginger, and red pepper flakes in a small bowl. Reserve. Heat half the oil in a large skillet set over medium-high heat; stir-fry the beef until brown, about 3 minutes. Remove from skillet and reserve. Add remaining oil to skillet and stir-fry broccoli, onion, pepper, and water chestnuts until crisp-tender, about 3 minutes. Stir in reserved chili sauce mixture and cook until thickened, about 5 minutes. Add beef and heat through, about 2 minutes. Serve over cooked noodles.

Courtesy of H.J. Heinz Company, L.P.

15-Minute Beef Stew

PREP: 5 minutes

COOK: 15 minutes

YIELD: 4 servings

Heat olive oil in 12-inch nonstick skillet over medium-high heat and brown steak. Stir in remaining ingredients. Bring to a boil over high heat. Reduce heat to low and simmer uncovered 10 minutes or until steak is tender.

VARIATION

Also terrific with **LIPTON® RECIPE SECRETS® Onion Soup Mix.**

Courtesy of Unilever

1 tablespoon olive oil

1 lb. boneless sirloin steak, cut into 1-inch cubes

1 envelope **LIPTON® RECIPE SECRETS® Onion Mushroom Soup Mix**

1 cup water

2 tablespoons tomato paste

1 (14 ½-oz.) can new potatoes, drained and cut into chunks

1 (10-oz.) package frozen green peas and carrots, thawed

Fiesta Beefy Enchilada Skillet

1 lb. ground beef

1 (16-oz.) jar **PACE® Picante Sauce**

8 (6-inch) corn tortillas, cut into 1-inch squares

1 cup shredded Cheddar cheese

Sour cream

Chopped green onion

PREP: 5 minutes

COOK: 10 minutes

YIELD: 4 servings

Cook the ground beef in a 10-inch skillet over medium-high heat until browned, stirring frequently to break up meat. Pour off any fat. Add the sauce, tortillas, and half the cheese. Heat to a boil. Reduce the heat to low. Cover and cook for 5 minutes or until hot and bubbling. Top with the remaining cheese. Serve with the sour cream and the green onions.

Courtesy of Campbell Soup Company

Easy Chow Mein

PREP: 5 minutes

COOK: 20 minutes

YIELD: 4 servings

Cook ground beef and onion in a large skillet over high heat, until no longer pink, about 8 minutes. Drain fat. Stir in cooked vegetables, soup, water, and soy sauce; cook over medium heat until heated through, 5 to 10 minutes. Season with ground black pepper. Serve garnished with chow mein noodles.

Courtesy of Birds Eye Foods, Inc.

1 lb. ground beef

½ medium onion, chopped

1 (12-oz.) package **BIRDS EYE® STEAMFRESH® Baby Broccoli Blend**, cooked according to package directions

1 (10.75-oz.) can 98% fat-free cream of mushroom soup

½ cup water

1 tablespoon soy sauce

Ground black pepper

Crunchy chow mein noodles

Cheeseburger Macaroni

PREP: 10 minutes

COOK: 20 minutes

YIELD: 6 servings

In a large skillet over high heat, cook ground chuck until browned; drain fat. Add cooked macaroni, vegetables, soup, milk, Cheddar cheese, ketchup, and mustard. Cook over medium heat until heated through, 5 to 10 minutes. Season with salt and pepper. Serve garnished with sliced pickles, if desired.

Courtesy of Birds Eye Foods, Inc.

1 lb. ground chuck

8 oz. dry elbow macaroni, cooked according to package directions and drained

8 oz. (½ of a 1-lb. bag) **BIRDS EYE® Classic Mixed Vegetables**, cooked according to package directions and drained

1 (10.75-oz.) can cheddar cheese soup

1 cup milk

1 cup shredded Cheddar cheese

¼ cup ketchup

2 tablespoons prepared mustard

Salt and pepper

Dill pickles, sliced (for garnish, optional)

Beef Macaroni and Cheese

1 lb. ground beef

1 cup chopped onion

Salt and pepper (optional)

1 (14 ½-oz.) can **DEL MONTE® Diced Tomatoes with Basil, Garlic & Oregano**

1 cup water

1 cup elbow macaroni

1 ½ cups shredded Cheddar cheese

PREP: 5 minutes

COOK: 20 minutes

YIELD: 4 servings

Brown meat and onion over medium-high heat in skillet; drain. Season with salt and pepper, if desired. Add tomatoes and water; bring to boil. Stir in macaroni. Cover and simmer 10 minutes or until cooked. Stir in cheese. Garnish with sour cream, if desired.

Courtesy of Del Monte Foods

Stovetop Beef & Penne Casserole

2 cups (8 oz.) dry penne pasta (or small pasta of your choice)

2 lbs. lean ground beef

1 medium onion, chopped

2 (12-fl oz.) cans **NESTLÉ® CARNATION® Evaporated Milk**

1 (15-oz.) can **LIBBY'S® 100% Pure Pumpkin**

1 (15-oz.) can tomato sauce

1 tablespoon brown sugar, packed

1 tablespoon paprika

1 tablespoon Worcestershire sauce

2 teaspoons salt

½ teaspoon garlic powder

½ teaspoon ground black pepper

2 cups frozen peas, thawed

PREP: 10 minutes

COOK: 20 minutes

YIELD: 12 servings

Cook pasta in large saucepan for 1 to 2 minutes less than package directions state (pasta should be slightly firm in texture); drain. Cook beef and onion in large saucepan over medium-high heat until beef is no longer pink; drain. Reduce heat to medium. Stir in evaporated milk, pumpkin, tomato sauce, brown sugar, paprika, Worcestershire sauce, salt, garlic powder, and pepper. Cook, stirring occasionally, until mixture begins to simmer. Add pasta and peas; stir until heated.

COOK'S TIP

Feed your family twice but only cook once! Each recipe is already doubled. Just serve your family half and freeze the rest for another meal. Thaw in refrigerator and reheat in microwave or on stovetop.

Courtesy of Nestlé USA

Mini Italian Meat Loaf Burgers

PREP: 10 minutes

COOK: 20 minutes

YIELD: 6 servings

Preheat oven to 375°F. Drain tomatoes, reserving ⅓ cup liquid. Combine reserved tomato liquid with remaining ingredients, except cheese, in large bowl. Shape into 6 patties; top with cheese. Place patties on a baking sheet. Bake for 20 minutes to desired doneness or until an internal temperature of 160°F is reached.

Courtesy of Del Monte Foods

1 (14 ½-oz.) can **DEL MONTE® Diced Tomatoes with Basil, Garlic & Oregano**

1 lb. ground beef

¾ cup Italian seasoned dry bread crumbs

½ medium green pepper, finely chopped

1 egg, beaten

1 cup shredded Mozzarella

Mini Meatloaf Burgers

PREP: 5 minutes

COOK: 14 minutes

YIELD: 4 servings

In a medium bowl, combine all ingredients. Add salt and pepper, if desired. Shape into four patties. In a large skillet, cook burgers over medium high heat for 5 to 7 minutes on each side to medium doneness (160°F), or until cooked through.

COOK'S TIP

Be sure to shake well before measuring out the Worcestershire sauce.

Courtesy of H.J. Heinz Company, L.P.

¼ cup **LEA & PERRINS® Worcestershire Sauce**

2 tablespoons **HEINZ® Tomato Ketchup**

1 lb. lean ground beef

¼ cup finely chopped onions or shallots

2 tablespoons plain dry bread crumbs

Salt and pepper (optional)

Mushroom Swiss Burgers

SAUTÉED MUSHROOMS

1 tablespoon olive oil

8 oz. mushrooms, sliced

1 small onion, sliced

¼ teaspoon salt

⅛ teaspoon ground black pepper

BURGERS

½ cup fresh bread crumbs
(1 slice bread)

3 tablespoons milk

1 lb. lean ground beef

1 egg yolk, beaten

½ teaspoon salt

¼ teaspoon ground black pepper

4 slices Swiss cheese

4 **COBBLESTONE MILL Potato Hamburger Rolls**

4 leaf lettuce leaves

PREP: 10 minutes

COOK: 14 minutes

YIELD: 4 servings

FOR THE SAUTÉED MUSHROOMS: Heat oil in large skillet over medium-high heat. Add mushrooms and onion. Cook about 10 minutes, stirring frequently. Stir in salt and pepper.

FOR THE BURGERS: Place bread crumbs and milk in large bowl; let stand 5 minutes. Add ground beef, egg yolk, salt, and pepper. Mix well. Shape into four ½-inch-thick patties. Place patties on preheated gas grill grid over medium heat. Grill, covered, 7 to 8 minutes to medium doneness (160°F), turning occasionally. Top burgers with cheese slices during last minute of grilling. About 2 minutes before burgers are done, place rolls, cut sides down, on grid. Grill until lightly toasted. Place lettuce on each roll bottom. Top with burger and ¼ of sautéed mushrooms. Close sandwiches.

Courtesy of Flowers Foods

Outside-In Bacon Cheeseburgers

1 lb. ground beef

1 cup shredded sharp Cheddar cheese

½ cup chopped onion

8 slices bacon, cooked crisp, crumbled

4 **NATURE'S OWN Honey Wheat Sandwich Buns**

4 lettuce leaves

4 slices tomato

PREP: 20 minutes

COOK: 8 minutes

YIELD: 4 servings

Preheat gas grill to medium heat. Combine ground beef, cheese, onion, and bacon in large bowl, mixing lightly but thoroughly. Shape into four ½-inch-thick patties. Place patties and rolls on grill grid; do not separate rolls. Grill rolls, covered, 2 to 3 minutes on each side or until crusts are crisp. Grill patties, covered, 7 to 8 minutes to medium doneness (160°F), turning occasionally. Place lettuce leaf on each roll bottom. Top with burger and tomato slice. Close sandwiches.

Courtesy of Flowers Foods

PACE® Black Bean Burgers

PREP: 10 minutes

COOK: 10 minutes

YIELD: 6 servings

Mix 1 cup salsa and the beef thoroughly in a large bowl. Shape the beef mixture firmly into six patties. Cook the patties in a 12-inch skillet or grill pan over medium-high heat for 10 minutes or until well browned on both sides and cooked through to medium doneness (160°F). Serve the burgers on the rolls with the remaining salsa.

VARIATIONS

• Top each burger with 1 slice Monterey Jack or Cheddar cheese during the last 3 minutes of cooking. Top with sliced avocado, tomato, and lettuce.

• Substitute 1¼ lbs. ground turkey for the ground beef and combine with ¾ cup salsa.

Courtesy of Campbell Soup Company

1 (16-oz.) jar **PACE® Black Bean & Roasted Corn Salsa**

1½ lbs. ground beef

6 sesame sandwich rolls

Burgers Parmigiana

1 lb. lean ground beef

8 oz. Italian sausage, removed from casings

½ cup grated Parmesan

3 tablespoons balsamic vinegar

1 tablespoon Italian seasoning

4 COBBLESTONE MILL Sandwich Rolls

½ cup marinara sauce

Additional grated Parmesan (optional)

Fresh basil leaves (optional)

PREP: 15 minutes

COOK: 15 minutes

YIELD: 4 servings

Preheat broiler. Combine ground beef, sausage, cheese, vinegar, and Italian seasoning in large bowl. Shape into four ¾-inch-thick patties. Place patties on rack in broiler pan. Broil 3 to 4 inches from heat source 14 minutes to medium doneness (160°F), turning once. About 3 minutes before burgers are done, place rolls, cut sides up, in single layer on baking sheet. Broil 2 minutes or until toasted. Turn rolls over; continue broiling 1 minute or until crusts are crisp. Meanwhile heat marinara sauce in microwave or on range top until hot. Place burger on each roll bottom. Top with marinara sauce; add cheese and basil, if desired. Close sandwiches.

Courtesy of Flowers Foods

Burgers with the West Coast Works

1 cup kalamata or Greek-style olives, pitted

2 tablespoons olive oil

1-inch wedge of onion

2 garlic cloves

1 heaping tablespoon capers

1 teaspoon balsamic vinegar or 2 teaspoons brandy

Freshly ground black pepper

4 ORGANIC PRAIRIE Ground Beef Patties (2 packages), thawed

4 crusty burger buns, split

Mayonnaise

16 fresh basil leaves

1 (6 ½-oz.) jar quartered, marinated artichoke hearts, drained and sliced

1 large roasted red pepper, seeded and sliced

PREP: 20 minutes

COOK: 10 minutes

YIELD: 4 servings

To make the tapenade, place olives in food processor or blender with olive oil, onion, garlic, capers, vinegar (or brandy), and pepper to taste (make it lots of pepper). Process until mixture is coarsely pureed. Grill or broil the burgers to desired doneness (160°F is recommended for food safety). Slather tapenade on top halves of buns. Spread mayonnaise on bottom halves; arrange basil leaves over mayonnaise. Add the burgers and top with artichokes and roasted red peppers.

COOK'S TIPS

• For even lustier California flavor, marinate the beef patties in a little red wine for 30 to 40 minutes before grilling. And pour a glass of that same good wine to go with the burgers.

• If you use olives with pits, pit them by smacking each one lightly on a cutting board with the flat side of a wide-bladed knife. This will "crack" the flesh open so you can easily remove the pits.

Copyright by Terese Allen; courtesy of Organic Valley Family of Farms

Teriyaki Meatballs and Rice

PREP: 5 minutes

COOK: 20 minutes

YIELD: 2 servings

In a saucepan over medium heat, combine prepared meatballs, rice, pineapple, teriyaki sauce, and water. Cook until heated through, about 5 minutes. Garnish with cashews before serving.

Courtesy of Birds Eye Foods, Inc.

12 fully cooked frozen meatballs, cooked according to package directions

1 (10-oz.) package **BIRDS EYE® STEAMFRESH® Long Grain White Rice with Mixed Vegetables**, cooked according to package directions

¼ cup drained pineapple tidbits

3 tablespoons teriyaki sauce

1 tablespoon water

Cashews

Sweet & Sour Meatball Stir-Fry

1 tablespoon **LAND O LAKES® Butter**

1 teaspoon freshly grated ginger root

1 (16-oz.) bag precut fresh stir-fry vegetables, cut into bite-size pieces

8 oz. (½ of a 16-oz. package) frozen meatballs, thawed

½ cup apricot preserves

¼ cup cocktail sauce

Chow mein noodles (optional)

PREP: 5 minutes

COOK: 10 minutes

YIELD: 4 (1 ¼-cup) servings

Melt butter in 12-inch skillet until sizzling; add ginger root. Cook over medium-high heat 1 minute. Add vegetables and meatballs. Continue cooking, stirring constantly, until vegetables are crisply tender and meatballs are heated through, 5 to 6 minutes. Combine preserves and cocktail sauce in small bowl. Stir into vegetable mixture; cook until heated through, 2 to 3 minutes. Serve over chow mein noodles, if desired.

COOK'S TIPS

- Is there a difference between cocktail sauce and chili sauce? Both use tomatoes as a base for the sauce but the cocktail sauce adds horseradish, lemon juice, and hot pepper sauce to give it a mild heat and spicy zing. Chili sauce is more salsa- or ketchup-like with chili powder, onions, green peppers, vinegar, and spices.

- Prepared sweet-and-sour sauce can be used in place of the apricot preserves and cocktail sauce.

Courtesy of Land O'Lakes, Inc.

Pepperoni Pizza Pasta

PREP: 10 minutes

COOK: 20 minutes

YIELD: 4 servings

In a large saucepan over medium heat, toss cooked macaroni, vegetables, spaghetti sauce, and pepperoni together. Cook until heated through, about 10 minutes. Sprinkle with cheese before serving.

Courtesy of Birds Eye Foods, Inc.

1 (16-oz.) package elbow macaroni, cooked according to package directions

1 (12-oz.) package **BIRDS EYE® STEAMFRESH® Specially Seasoned Garlic Baby Peas and Mushrooms**, cooked according to package directions

1 (24-oz.) jar spaghetti sauce

3 oz. pepperoni, cut into thin strips

1 cup Italian blend cheese, shredded

Pepperoni Pizza

1 (12-inch) prepared pizza crust

½ cup pizza sauce or spaghetti sauce

1 ½ cups **KRAFT Shredded Mozzarella Cheese**

1 (6-oz.) package **OSCAR MAYER Pepperoni**

PREP: 5 minutes

COOK: 12 minutes

YIELD: 6 servings

Preheat oven to 450°F. Place pizza crust on baking sheet. Spread crust with pizza sauce; top with cheese and pepperoni slices. Bake 10 to 12 minutes or until cheese is melted and crust is golden brown.

Courtesy of Kraft Foods

Hot Italian Subs

PREP: 5 minutes

COOK: 25 minutes

YIELD: 4 servings

Simmer sausage in water 10 minutes; drain. Heat 1 tablespoon olive oil in heavy skillet over medium heat. Add onion and pepper; sauté until vegetables are limp. Season to taste with salt and pepper. Push vegetables to one side; add sausages and brown them, adding more oil if necessary. Stir in pasta sauce and olives; simmer 10 minutes. Slice open the bread loaf halves or buns and place an Italian sausage in each one. Pile on the vegetable mixture—and pass the napkins!

COOK'S TIP

If you've got a crowd coming over, the recipe may be doubled, tripled, quadrupled, or more.

Copyright by Terese Allen; courtesy of Organic Valley Family of Farms

4 links **ORGANIC PRAIRIE Italian pork sausage**

Olive oil

1 medium onion, thinly sliced

1 large or 2 small bell peppers, thinly sliced

Salt

Pepper

1 ½ cups chunky pasta sauce

¼ cup sliced black or green imported olives

2 (14-inch) loaves Italian bread, cut in half crosswise, or 4 bratwurst buns

Wild Porcini Mushroom Risotto with Italian Sausage and Spinach

1 (5.9-oz.) box **LUNDBERG® Wild Porcini Mushroom Risotto**

1 lb. Italian sweet sausage, casings removed, crumbled into ½-inch pieces

2 ½ cups water

½ tablespoon olive oil

1 cup stemmed baby spinach, chopped

Grated Parmesan

COOK: 25 minutes

YIELD: 4 servings

Prepare **LUNDBERG® Wild Porcini Mushroom Risotto** according to box directions. While risotto is cooking, heat a large nonstick skillet over medium-high heat. Add sausage and sauté until browned, about 10 minutes. Drain off fat. Stir in spinach or other greens and lightly cook until wilted. Stir sausage and spinach mixture into cooked risotto. Serve with grated Parmesan.

Courtesy of Lundberg Family Farms

Bow Ties in Sausage and Pepper Sauce

6 oz. dried bow tie pasta

12 oz. sweet Italian sausage links, cut into ¾-inch slices

1 onion, cut into thin wedges

2 green, yellow, and/or red sweet peppers, cut into thin strips

1 (14.5-oz.) can **CONTADINA® Recipe Ready Diced Tomatoes**

1 (8-oz.) can **CONTADINA Garlic & Onion Tomato Sauce**

2 tablespoons grated Parmesan

Toasted pine nuts or almonds (for garnish)

PREP: 5 minutes

COOK: 25 minutes

YIELD: 6 servings

Cook pasta according to package directions; drain. Cook sausage and onion in large nonstick skillet until sausage is lightly browned; drain. Add peppers; cook and stir 2 minutes more. Stir in undrained tomatoes and tomato sauce. Bring to boil; reduce heat. Simmer, uncovered, 5 minutes. Stir in cooked pasta; heat through. Sprinkle with cheese. Sprinkle with toasted pine nuts or almonds, if desired.

Courtesy of Del Monte Foods

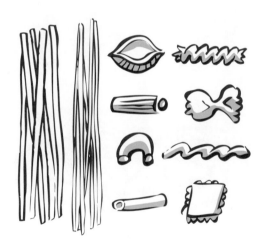

Caribbean Pork and Rice with Vegetables

PREP: 10 minutes

COOK: 20 minutes

YIELD: 4 servings

In a large skillet over high heat, heat olive oil. Add sliced pork; season with salt and pepper and cook until no longer pink, about 10 minutes. Stir in cooked rice, vegetables, jerk marinade, and water. Cook until thickened and heated through, about 10 minutes. Season with salt and pepper.

Courtesy of Birds Eye Foods, Inc.

1 tablespoon olive oil

1 lb. boneless pork chops, cut into strips

Salt and pepper

1 (10-oz.) package **BIRDS EYE® STEAMFRESH® Long Grain White Rice**, cooked according to package directions

1 (12-oz.) package **BIRDS EYE® STEAMFRESH® Asparagus, Gold and White Corn, Baby Carrots**, cooked according to package directions

1 cup prepared Caribbean jerk marinade

¼ cup water

Honey Cashew Five-Spice Pork with Brown Rice

8 to 10 oz. (¾-inch-thick) **SMITHFIELD® Boneless Pork Chops**, cut into ½-inch-wide strips

¾ teaspoon five-spice powder

¼ teaspoon salt

1 tablespoon reduced-sodium soy sauce

1 tablespoon honey

1 tablespoon vegetable oil

¼ cup unsalted roasted cashews or peanuts

1 cup hot, cooked quick-cooking or ready-to-serve brown rice

PREP: 13 minutes

COOK: 6 minutes

YIELD: 2 servings

Place pork on a piece of wax paper. Combine five-spice powder and salt; sprinkle on pork and toss well to coat strips. Stir together soy sauce and honey; set aside. Heat oil in a large, nonstick skillet over medium-high heat. Add pork and cook until browned on all sides and no longer pink in center, about 4 to 5 minutes. Add cashews; drizzle with soy sauce mixture, stirring to coat; immediately remove from heat. Serve on brown rice.

COOK'S TIP

Five-spice powder is a Chinese spice mixture of cinnamon, cloves, star anise, fennel, and pepper. It is a strongly flavored, fragrant spice, so use it sparingly at first. The blend works well in savory dishes that benefit from the addition of ground cinnamon as an ingredient.

Courtesy of Smithfield Foods

Asian Noodles with Pork and Peanut Sauce

4 oz. soba (thin buckwheat) noodles or whole wheat spaghetti, uncooked

¼ cup creamy peanut butter (not natural)

2 tablespoons soy sauce

1 teaspoon dark sesame oil

1 teaspoon Chinese chili garlic paste (preferably Lan Chi) or sriracha (Southeast Asian chile sauce)

2 teaspoons vegetable oil

8 to 10 oz. (¾-inch-thick) **SMITHFIELD® Boneless Pork Chops**, cut into ½-inch-wide strips

1 medium zucchini, cut into julienne strips

1 small red bell pepper, cut into thin strips (optional)

2 tablespoons chopped cilantro

PREP: 5 minutes

COOK: 25 minutes

YIELD: 2 servings

Cook noodles in boiling water until just tender according to package directions. Drain, reserving ¼ cup cooking water. Keep noodles warm. Stir together reserved cooking water, peanut butter, soy sauce, sesame oil, and chili garlic paste. Set aside. Heat oil in a large, nonstick skillet over medium-high heat. Add pork and sauté until browned on all sides and no longer pink in center, 4 to 5 minutes. Transfer to a plate and set aside. Add zucchini and pepper, if using, to skillet; sauté until just tender. Transfer to plate of pork. Return skillet to heat; pour in reserved peanut butter mixture. Add pork and vegetables; bring to a simmer over medium heat, stirring constantly. Serve over noodles; sprinkle with cilantro.

Courtesy of Smithfield Foods

Peachy Pork Picante

PREP: 5 minutes

COOK: 25 minutes

YIELD: 4 servings

1 lb. boneless pork loin, cut into ¾-inch cubes

1 to 2 tablespoons taco seasoning mix

2 teaspoons vegetable oil

1 (8-oz.) bottle chunky-style salsa

⅓ cup peach preserves

Hot cooked rice (optional)

Coat pork cubes with taco seasoning. Heat oil in large nonstick skillet over medium-high heat; add pork and cook to brown, stirring occasionally. Add salsa and preserves to pan, lower heat, cover, and simmer for 15 to 20 minutes. Serve over rice, if desired.

SERVING SUGGESTIONS

Peachy Pork Picante is one of those dishes that sounds really different but all the flavors work really well. It is best served over hot steamed rice, but works over couscous as well.

Courtesy of National Pork Board

Skillet Pork Hash

1 tablespoon olive oil

1 lb. boneless pork loin, cut into ½-inch cubes

1 (16-oz.) package refrigerated cooked, peeled, and diced potato

1 cup chopped onion

1 cup chopped green bell pepper

1 clove garlic, crushed

⅓ cup chicken broth

1 teaspoon dried thyme

1 teaspoon salt

¼ teaspoon pepper

2 tablespoons chopped fresh parsley

PREP: 10 minutes

COOK: 20 minutes

YIELD: 4 servings

Heat oil in large ovenproof skillet over medium-high heat. Cook pork 3 to 4 minutes, until slightly brown. Stir in potato, onion, green pepper, garlic, broth, thyme, salt, and pepper. Cover, lower heat, and simmer for 8 to 10 minutes. Place skillet under broiler 4 to 5 inches from heat source. Broil until surface of hash is crisp and golden brown, about 2 minutes. Sprinkle with parsley.

COOK'S TIP

Have some leftover pork roast and potatoes? Cut up and toss together for a hearty winter breakfast—or supper—treat. For dinner, serve with crusty hard rolls and a fruit salad. As part of a morning menu, serve with fresh fruit and muffins.

Courtesy of National Pork Board

Apricot Glazed Pork Kabobs

PREP: 15 minutes

MARINATE: 30 minutes

COOK: 15 minutes

YIELD: 4 to 6 servings

1 (10-oz.) jar apricot preserves

4 tablespoons orange liqueur or orange juice

2 tablespoons butter

1 lb. boneless pork loin, cut into 1-inch cubes

Stir together preserves, liqueur, and butter in a small saucepan and simmer until butter is melted (or combine ingredients in a 2-cup glass measure and microwave on high 1 minute). Place pork cubes in heavy resealable plastic bag; pour ¾ cup of the apricot mixture over to coat. Marinate at least 30 minutes. Thread pork onto 4 to 6 skewers. Grill over hot coals 10 to 12 minutes, turning occasionally and basting with marinade. Heat remaining apricot sauce to boiling and serve alongside kabobs, if desired.

SERVING SUGGESTION

This is a fun recipe for summer gatherings. Serve the kabobs with corn on the cob, your favorite baked beans, and potato salad.

Courtesy of National Pork Board

Smoky Citrus Kabobs

PREP: 15 minutes

COOK: 12 minutes

YIELD: 4 servings

Thread tenderloin cubes onto skewers (if using bamboo skewers, soak in water for 30 minutes before using to prevent burning). Stir together remaining ingredients for basting sauce. Place kabobs over medium-hot coals, brushing generously with basting sauce. Grill and turn to brown evenly, brushing frequently with sauce just until done, 10 to 12 minutes.

Courtesy of National Pork Board

1 lb. **SMITHFIELD® Pork Tenderloin**, cut into ¾-inch cubes

⅓ cup smoky barbecue sauce

⅓ cup orange marmalade

2 tablespoons prepared horseradish

Parmesan Pork Tenderloin

1 lb. pork tenderloin

3 tablespoons fine dry bread crumbs

1 tablespoon grated Parmesan

1 teaspoon salt

⅛ teaspoon pepper

2 teaspoons vegetable oil

1 small onion, thinly sliced

1 clove garlic, minced

2 small zucchini or summer squash, thinly sliced

PREP: 18 minutes

COOK: 12 minutes

YIELD: 4 servings

Cut tenderloin crosswise into 12 slices, approximately ¾-inch thick. Place each slice on its cut surface and flatten with heel of hand to ½-inch thickness. Combine crumbs, Parmesan, salt, and pepper; dredge pork slices to coat. Heat oil over medium-high heat in nonstick pan. Sauté pork for 2 to 3 minutes per side; remove and keep warm. Add onion, garlic, and zucchini or squash to skillet and sauté 5 minutes or until tender.

COOK'S TIP

Add seasoned bread crumbs to add more kick to this dish. Serve these breaded pork medallions with tortellini and sautéed summer squash.

Courtesy of National Pork Board

Pork Tenderloin with Creamy Mustard Sauce

1 lb. pork tenderloin

Salt and ground black pepper (optional)

1 teaspoon vegetable oil

½ cup **NESTLÉ® CARNATION® Evaporated Fat Free Milk**

2 tablespoons Dijon mustard

2 or 3 green onions, sliced

PREP: 15 minutes

COOK: 10 minutes

YIELD: 4 servings

Cut pork into 1-inch-thick slices. Place pork between two pieces of plastic wrap. Flatten to ¼-inch thickness using meat mallet or rolling pin. Season with salt and ground black pepper, if desired. Heat oil in large nonstick skillet over medium-high heat. Add half of the pork; cook on each side for 2 minutes or until browned and cooked through. Remove from skillet; set aside and keep warm. Repeat with remaining pork. Reduce heat to low. Add evaporated milk; stir to loosen brown bits from bottom of skillet. Stir in mustard and green onions. Return pork to skillet. Cook for 1 to 2 minutes or until sauce is slightly thickened, turning pork to coat with sauce.

Courtesy of Nestlé USA

Honey-Mustard Tenderloin

COOK: 30 minutes

YIELD: 4 servings

Preheat oven to 450°F. Combine all ingredients but tenderloin; coat tenderloin well with sauce. Roast for 20 to 30 minutes, basting occasionally, until meat thermometer inserted in thickest part of tenderloin registers 155°F to 160°F. Slice thinly to serve.

COOK'S TIP

A simple way to turn a weekday meal into something special. Serve with wild rice mix and steamed fresh asparagus.

Courtesy of National Pork Board

4 tablespoons honey

2 tablespoons cider vinegar

2 tablespoons brown sugar

1 tablespoon Dijon mustard

1 whole (1-lb.) pork tenderloin

Cranberry Pork Chops

PREP: 10 minutes

COOK: 15 minutes

YIELD: 4 servings

Season pork with salt and ground black pepper, if desired. Heat oil in large nonstick skillet over medium-high heat. Add pork and onion; cook pork quickly on both sides until browned. Remove pork from skillet. Add **JUICY JUICE®** and sugar to skillet; stir until sugar is dissolved. Stir in cranberries, garlic, and thyme; cook, stirring occasionally, for 2 minutes. Return pork to skillet; reduce heat to low. Cover; cook for 5 minutes or until pork is no longer pink in center. Sprinkle with nuts, if using, before serving.

Courtesy of Nestlé USA

4 (¾-inch-thick) boneless pork loin chops (about 1 ½ lbs. total)

Salt and pepper (optional)

2 teaspoons vegetable oil

1 medium onion, thickly sliced

¾ cup **Apple NESTLÉ® JUICY JUICE® All Natural 100% Juice**

2 to 3 tablespoons granulated sugar

¾ cup fresh cranberries

1 large clove garlic, finely chopped

¾ teaspoon chopped fresh thyme or ¼ teaspoon crushed dried thyme

¼ cup coarsely chopped walnuts, toasted (optional)

Pork Chop and Fresh Apple Sauté

⅓ cup low-salt chicken broth

2 tablespoons raisins

1 tablespoon unseasoned rice vinegar

2 medium apples, peeled

2 tablespoons unsalted butter, divided

1 ½ teaspoons sugar

2 (¾-inch-thick) **SMITHFIELD Pork Chops**

Salt and freshly ground pepper

PREP: 10 minutes

COOK: 20 minutes

YIELD: 2 servings

Combine chicken broth, raisins, and vinegar in a small bowl and set aside. Thinly slice apples. Place a large, heavy skillet over medium-high heat until very hot. Add 1 tablespoon of the butter. When butter is melted and sizzling, add apples and sprinkle with sugar. Sauté until apple slices are golden brown, 6 to 8 minutes. Add broth mixture all at once; simmer until liquid is syrupy and reduced to about 3 tablespoons, about 1 minute. Transfer mixture to a bowl. Wipe skillet clean. Pat pork chops dry and season with salt and pepper. Place skillet back over medium-high heat until very hot. Add remaining 1 tablespoon butter. When butter is melted and sizzling, add chops and sear until browned on bottom, 3 to 4 minutes; turn chops and sear until browned and pork is cooked through, 3 to 4 minutes. Transfer chops to serving plates and spoon apple mixture over.

Courtesy of Smithfield Foods

Pineapple Glazed Pork Chops

PREP: 5 minutes

COOK: 20 minutes

YIELD: 4 servings

Brown chops with garlic in margarine in large skillet. Remove chops from skillet. Spoon off fat. Add crushed pineapple, jelly, cinnamon, and ginger to skillet. Cook, over medium heat, until jelly melts. Return chops to skillet; spoon sauce over chops. Reduce heat to low. Cover; cook 10 minutes or until chops are no longer pink in center. Remove chops to serving platter; keep warm. Stir together water and cornstarch; add to skillet. Cook, stirring, until thickened. Spoon sauce over chops.

Courtesy of Dole Food Company

4 (¾- to 1-inch-thick) pork loin chops

1 clove garlic, finely chopped or ¼ teaspoon garlic powder

1 tablespoon margarine

1 (8-oz.) can **DOLE® Crushed Pineapple**, undrained

½ cup apple jelly

¼ teaspoon ground cinnamon

¼ teaspoon ground ginger

1 tablespoon water

1 teaspoon cornstarch

Golden Onion-Baked Pork Chops

1 envelope **LIPTON® RECIPE SECRETS® Golden Onion Soup Mix**

⅓ cup plain dry bread crumbs

4 (1-inch-thick) bone-in pork chops

1 egg, well beaten

PREP: 10 minutes

COOK: 20 minutes

YIELD: 4 servings

Preheat oven to 400°F. Combine **LIPTON® RECIPE SECRETS® Golden Onion Soup Mix** with bread crumbs in small bowl. Dip chops in egg, then bread crumb mixture, until evenly coated. Arrange chops on baking sheet. Bake uncovered 20 minutes or until done.

VARIATION

Also terrific with **LIPTON® RECIPE SECRETS® Onion and Savory Herb with Garlic Soup Mix**.

Courtesy of Unilever

Bruschetta Pork Chops

2 boneless butterflied pork chops

2 tablespoons (¼ of a packet) **SHAKE 'N BAKE Original Pork Seasoned Coating Mix**

1 large plum tomato, chopped

¼ cup **KRAFT Sun-Dried Tomato Dressing**

½ cup **KRAFT Shredded Low-Moisture Part-Skim Mozzarella Cheese**

PREP: 5 minutes

COOK: 25 minutes

YIELD: 2 servings

Heat oven to 425°F. Coat chops with coating mix as directed on package. Place on baking sheet sprayed with cooking spray. Bake for 20 minutes or until chops are done (a thermometer inserted in thickest part registers 160°F). Meanwhile, combine tomato and dressing. Top chops with tomato mixture and cheese. Bake 5 minutes or until cheese is melted.

Courtesy of Kraft Foods

Pork with Mushroom Dijon Sauce

COOK: 25 minutes

YIELD: 2 servings

Season chops with lemon pepper. Heat oil in skillet. Add chops and cook until browned. Remove chops. Add mushrooms and cook until tender. Add soup, milk, wine, and mustard. Heat to a boil. Add chops. Cover and cook over low heat 10 minutes or until done.

Courtesy of Campbell Soup Company

4 (¾-inch-thick) boneless pork chops

½ teaspoon lemon pepper seasoning

1 tablespoon vegetable oil

1 cup sliced mushrooms

1 (10 ¾-oz.) can **CAMPBELL'S® Condensed Cream of Mushroom Soup (Regular, 98% Fat Free, or 25% Less Sodium)**

¼ cup milk

2 tablespoons Chablis or other dry white wine

1 tablespoon Dijon-style mustard

Coriander-Pepper Chops

PREP: 5 minutes

COOK: 8 minutes

MARINATE: 30 minutes

YIELD: 4 servings

2 cloves garlic, crushed

1 tablespoon crushed coriander seeds

1 tablespoon coarsely ground black pepper

1 tablespoon brown sugar

3 tablespoons soy sauce

4 (1-inch-thick) boneless pork chops

Combine all ingredients except pork chops. Place chops in a shallow dish and pour marinade over; let marinate 30 minutes. Prepare medium-hot coals in grill bed (or preheat broiler). Remove pork from marinade, discarding marinade. Grill chops (or broil 3 to 4 inches from heat source) for 7 to 8 minutes, turning once.

COOK'S TIP

Create savory, sweet chops on the grill with a marinade made with soy sauce and brown sugar.

Courtesy of National Pork Board

Cinnamon-Maple Pork Chops

2 cups **HEINZ® Tomato Ketchup**

½ cup maple syrup

1 tablespoon ground cinnamon

1 tablespoon chopped fresh thyme

2 teaspoons hot pepper sauce

¼ teaspoon ground cumin

¼ teaspoon ground coriander

2 cloves garlic, minced

3 green onions, finely chopped

6 thick pork chops (3 lbs. total)

½ teaspoon salt

½ teaspoon pepper

PREP: 5 minutes

COOK: 25 minutes

YIELD: 6 servings

Combine the ketchup, maple syrup, cinnamon, thyme, hot pepper sauce, cumin, coriander, and garlic in a saucepan; bring to a boil over medium-high heat. Reduce heat to low and simmer for 10 minutes or until sauce is very thick. Cool completely; stir in onions. Preheat the grill to medium-high and grease lightly. Sprinkle pork chops evenly with salt and pepper; coat all over with half the sauce. Grill chops, basting often with remaining sauce, for about 7 minutes per side or until only slightly pink in the center.

Courtesy of H.J. Heinz Company, L.P.

Honey-Hot Chops

PREP: 5 minutes

COOK: 10 minutes

YIELD: 4 servings

6 tablespoons honey

2 tablespoons hot pepper sauce

4 (¾- to 1-inch-thick) pork chops

Salt and pepper, to taste

Prepare medium-hot fire in kettle-style grill. In small bowl stir together honey and hot pepper sauce. Season chops with salt and pepper and grill over direct heat, turning and basting with honey-pepper sauce mixture, until chops are nicely browned, 8 to 10 minutes.

COOK'S TIP

Fire up the grill and dinner is ready in fewer than 15 minutes with pork chops that are finished with a sweet-hot glaze. Pair the chops with baked sweet potatoes, a green salad, and warm dinner rolls.

Courtesy of National Pork Board

Pan-Seared Lamb Chops

8 lamb loin chops, excess fat removed

Salt and pepper (optional)

2 tablespoons butter, divided

⅓ cup **LEA & PERRINS® Worcestershire Sauce**

2 tablespoons freshly squeezed lemon juice

1 tablespoon chopped fresh mint

Mint sprigs (for garnish)

Lemon zest (for garnish)

PREP: 5 minutes

COOK: 10 minutes

YIELD: 4 to 8 servings

Season chops with salt and pepper, if desired. In a large skillet over medium-high heat, brown chops in 1 tablespoon of the butter for about 4 minutes each side for medium-rare. Reduce heat to medium and stir in Worcestershire sauce and lemon juice. When sauce bubbles, remove pan from heat and place chops on serving dish. Add remaining 1 tablespoon butter and mint, stirring constantly, until butter has melted and the sauce has a light creamy sheen. Spoon sauce over the chops, and garnish with mint sprigs and lemon zest.

COOK'S TIP

Although lamb loin chops are especially tender, they can be expensive. Shoulder chops can also be used and are less pricey.

Courtesy of H.J. Heinz Company, L.P.

Lemony Walnut-Crusted Fish Fillets

PREP: 15 minutes

COOK: 15 minutes

YIELD: 4 servings

Preheat oven to 425°F. Arrange cod on baking sheet, then drizzle with lemon juice; set aside. Process bread in food processor until fine crumbs form. Add parsley, lemon zest, and salt and process until chopped. Add **I CAN'T BELIEVE IT'S NOT BUTTER!®** and pulse just until combined. Combine bread mixture with walnuts in small bowl. Evenly top cod with crumb mixture. Bake 15 minutes or until cod flakes with a fork and crumbs are golden.

Courtesy of Unilever

1 lb. cod or halibut fillet, about 1-inch thick

1 tablespoon lemon juice

2 small slices whole wheat bread

¼ cup loosely packed fresh parsley leaves

1 teaspoon grated lemon zest

⅛ teaspoon salt

2 tablespoons **I CAN'T BELIEVE IT'S NOT BUTTER!® Cooking & Baking Stick**

¼ cup finely chopped walnuts

Fish Fillet with a Creamy Sauce and Almonds

PREP: 7 minutes

COOK: 15 minutes

YIELD: 4 servings

In a bowl combine grape juice, lemon juice, and fish stock. Set aside. In a skillet, heat oil and brown garlic and onion. Lightly flour the fish and add to skillet. Sprinkle one additional tablespoon of flour on top of fish and cook until the underside of fish is browned. Turn fish over and add juice/fish stock mixture a little at a time. Let cook until sauce thickens a little, then add peas. Continue cooking for a few more minutes until fish is cooked through and no longer transparent. Transfer to serving platter. Sprinkle with minced parsley and garnish with almonds.

Courtesy of Welch Foods Inc., A Cooperative

½ cup **WELCH'S White Grape Juice***

3 tablespoons lemon juice

½ cup seafood or fish stock

1 to 2 tablespoons extra virgin olive oil

4 garlic cloves, minced

1 onion, minced

Flour

1 ¼ lbs. fish fillet (halibut, cod, tilapia)

1 cup frozen peas

1 tablespoon minced parsley

2 tablespoons sliced almonds (for garnish)

Salt to taste

*Or use ½ cup white wine and omit lemon juice. Combining grape juice with lemon juice makes a good substitute in recipes calling for wine; use purple grape juice for red wine and white grape juice for white wine.

Cod with Peas & Bacon

COOK: 30 minutes

YIELD: 4 servings

Cook the bacon in a single layer in a large skillet over medium heat, turning the strips often, until browned and crisp, about 10 minutes. Drain the bacon on paper towels and pour off all but about 2 tablespoons of the bacon fat from the skillet. Return the skillet with the bacon fat to medium heat and add butter. When the butter has melted, add the cod and cook until browned on each side and just cooked through, about 4 minutes per side. Transfer the fish to a plate and set aside. Add the chopped white parts of the scallions and the peas to the skillet and cook for 1 minute. Stir in the wine, scraping any browned bits stuck to the bottom of the skillet with a wooden spoon. Let the sauce boil for 1 minute, then stir in the cream. Boil the sauce until slightly thickened, 8 to 10 minutes. Return the fish to the skillet and let cook until heated through, about 2 minutes. Add the chopped scallion greens and season to your taste with salt and pepper. Crumble the bacon over the fish just before serving.

COOK'S TIP

In the Applegate Kitchen, we love using fresh peas when they are in season. We blanch them in boiling salted water until just tender before adding them to the skillet.

Courtesy of Applegate Farms, an Organic & Natural Meat Company

6 oz. **APPLEGATE FARMS Sunday Bacon**, strips separated

2 tablespoons butter

4 (6-oz.) skinless cod fillets

1 bunch scallions, trimmed, white and green parts chopped separately

2 cups frozen peas, thawed

¼ cup white wine

1 cup heavy cream

Salt and freshly ground black pepper

Pan-Browned Tilapia

2 tablespoons extra virgin olive oil

1 lb. tilapia fillets

Flour for dredging

Salt and pepper to taste

2 garlic cloves, crushed

⅓ cup **WELCH'S White Grape Juice**

2 tablespoons lemon juice

¼ cup minced parsley

3 scallions, white part sliced thin

⅓ cup chicken broth

PREP: 5 minutes

COOK: 20 minutes

YIELD: 4 servings

In a 10-inch skillet, heat olive oil over medium-high heat for 1 minute. Dredge the top side of the fillets in flour. Cook the fillets, floured side down, until they are browned, 3 to 4 minutes. Turn them and season with salt and pepper. (See note if using a thick fillet). Add garlic, grape juice, lemon juice, parsley, and scallions. Cook for 3 to 4 minutes or until fish begins to flake. Transfer fish to platter. Add chicken broth to skillet and cook for a few minutes. Pour this sauce over fish.

VARIATION

Try this recipe with cod, haddock, or other whitefish. To prepare a thick fillet such as cod, turn fish over; add garlic, wine, and scallions, and place in a preheated 400°F oven (use an ovenproof skillet) for 5 to 7 minutes. Use ½ cup of dry white wine instead of the grape juice and lemon juice.

Courtesy of Welch Foods Inc., A Cooperative

Grilled Ginger-Lime Swordfish & Vegetables

PREP: 10 minutes

GRILL: 16 minutes

YIELD: 4 servings

Preheat grill to medium heat. Mix mayo, juice, and seasonings. Remove ¼ cup of the mayo mixture for later use; brush remaining mayo mixture evenly onto the fish and vegetables. Place on grate of grill; cover with lid. Grill 5 to 8 minutes on each side or until fish flakes easily with fork and vegetables are crisp-tender. Serve over the rice; top evenly with the reserved mayo mixture.

Courtesy of Kraft Foods

¾ cup **KRAFT Real Mayo Mayonnaise**

2 tablespoons lime juice

1 ½ teaspoons finely chopped peeled ginger root

¼ teaspoon ground red pepper (cayenne)

4 swordfish steaks, each 1 ½ inches thick (2 lbs.)

2 red, yellow, or green bell peppers, cut into quarters

2 small zucchini, cut in half lengthwise

2 cups hot cooked rice

Sautéed Trout with Almond-Butter Sauce

PREP: 15 minutes

COOK: 15 minutes

YIELD: 4 servings

Preheat oven to 250°F. In a bowl, combine 3 tablespoons of the soymilk, lemon juice, almond butter, ¼ teaspoon of the salt, and ⅛ teaspoon of the pepper. In a shallow bowl, lightly beat the egg and the remaining soymilk. In another shallow bowl, combine the flour, remaining salt, and remaining pepper. Dip the trout into the egg mixture, then into the flour. In a large nonstick skillet, heat 1 tablespoon of the oil over medium heat. Cook the fish in batches, skin side up, until the first side is browned, 2 to 3 minutes. Then cook the second side until opaque, 3 to 4 minutes. Keep warm on a baking sheet in the oven. Add the remaining oil for the next batch. Serve with the almond-butter sauce.

Courtesy of Hain Celestial Group

5 tablespoons **WESTSOY® Unsweetened Soymilk**, divided

2 tablespoons lemon juice

1 ½ tablespoons **ARROWHEAD MILLS® Creamy Almond Butter**

½ teaspoon **HAIN PURE FOODS® Sea Salt**, divided

¼ teaspoon ground black pepper, divided

1 large egg

⅓ cup **ARROWHEAD MILLS® Stoneground Whole Wheat Flour**

4 (6-oz.) trout fillets, each ½-inch thick

2 tablespoons **HAIN PURE FOODS® Canola Oil** or **Spectrum Naturals Canola Oil**

Quick Tuna & Vegetable Casserole

2 ½ cups water

1 (5.7-oz.) package **KNORR® Rice Sides™ Cheddar Broccoli**

1 cup frozen green peas, partially thawed, or 1 (8 ¼-oz.) can green peas, drained

1 (6-oz.) can tuna, drained and flaked

2 tablespoons **I CAN'T BELIEVE IT'S NOT BUTTER!® Spread**

PREP: 5 minutes

COOK: 16 minutes

YIELD: 4 servings

Bring water to a boil in 12-inch skillet; stir in remaining ingredients. Reduce heat to low and simmer, stirring occasionally, 12 minutes or until rice is tender.

To microwave: Decrease water to 2 ¼ cups. Combine all ingredients in 2-quart microwave-safe casserole. Microwave uncovered at high 16 minutes or until rice is tender; stir.

Courtesy of Unilever

Baked Salmon with Black Olive Salsa

PREP: 10 minutes

COOK: 20 minutes

YIELD: 6 servings

Preheat oven to 400°F. Place salmon, skin side down, on foil-lined baking sheet. Combine remaining ingredients; spoon over salmon. Bake 18 to 20 minutes or until salmon flakes easily with fork.

Courtesy of Kraft Foods

1 (1 ½-lb.) salmon fillet

¼ cup sliced pitted black olives

¼ cup chopped green pepper

¼ cup chopped red onion

5 cherry tomatoes, quartered

¼ cup **KRAFT Sun-Dried Tomato Dressing**

Salmon with Scallions & Bacon

8 pieces **APPLEGATE FARMS Peppered Bacon**

1 lb. wild salmon fillet, cut into 4 pieces

1 tablespoon extra virgin olive oil

Salt and freshly ground pepper

1 bunch scallions, trimmed and coarsely chopped

White wine (optional)

PREP: 5 minutes

COOK: 20 minutes

YIELD: 4 servings

Cook the bacon in a large nonstick skillet over medium heat, turning the slices occasionally, until brown and crisp. Remove from the pan and drain on paper towel. Pour off most of the bacon grease and set the skillet aside. Rub the salmon pieces with the olive oil. Sprinkle with salt and a little pepper on all sides. Using the same skillet, brown the salmon on both sides over medium heat. Add the scallions, scattering them around the salmon. Cover and cook for about 5 minutes. Transfer salmon to a platter or plates then spoon the scallions on top of each piece. Add a splash of wine or water to the skillet and cook, stirring with a wooden spoon and scraping up any browned bits, for about 1 minute. Spoon the sauce over the salmon. Garnish the salmon with the bacon.

COOK'S TIP

Choose wild salmon over farm-raised. Farmed fish are fed mainly on soy-based pellets and tend to have a milder flavor.

Courtesy of Applegate Farms, an Organic & Natural Meat Company

Salmon Fillets with Creamy Corn & Dill

Nonstick cooking spray

6 (4-oz.) salmon fillets (about 1 ½ lbs. total)

½ teaspoon salt, divided

½ teaspoon ground black pepper, divided

1 (16-oz.) package frozen corn, thawed, *or* 1 lb. fresh corn kernels

1 (12-fl. oz.) can **NESTLÉ® CARNATION® Evaporated Lowfat 2% Milk**

1 tablespoon all-purpose flour

¾ teaspoon garlic powder

2 tablespoons fresh chopped dill or 1 ½ teaspoons dried dill, divided

PREP: 5 minutes

COOK: 25 minutes

YIELD: 6 servings

Preheat oven to 325°F. Line baking sheet with foil. Spray foil with nonstick cooking spray. Spray large nonstick skillet with nonstick cooking spray; heat over medium-high heat. Place salmon in skillet. Cook, turning once, for about 3 minutes or until lightly browned. Remove from skillet; place salmon skin side down on prepared baking sheet. Sprinkle with ¼ teaspoon of the salt and ¼ teaspoon of the pepper. Bake for 15 to 20 minutes or until salmon flakes easily when tested with a fork. Do not overbake. Baking time will vary slightly with thickness of fillets. Meanwhile, combine corn, evaporated milk, flour, garlic powder, remaining ¼ teaspoon salt, and remaining ¼ teaspoon pepper in skillet. Cook over medium-high heat, stirring occasionally, until mixture comes to a gentle boil. Reduce heat to medium-low; cook, stirring occasionally, for 5 to 7 minutes or until slightly thickened. Remove from heat; stir in half of dill. To serve, pour corn mixture on serving platter or divide mixture between six plates. Top with salmon. Sprinkle salmon with remaining dill.

Courtesy of Nestlé USA

Sweetheart Salmon Fillets

4 (4- to 6-oz.) salmon fillets

¼ cup flour

Salt and pepper to taste

3 tablespoons butter or margarine

½ cup **WELCH'S 100% Grape Juice made from Concord grapes**

½ cup chicken broth

½ teaspoon dill

¼ cup half-and-half

1 to 2 teaspoons freshly squeezed lemon juice

Lemon slices (for garnish)

Parsley (for garnish)

PREP: 5 minutes

COOK: 25 minutes

YIELD: 4 servings

Dust salmon fillets generously with mixture of flour, salt, and pepper to coat. Melt butter in broad skillet. Add fillets; cook over medium-high heat for 5 to 10 minutes per side until filets are opaque or just beginning to flake in thickest part. Remove to warm plate. Deglaze pan with grape juice and broth, loosening browned particles. Stir in dill and half-and-half. Cook just until slightly thickened. Season with salt and pepper; add lemon juice to taste. To serve, spoon sauce over fillets. Garnish with lemon slices and parsley, if desired.

Recipe courtesy of the New York Wine & Grape Foundation and the National Grape Cooperative. Courtesy of Welch Foods Inc., A Cooperative

Sesame-Encrusted Salmon

PREP: 10 minutes

COOK: 10 minutes

YIELD: 6 servings

Preheat broiler to high. Line a baking sheet with non-stick foil. Arrange the salmon fillets on the baking sheet. Sprinkle with salt and pepper. Bring the ketchup, soy sauce, lemon juice, honey, lemon zest, and garlic to a boil in a small saucepan; stir occasionally. Brush half the ketchup mixture over the top of the salmon. Broil the salmon for 2 minutes. Remove the pan from the oven. Carefully turn the salmon over. Brush with the remaining glaze. Broil for 2 minutes. Sprinkle the tops of the salmon fillets evenly with sesame seeds to create a crust. Broil for an additional 2 to 3 minutes or until fish flakes easily with a fork.

Courtesy of H.J. Heinz Company, L.P

6 skinless, boneless salmon fillets

½ teaspoon salt

½ teaspoon pepper

⅓ cup **HEINZ® Tomato Ketchup**

2 tablespoons soy sauce

2 tablespoons lemon juice

1 tablespoon honey

½ teaspoon finely grated lemon zest

1 clove garlic, minced

3 tablespoons sesame seeds

Tarragon-Encrusted Salmon

4 tablespoons butter, softened

2 tablespoons lemon juice

1 (0.7-oz.) package **SIMPLY ORGANIC Steak Marinade Mix**

1 to 1 ½ lbs. salmon steaks, at least 1-inch thick

Fresh tomato slices (for garnish, optional)

PREP: 5 minutes

COOK: 10 minutes

YIELD: 4 servings

Preheat broiler to high or warm up grill. In a small bowl blend butter, lemon juice, and Steak Marinade. Lay salmon on broiler pan or grill, skin side down. Spread a thin layer of butter mixture on steaks. Broil 8 to 10 minutes or grill until salmon is just flaky. Garnish with tomato slices, if desired.

Courtesy of Simply Organic

Grilled Teriyaki Salmon

PREP: 5 minutes

MARINATE: 1 to 2 hours

COOK: 14 minutes

YIELD: 4 servings

Combine first six ingredients and pour into shallow nonaluminum baking dish. Place salmon steaks in dish, cover, and refrigerate 1 to 2 hours, turning salmon halfway through marination. Remove from marinade and grill on BBQ grill that has been lightly greased with vegetable oil. Cook on medium-high heat (350°F) 5 to 7 minutes per side or until salmon is just barely opaque throughout and has attractive grill marks on outside. Serve immediately with fresh mango salsa.

Courtesy of Frontier Natural Products Co-op

½ cup soy sauce

2 tablespoons vegetable oil

2 tablespoons finely minced fresh ginger root

2 teaspoons **FRONTIER** crushed red chili peppers

1 tablespoon **FRONTIER** garlic flakes

2 tablespoons brown sugar

4 (½-lb. each) salmon steaks

Fresh mango salsa

Grilled Dilled Salmon

2 tablespoons melted unsalted butter

½ teaspoon **FRONTIER** dillweed

¼ teaspoon **FRONTIER** onion powder

1 tablespoon lemon juice

⅛ teaspoon **FRONTIER** black pepper, medium grind

1 lb. salmon fillets

PREP: 10 minutes

COOK: 15 minutes

YIELD: 4 servings

Prepare grill. Combine all ingredients but fish in a bowl and set aside. Arrange salmon in a tray made of heavy-duty foil with 1-inch sides. Spread butter mixture over fillets. Place on grill over hot coals. Cover lightly with foil and cook about 15 minutes, until fish flakes when tested with a fork.

Courtesy of Frontier Natural Products Co-op

Grilled Salmon with Mediterranean Salsa

PREP: 15 minutes

COOK: 10 minutes

YIELD: 4 servings

Preheat grill to medium heat. Mix parsley, tomatoes, cheese, olives, oil, and lemon juice until well blended. Let stand at room temperature until ready to use. Grill salmon 5 minutes on each side or until salmon flakes easily with fork. Serve each fillet topped with ¼ cup of the tomato salsa.

Courtesy of Kraft Foods

½ cup chopped fresh parsley

⅓ cup chopped plum tomatoes

¼ cup **ATHENOS Traditional Crumbled Feta Cheese**

¼ cup coarsely chopped pitted kalamata olives

2 tablespoons olive oil

1 tablespoon lemon juice

4 (4-oz.) salmon fillets

Honey Mustard Glazed Salmon with Tropical Fruit Salsa

PREP: 20 minutes

COOK: 10 minutes

YIELD: 4 servings

Stir together mustard, honey, hot pepper sauce, and ½ teaspoon of the salt in small bowl. Heat outdoor or stove-top grill to medium-high. Combine tropical fruit salad, avocado, onion, bell pepper, lime juice, and remaining ¼ teaspoon salt. Cover; refrigerate salsa until ready to serve. Grill salmon 4 to 5 minutes. Turn and brush with honey-mustard glaze. Grill 4 to 5 minutes more or until desired doneness. Serve salmon with tropical salsa.

Courtesy of Dole Food Company

3 tablespoons spicy brown mustard

2 tablespoons honey

¼ teaspoon hot pepper sauce

¾ teaspoon salt, divided

1 (15.25-oz.) can **DOLE® Tropical Mixed Fruit**, diced

1 **DOLE Avocado**, peeled, diced

¼ cup chopped **DOLE Red Onion**

⅓ cup diced **DOLE Red Bell Pepper**

1 tablespoon lime juice

1 ⅓ lbs. salmon fillets

Moroccan Spiced Salmon

GLAZE

½ cup **HEINZ® Tomato Ketchup**

2 tablespoons lime juice

1 tablespoon brown sugar

2 teaspoons ground cinnamon

2 teaspoons ground ginger

1 teaspoon ground coriander

½ teaspoon each ground cumin

½ teaspoon black pepper

SALMON

6 boneless, skinless salmon fillets

1 tablespoon vegetable oil

Lime wedges

PREP: 15 minutes

COOK: 10 minutes

YIELD: 6 servings

Stir the ingredients for the glaze until smooth. Heat on high in the microwave for 2 minutes; stop to stir twice. Preheat the grill to medium-high; grease the grate well. Brush the salmon with the oil. Place the salmon on the grill. Grill for 3 minutes. Turn and brush liberally with the glaze mixture, reserving some glaze for serving. Reduce the heat to medium. Close the lid and cook for 3 to 4 minutes or until just barely coral on the inside when tested with a knife. Brush with additional glaze. Serve with lime wedges.

Courtesy of H.J. Heinz Company, L.P.

Dilled Salmon Cakes

PREP: 22 minutes

COOK: 8 minutes

YIELD: 6 servings

Combine all ingredients for sauce in small bowl; mix well. Cover and chill while making salmon cakes. Combine all ingredients for salmon cakes in medium bowl; mix well. Let stand 5 minutes. Shape into 5 oval patties about 1-inch thick. Lightly spray nonstick skillet with nonstick cooking spray. Cook salmon cakes over medium heat 3 to 4 minutes on each side or until golden brown and heated through. Serve with sauce.

Courtesy of The Quaker Oats Company

SAUCE

½ cup plain nonfat yogurt

⅓ cup seeded, chopped tomato

⅓ cup seeded, chopped cucumber

1 tablespoon finely chopped onion

1 tablespoon finely chopped fresh dill or 1 teaspoon dried dillweed

SALMON CAKES

1 (14 ¾-oz.) can pink salmon, drained, skin and bones removed

¾ cup **QUAKER® Oats** (quick or old-fashioned, uncooked)

⅓ cup fat-free milk

2 egg whites, lightly beaten

2 tablespoons finely chopped onion

1 tablespoon finely chopped fresh dill or 1 teaspoon dried dillweed

¼ teaspoon salt (optional)

Herbed Crab Cakes

1 ½ cups **PEPPERIDGE FARM® Herb Seasoned Stuffing**

2 eggs, beaten

⅓ cup mayonnaise

2 teaspoons Dijon-style mustard

1 teaspoon Worcestershire sauce

1 tablespoon chopped fresh parsley or 1 teaspoon dried parsley flakes

1 (16-oz.) can refrigerated pasteurized crabmeat

2 tablespoons butter or margarine

Lemon wedges

PREP: 15 minutes

COOK: 10 minutes

YIELD: 6 servings

Crush ½ cup stuffing. Mix lightly remaining stuffing, eggs, mayonnaise, mustard, Worcestershire sauce, parsley, and crabmeat. Shape into 6 patties ½-inch thick. Coat with crushed stuffing. Heat butter in skillet. Cook patties 5 minutes or until hot. Serve with lemon wedges.

Courtesy of Campbell Soup Company

Lobster Pasta with Mushrooms and Artichoke

PREP: 10 minutes

COOK: 20 minutes

YIELD: 8 servings

Cook pasta according to instructions on package and toss with olive oil. In a large skillet, melt butter. Add shallots, stirring over moderate heat for 2 minutes. Add mushrooms and artichoke hearts. Continue stirring until mushrooms are softened. Stir in white wine and stock; let simmer for 3 minutes. Reduce heat to low. Temper yogurt by adding some of the mushrooms and artichokes hearts and mixing (this will ensure the yogurt doesn't curdle); add to skillet. Add ½ cup asiago, 2 tablespoons parsley, thyme, salt, and pepper. Stir in pasta and lobster. Garnish with remaining asiago and parsley.

Courtesy of Stonyfield Farm

½ lb. rigatoni or other pasta

4 tablespoons olive oil

3 tablespoons unsalted butter

2 shallots, minced

2 cups sliced mushrooms

2 (14-oz.) cans artichoke hearts, halved

¼ cup dry white wine

½ cup chicken or vegetable stock

2 cups **STONYFIELD FARM Plain Yogurt**

1 cup grated asiago, divided

2 ½ tablespoons chopped fresh parsley, divided

2 teaspoons fresh thyme leaves

Salt and pepper to taste

2 lbs. fresh lobster meat, cooked

Butternut Squash Risotto with Pan-Seared Scallops

1 (5.8-oz.) box **LUNDBERG® Butternut Squash Risotto**

1 lb. (12 to 14) large sea scallops

1 tablespoon olive oil

2 tablespoons butter

2 tablespoons chopped fresh sage

COOK: 25 minutes

YIELD: 4 servings

Prepare **LUNDBERG® Butternut Squash Risotto** according to box directions. While risotto is cooking, pat scallops dry. Heat oil in a 12-inch nonstick skillet over moderately high heat until hot, then sauté scallops until golden brown, 6 to 8 minutes. Transfer to a bowl with a slotted spoon; cover and keep warm. Discard any oil remaining in skillet. Cook butter in same skillet over moderate heat until it foams and turns light brown. Add sage and cook, stirring, 1 minute. Remove from heat. Mound risotto in the center of a wide bowl; arrange scallops around risotto and drizzle with sage butter.

Courtesy of Lundberg Family Farms

Cajun Shrimp

PREP: 10 minutes

COOK: 10 minutes

YIELD: 4 servings

Melt butter in skillet over medium-high heat. Add garlic, Worcestershire sauce, Cajun seasoning, green onions, and stock. Stir while cooking 3 to 5 minutes or until the sauce has thickened slightly. Add the shrimp and cook, stirring until shrimp are pink and just cooked through, approximately 2 to 3 minutes more. Serve immediately over cooked rice.

Courtesy of Frontier Natural Products Co-op

½ stick unsalted butter

3 cloves garlic, minced

2 teaspoons Worcestershire sauce

2 tablespoons **FRONTIER Cajun Seasoning**

1 bunch green onions, thinly sliced

1 cup vegetable stock or chicken stock

1 lb. large shrimp, peeled and deveined

Cooked rice

Sautéed Spicy Shrimp

PREP: 15 minutes

COOK: 8 minutes

YIELD: 4 servings

1 packet **OVEN FRY Fish Fry Seasoned Coating Mix for Fish**

¼ teaspoon ground red pepper

1 lb. shrimp, cleaned

1 egg, beaten

2 tablespoons oil

2 tablespoons butter or margarine

Combine coating mix and red pepper. Dip shrimp in egg; cover with coating mix. Discard any remaining coating mix. Heat oil and butter in large skillet on medium-high heat. Add shrimp in single-layer batches; cook 2 to 3 minutes or until golden brown, turning once. Add more oil and butter to skillet, if necessary, to cook remaining batches of shrimp.

Courtesy of Kraft Foods

Spicy Shrimp & Zucchini Sauté

1 cup **LEA & PERRINS®** **Marinade for Chicken**

1 cup **CLASSICO®** **Spicy Tomato & Basil Sauce**

1 lb. medium raw shrimp, peeled and deveined

1 medium onion, diced

3 small zucchini, cut lengthwise and sliced

4 cups cooked pasta, such as bow tie, elbow, or rotini, or 8 oz. dry pasta, cooked according to package instructions

PREP: 10 minutes

MARINATE: 10 minutes

COOK: 10 minutes

YIELD: 6 to 8 servings

In a medium bowl, mix together the Marinade, Spicy Tomato & Basil Sauce, and shrimp, and lightly toss until well coated. Cover and allow to marinate in refrigerator for 10 minutes. In a large skillet sprayed with nonstick cooking spray, over medium-high heat, sauté onion for 1 minute. Add zucchini and continue cooking for 3 to 4 minutes, or until crisp-tender, adding more cooking spray if needed. Add shrimp and marinade, and cook for an additional 3 to 4 minutes, or until shrimp are cooked through, stirring frequently. Add cooked pasta and lightly toss.

Courtesy of H.J. Heinz Company, L.P.

Prawns Peri Peri with Rice

3 tablespoons butter

1 tablespoon olive oil

1 tablespoon minced garlic

½ fresh lemon, juiced

1 teaspoon minced dried red chili

1 lb. (16 to 20) large shrimp, thawed, peeled, and deveined

1 (10-oz.) box **BIRDS EYE® Rice Pilaf in Herbed Butter Sauce**, cooked according to box directions

Salt and pepper

Lemon zest (for garnish)

PREP: 10 minutes

COOK: 15 minutes

YIELD: 4 servings

In a large skillet, heat butter and olive oil over medium heat. Add garlic, lemon juice, dried red chili, and shrimp. Cook until shrimp are opaque and firm, about 5 to 7 minutes. Stir in cooked **BIRDS EYE® Rice Pilaf in Herbed Butter Sauce** and continue cooking until heated through, about 3 minutes. Season with salt and pepper. Garnish with lemon zest before serving.

Courtesy of Birds Eye Foods, Inc.

Paella with Sausage and Shrimp

PREP: 5 minutes

COOK: 25 minutes

YIELD: 6 (1-cup) servings

On medium-high heat, warm olive oil in a large skillet. Sauté sausage and shrimp in oil. Add water, broth powder, saffron, and Garlic Pasta Sauce Mix and stir. Then add tomatoes and rice. Cover with lid and let simmer 15 to 20 minutes on low.

COOK'S TIP

Substitute chicken or add other seafood in place of the sausage.

Courtesy of Simply Organic

2 tablespoons olive oil

½ lb. sliced sausage, like chorizo

½ lb. medium (40 to 50 count) uncooked shrimp

2 cups water

2 tablespoons chicken-flavored broth powder

8 to 10 strands saffron

1 (1.13-oz.) package **SIMPLY ORGANIC Roasted Garlic Pasta Sauce Mix**

1 (14.5-oz.) can diced tomatoes

2 cups instant rice

Sautéed Shrimp with Spices

2 tablespoons extra virgin olive oil, divided

1 tablespoon sesame oil

1 or 2 garlic cloves, pureed or finely minced

1 tablespoon grated ginger

1 sprig fresh thyme

1 ½ lbs. shrimp, cleaned and deveined

¼ cup white wine

¼ cup **WELCH'S White Grape Juice**

2 tablespoons lemon juice, plus 1 tablespoon for reducing pan juices

2 tablespoons parsley, minced

Salt and pepper to taste

PREP: 10 minutes

COOK: 12 minutes

YIELD: 4 servings

Heat 1 tablespoon olive oil over medium heat in a large skillet. Add sesame oil, garlic, ginger, and thyme. Add shrimp and cook for about 2 minutes. Pour in wine, grape juice, and 2 tablespoons lemon juice, and cook for 3 to 4 minutes, basting with pan liquid at the same time. Shrimp are done when they turn pink. Season with salt and pepper to taste. Remove shrimp from liquid. Transfer to serving platter. In the same skillet, stir in 1 tablespoon of olive oil and the remaining 1 tablespoon of lemon juice and cook liquid down for about 3 to 5 minutes. Pour over shrimp and toss with parsley. Serve warm.

COOK'S NOTE

If desired, replace the wine with additional grape juice. Increase grape juice to ½ cup and lemon juice to 4 tablespoons.

Courtesy of Welch Foods Inc., A Cooperative

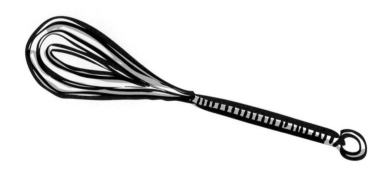

Greek-Style Pasta with Shrimp

PREP: 10 minutes

COOK: 20 minutes

YIELD: 4 servings

Heat oil in a large skillet over medium heat. Add garlic and sauté 30 seconds. Add shrimp, artichokes, feta, tomatoes, lemon juice, parsley, oregano, crushed red pepper, and kalamata olives and sauté until shrimp are cooked through, about 3 minutes. Add shrimp mixture to cooked spaghetti and toss to mix.

Courtesy of Lundberg Family Farms

1 tablespoon olive oil

4 teaspoons minced garlic

1 lb. uncooked medium shrimp, peeled and deveined

1 ½ cups canned artichoke hearts, drained

½ cup crumbled feta (4-oz. block)

1 large tomato, chopped

3 tablespoons fresh lemon juice

3 tablespoons chopped fresh parsley

2 tablespoons chopped fresh oregano or 1 ½ teaspoons dried oregano

⅛ teaspoon crushed red pepper flakes (optional)

¼ cup pitted kalamata olives

1 (10-oz.) box **LUNDBERG® Spaghetti Brown Rice Pasta**, cooked and drained

Garlic Shrimp & Pasta

2 tablespoons cornstarch

1 ¾ cups **SWANSON® Chicken Broth**

2 cloves garlic, minced

3 tablespoons chopped fresh parsley or 1 tablespoon dried parsley flakes

2 tablespoons lemon juice

⅛ teaspoon ground red pepper

1 lb. medium shrimp, shelled and deveined

4 cups hot cooked thin spaghetti, cooked without salt

PREP: 5 minutes

COOK: 20 minutes

YIELD: 4 servings

Mix cornstarch, broth, garlic, parsley, lemon juice, and red pepper in saucepan. Heat to a boil. Cook and stir until mixture boils and thickens. Add shrimp. Cook 5 minutes or until shrimp is done. Toss with spaghetti.

VARIATION

This recipe is also great using **SWANSON® Natural Goodness™** or **Certified Organic Chicken Broth** in place of the regular chicken broth.

Courtesy of Campbell Soup Company

Shrimp and Grits

PREP: 5 minutes

COOK: 25 minutes

YIELD: 6 servings

Melt butter in large saucepan. Add garlic, scallions, precooked spinach, and thyme. Cook for about 2 minutes. Add grits and cook for 2 minutes, stirring constantly. One at a time, whisk in broth, yogurt, salt, pepper, and hot sauce. Simmer for 6 minutes. Add shrimp and goat cheese; cook until shrimp is bright pink. Cover and remove from heat, let sit with cover on for 5 minutes (do not remove cover). Garnish with sprigs of fresh thyme.

Courtesy of Stonyfield Farm

2 tablespoons butter

3 cloves garlic, chopped

3 scallions, chopped

1 cup spinach, cooked and drained

2 teaspoons fresh thyme, plus a few sprigs for garnish

1 cup quick-cooking grits

3 ½ cups low-sodium chicken broth

1 cup **STONYFIELD FARM Plain Yogurt**

½ teaspoon salt or to taste

½ teaspoon freshly ground black pepper

2 teaspoons hot sauce

30 uncooked large shrimp, peeled and deveined

1 cup crumbled goat cheese

Acapulco Grilled Shrimp

1 (14.5-oz.) can **DEL MONTE®
Diced Tomatoes with Green
Pepper and Onion**, undrained

1 orange, peeled and chopped

¼ cup cilantro, chopped

2 teaspoons olive oil

1 to 2 teaspoons minced
jalapeño

1 garlic clove, crushed

1 lb. medium shrimp, peeled
and deveined

Salt and pepper (optional)

Cooked rice

PREP: 20 minutes

COOK: 6 minutes

YIELD: 4 servings

Combine tomatoes, orange, cilantro, oil, jalapeño, and garlic in medium bowl. Thread shrimp on skewers. Season to taste with salt and pepper, if desired. Brush grill with oil. Cook over hot coals about 3 minutes per side or until shrimp just turns opaque. Serve over rice with tomato mixture on side.

COOK'S TIP

Use cayenne pepper or hot pepper sauce in place of jalapeño.

Courtesy of Del Monte Foods

Thai Pineapple-Shrimp Curry with Jasmine Rice and Fragrant Herbs

1 tablespoon canola oil

1 to 2 tablespoons canned Thai red or yellow curry paste

2 cups **DOLE® Pineapple Juice**

3 tablespoons Thai or Vietnamese fish sauce

12 oz. fresh large shrimp, peeled and deveined

2 cups fresh **DOLE Tropical Gold® Pineapple**, cut in chunks

1 (6-oz.) package **DOLE Baby Spinach**

2 cups cooked Thai jasmine rice

¼ cup **DOLE Green Onions**, thinly sliced

¼ cup slivered fresh mint leaves

PREP: 16 minutes

COOK: 14 minutes

YIELD: 4 servings

Heat oil in large saucepan over medium heat. Add curry paste and cook, stirring constantly, until very fragrant, about 3 minutes. Stir pineapple juice and fish sauce into the curry paste mixture and let come to a simmer. Add shrimp and pineapple chunks to the simmering curry and cook just until shrimp turns opaque, about 5 minutes. Remove from heat, add spinach, and stir just until spinach wilts. Scoop ½ cup rice into the centers of each 4 serving bowls. Ladle equal portions of curry shrimp mixture into each bowl around the rice, and sprinkle each serving with equal portions of green onions and mint.

Courtesy of Dole Food Company

Bacon-Wrapped BBQ-Shrimp Kabobs

PREP: 10 minutes

COOK: 8 minutes

YIELD: 5 servings (2 kabobs each)

Heat grill to medium heat. Wrap one bacon piece around each shrimp. Thread two each shrimp, zucchini slices, and pepper pieces alternately on 10 skewers. Grill 3 to 4 minutes on each side or until shrimp turn pink, turning and brushing occasionally with barbecue sauce.

Courtesy of Kraft Foods

10 slices **OSCAR MAYER Fully Cooked Bacon**, cut in half

20 to 30 uncooked large shrimp (about 1 lb.), peeled and deveined

2 zucchini, trimmed, cut into 10 slices each

2 yellow peppers, cut into 10 pieces each

1 cup **BULL'S EYE Original Barbecue Sauce**

Grilled Butterflied Jumbo Shrimp

¼ cup **HEINZ® Chili Sauce**

¼ cup melted butter

¼ cup orange juice

⅓ cup dark rum

2 tablespoons chopped fresh chives, divided

2 tablespoons chopped fresh coriander, divided

2 teaspoons **HEINZ® Mustard**

½ teaspoon vanilla extract

2 cloves garlic, minced

2 lbs. jumbo shrimp, in shells

PREP: 17 minutes

COOK: 13 minutes

COOL: 15 minutes

YIELD: 8 servings

Whisk the chili sauce with the melted butter and orange juice in a saucepan set over medium heat. Bring to a boil. Stir in the rum, half each of the chives and the coriander, mustard, vanilla, and garlic. Remove from the heat and cool completely. Slice lengthwise through the top of each shrimp shell and almost all the way through the meat of each shrimp so that they can lie flat. Toss the shrimp with half the sauce mixture. Set aside. Preheat the grill to medium-high and grease lightly. Grill shrimp for 3 to 5 minutes per side or until cooked through. Baste shrimp often with the reserved sauce. Gently toss hot, cooked shrimp with any remaining sauce mixture. Sprinkle with remaining chives and coriander.

Courtesy of H.J. Heinz Company, L.P.

Side Dishes

Stir-Fried Vegetables

2 tablespoons vegetable oil

1 medium onion, sliced

6 stalks celery, cut in 1-inch slices

6 green onions, cut in half lengthwise

2 large bell peppers, sliced

½ cup water

⅓ cup salt-free soy sauce

2 tablespoons honey

2 teaspoons **FRONTIER Oriental Seasoning**

2 cups fresh mung bean sprouts

½ lb. fresh mushrooms, sliced

Crushed red pepper (optional)

Hot cooked rice

PREP: 15 minutes

COOK: 15 minutes

YIELD: 4 servings

Heat oil in a wok or skillet. Add onion, celery, green onions, and peppers. Cover and simmer for 5 minutes, stirring frequently. Mix together water, soy sauce, honey, and **FRONTIER Oriental Seasoning**. Pour this sauce over the vegetables, cover, and cook for 5 minutes. Stir in mung bean sprouts, mushrooms, and red pepper, if desired, and cook another 5 minutes. Serve over hot rice.

Courtesy of Frontier Natural Products Co-op

Oven-Roasted Vegetables

PREP: 10 minutes

COOK: 20 minutes

YIELD: 4 (½-cup) servings

Preheat oven to 450°F. In 13 x 9-inch baking or roasting pan, combine all ingredients until evenly coated. Bake, stirring once, for 20 minutes or until vegetables are tender.

VARIATION

Spray pan lightly with nonstick cooking spray and replace oil with 2 tablespoons water.

COOK'S TIP

Also terrific with **LIPTON® RECIPE SECRETS® Onion Soup Mix** or **LIPTON® RECIPE SECRETS® Golden Onion Soup Mix.**

Courtesy of Unilever

1 envelope **LIPTON® RECIPE SECRETS® Savory Herb with Garlic Soup Mix**

1 ½ lbs. assorted sliced fresh vegetables, such as zucchini, yellow squash, red, green or yellow bell peppers, carrots, celery, onion, mushrooms

2 tablespoons olive oil

Grilled Parmesan Vegetables

PREP: 10 minutes

COOK: 10 minutes

YIELD: 8 servings

Preheat grill to medium heat. Arrange vegetables on grate of grill. Grill 10 minutes or until crisp-tender, turning occasionally. Place in large bowl. Add dressing; toss to coat. Sprinkle with cheese.

Courtesy of Kraft Foods

2 each medium zucchini and yellow squash, cut into ½-inch-thick slices

2 each medium red, green, and yellow peppers, cut into 1 ½-inch-thick slices

⅓ cup **KRAFT Light Zesty Italian Dressing**

¼ cup **KRAFT Grated Parmesan Cheese**

Roasted Asparagus Spears

2 lbs. asparagus, ends trimmed

1 ½ tablespoons **EDEN Extra Virgin Olive Oil**

2 cloves garlic, very finely minced or grated

1 tablespoon **EDEN Shoyu Soy Sauce**

2 tablespoons freshly squeezed lemon

PREP: 5 minutes

COOK: 20 minutes

YIELD: 4 servings

Preheat oven to 400°F. In a medium-size mixing bowl, toss the asparagus with the olive oil, garlic, shoyu soy sauce, and lemon juice. Place the asparagus on a baking sheet, evenly spreading the spears. Roast for 15 to 20 minutes, depending on the thickness of the spears. Test with a fork periodically.

Courtesy of Eden Foods

Asparagus with Toasted Hazelnut Butter

3 tablespoons chopped hazelnuts

1 lb. fresh asparagus spears, trimmed

Water

3 tablespoons **LAND O LAKES® Butter**, softened

Salt and pepper

1 tablespoon chopped fresh basil leaves or 1 teaspoon dried basil leaves

PREP: 10 minutes

COOK: 15 minutes

YIELD: 6 servings

Toast hazelnuts in 10-inch skillet over medium heat, stirring constantly, until golden brown, 4 to 5 minutes. Remove from skillet; set aside. Place asparagus and enough water to cover in same skillet. Cook over high heat until water comes to a boil, 4 to 6 minutes. Reduce heat to medium; cook until asparagus is crisply tender, 2 to 4 minutes. Drain. Add toasted hazelnuts and butter; toss lightly until butter is melted. Season with salt and pepper. Sprinkle with basil.

Courtesy of Land O'Lakes, Inc.

Green Beans and Potatoes with Pesto

PREP: 5 minutes

COOK: 10 minutes

YIELD: 4 servings

Cook the potatoes in boiling salted water for 6 to 8 minutes or until tender. Toast the almonds in a small skillet until golden. When the potatoes are tender, add the green beans and cook 1-2 minutes longer. Drain and toss in a bowl with the pesto. Season to taste with salt and pepper. Top with the almonds before serving.

Courtesy of Birds Eye Foods, Inc.

¾ lb. small red potatoes, washed and cut in half

1 (8-oz.) box **BIRDS EYE® Green Beans & Almonds**

⅓ cup pesto, store-bought or homemade

Salt and black pepper

Glazed Lima Beans and Carrots

PREP: 5 minutes

COOK: 6 minutes

YIELD: 4 to 6 servings

Cook carrots in water in 9-inch skillet over high heat until water has evaporated, about 2 minutes. Stir in syrup, butter, and lemon juice. Cook over high heat, stirring occasionally, until thick and syrupy. Stir in beans; heat through. Sprinkle with nuts, if desired.

Courtesy of Del Monte Foods

1 cup diced carrot

¼ cup water

3 tablespoons maple syrup

1 tablespoon butter or margarine

1 tablespoon lemon juice

1 (15 ¼-oz.) can **DEL MONTE®
Green Lima Beans**, drained

¼ cup toasted chopped walnuts (optional)

Broccoli & Peppers in Browned Butter

¼ cup **LAND O LAKES®
Butter**

2 tablespoons coarsely chopped shallots or onion

2 teaspoons chopped garlic

1 tablespoon balsamic vinegar

3 teaspoons olive oil

7 cups broccoli florets

1 medium red bell pepper, cut into 1-inch pieces (1 cup)

1 teaspoon salt

¼ teaspoon pepper

3 tablespoons water

2 tablespoons toasted sesame seed (optional)

PREP: 15 minutes

COOK: 15 minutes

YIELD: 8 (½-cup) servings

Melt butter in 2-quart heavy saucepan over medium heat. Cook, stirring constantly and watching closely, until butter turns golden brown, 4 to 6 minutes. Remove from heat; stir in shallots, garlic, and vinegar. Set aside. Place all remaining ingredients except water and sesame seed in 12-inch deep skillet. Cook over medium-high heat, stirring occasionally, 3 minutes. Add water; reduce heat to medium. Cover; continue cooking until broccoli is crisply tender, 4 to 5 minutes. Remove from heat. Stir browned butter mixture into broccoli. Sprinkle with toasted sesame seed, if desired.

COOK'S TIP

Toasted sesame seeds can be purchased in the ethnic (Asian) aisle of the supermarket. To toast raw sesame seeds, bake in a shallow baking pan at 350°F for 6 to 8 minutes or until lightly browned.

Courtesy of Land O'Lakes, Inc.

Apple Glazed Carrots

PREP: 5 minutes

COOK: 20 minutes

YIELD: 4 servings

Combine **JUICY JUICE®** and cornstarch in small bowl; mix until smooth. Cook carrots in boiling water for 10 minutes or until crisp-tender; drain. Return to pan; add butter, honey, and salt. Add **JUICY JUICE®** mixture; cook over low heat, stirring occasionally, for 5 minutes or until glaze is thickened.

Courtesy of Nestlé USA

1 cup **Apple NESTLÉ® JUICY JUICE® All Natural 100% Juice**

1 ½ teaspoons cornstarch

1 lb. baby carrots

1 tablespoon butter or margarine

1 teaspoon honey

¼ teaspoon salt

Broiled Cauliflower with Miso Sauce

6 tablespoons organic roasted tahini (sesame butter)

1 tablespoon **EDEN ORGANIC Genmai Miso**

1 clove garlic, minced

½ cup water

1 medium head cauliflower, trimmed and rinsed, leave whole

1 tablespoon **EDEN Extra Virgin Olive Oil**

1 cup unseasoned whole wheat bread crumbs

¼ cup minced fresh parsley

1 tablespoon freshly squeezed lemon juice

PREP: 10 minutes

COOK: 20 minutes

YIELD: 6 servings

Mix the tahini, miso, garlic, and water together in a blender. Boil the whole head of cauliflower in 2 inches of water for 10 to 15 minutes just until tender. Do not overcook. Heat the oil in a skillet and sauté the bread crumbs and parsley. Place the head of cauliflower on an oiled baking sheet or pan (do not use glass, which will break under the broiler). Pour the tahini mixture evenly over the cauliflower. Sprinkle with bread crumbs. Broil for 3 to 5 minutes until golden. Be careful not to burn the bread crumbs. Remove and slice into wedges. Sprinkle with the lemon juice before serving.

Courtesy of Eden Foods

Cilantro Lime Corn

PREP: 10 minutes

COOK: 10 minutes

YIELD: 4 servings

In a small bowl, combine butter, lime juice, cilantro, black pepper, and salt. Mix until well blended. Melt butter mixture in a sauté pan over medium-high heat. Add onion, bell pepper, and jalapeño and sauté until onion is transparent and pepper is soft. Add corn and cook until heated through.

SERVING SUGGESTION

Serve as a hot side dish or with chips as a great appetizer.

Courtesy of Birds Eye Foods, Inc.

3 tablespoons butter

2 tablespoons lime juice

1 tablespoon chopped fresh cilantro

¼ teaspoon cracked black pepper

Pinch salt

¼ cup diced onion

1 red bell pepper, seeded and diced

1 jalapeño, seeded and diced

1 (1-lb.) bag **BIRDS EYE® Sweet Kernel Corn**, thawed and drained

Festive California Corn

1 (15.25-oz.) can **DEL MONTE® Whole Kernel Golden Sweet Corn**

1 cup broccoli florets

½ cup thinly sliced zucchini

½ cup thinly sliced red pepper

1 carrot, julienned

¼ cup plain nonfat yogurt, room temperature

⅛ teaspoon dillweed

Sliced green onion or fresh dill (for garnish)

PREP: 15 minutes

COOK: 8 minutes

YIELD: 6 servings

Drain corn, reserving 3 tablespoons liquid in saucepan. Add broccoli to liquid. Cover and cook 3 minutes. Add corn, zucchini, pepper, and carrot. Cover and cook 4 to 5 minutes or until heated through; drain. Combine yogurt and dillweed. Spoon over vegetables. Garnish with sliced green onion or fresh dill.

Courtesy of Del Monte Foods

Roasted Rosemary Garlic Potatoes

PREP: 5 minutes

COOK: 25 minutes

YIELD: 4 servings

Preheat oven 400°F. Cook whole potatoes in microwave oven at high for 30 seconds. Cut into ½-inch chunks and place in a 1-quart baking dish. In a small bowl, mix together marinade, butter, rosemary, and garlic. Pour over potatoes and toss to coat evenly. Sprinkle with freshly ground pepper, if desired. Roast in 400°F oven for 20 to 25 minutes or until tender and slightly browned, stirring halfway through.

Courtesy of H.J. Heinz Company, L.P.

1 lb. small red potatoes

½ cup **LEA & PERRINS® Marinade for Chicken**

2 tablespoons melted butter

2 teaspoons chopped fresh rosemary or ½ teaspoon dried rosemary

2 teaspoons minced garlic

Freshly ground pepper (optional)

Cajun-Parmesan Potato Slices

PREP: 10 minutes

COOK: 15 minutes

YIELD: 2 servings

Slice potatoes ¼-inch thick. Mix melted butter and Cajun Seasoning; brush on both sides of potato slices. Place on cookie sheet and broil 7 to 9 minutes or until they start to brown. Turn potatoes over and sprinkle with Parmesan. Broil additional 5 minutes or until tender.

Recipe by Deb Sullivan; courtesy of Frontier Natural Products Co-op

2 baking potatoes

2 tablespoons melted butter

2 ½ teaspoons **FRONTIER Cajun Seasoning**

¼ cup Parmesan

Crispy Pesto Potatoes

1 ½ lbs. baby red potatoes, halved, cooked, and drained

¼ cup **BUITONI Refrigerated Pesto with Basil**

PREP: 20 minutes

COOK: 5 minutes

YIELD: 6 servings

Preheat broiler. Line baking sheet with heavy-duty foil. Place hot potatoes and pesto in large bowl; toss to coat. Spread potatoes on prepared baking sheet. Broil for 4 to 5 minutes or until potatoes are lightly browned.

VARIATION

Substitute **BUITONI Refrigerated Reduced Fat Pesto with Basil.**

Courtesy of Nestlé USA

Scrumptious Cheddar Bacon Scalloped Potatoes

2 to 2 ½ lbs. (about 6 medium) potatoes, unpeeled and thinly sliced

3 tablespoons butter or margarine

3 tablespoons all-purpose flour

½ teaspoon salt

¼ teaspoon ground black pepper

1 (12-fl. oz.) can **NESTLÉ® CARNATION® Evaporated Lowfat 2% Milk**

1 cup water

6 slices turkey bacon, cooked and chopped, divided

2 cups (8-oz. package) shredded 2% Cheddar cheese, divided

2 green onions, sliced

PREP: 10 minutes

COOK: 20 minutes

YIELD: 16 servings

Place potatoes in large saucepan. Cover with water; bring to a boil. Cook over medium-high heat for 8 to 10 minutes or just until fork-tender; drain. Meanwhile, heat butter in medium saucepan over medium heat. Stir in flour, salt, and pepper. Gradually stir in evaporated milk, water, and ⅓ cup bacon. Cook, stirring constantly, for 8 to 10 minutes or until mixture comes to a boil. Remove from heat. Stir in 1 ½ cups of the cheese and the green onions. Layer half of potatoes in ungreased 3-quart microwave-safe dish. Pour half of sauce over potatoes. Top with remaining potatoes and sauce. Top with remaining ½ cup cheese and bacon. Microwave uncovered on high (100%) power for 2 to 3 minutes or until cheese is melted.

Courtesy of Nestlé USA

Super Smashed Potatoes

2 onions, peeled and very thickly sliced

½ cup **HEINZ® Tomato Ketchup**

1 tablespoon vegetable oil

2 teaspoons chili powder

1 teaspoon **HEINZ® Worcestershire Sauce**

5 Yukon Gold potatoes, peeled and quartered

2 cups grated aged Cheddar cheese

½ cup milk or sour cream

Salt and pepper (optional)

PREP: 10 minutes

COOK: 20 minutes

YIELD: 6 servings

Preheat grill to medium and line with perforated, nonstick foil or a grill basket. Toss the onions with the ketchup, vegetable oil, chili powder, and Worcestershire sauce. Grill for 10 to 12 minutes or until lightly charred and softened. Cool and chop. Reserve. Meanwhile, place potatoes in a pot and cover with salted water. Bring to a boil. Reduce heat to medium and simmer for 20 minutes or until potatoes are cooked. Drain potatoes and return to the pot. Add cheese, milk, and reserved onions; smash into potatoes using a potato masher or a large fork. Season with salt and pepper, if necessary. Serve immediately.

Courtesy of H.J. Heinz Company, L.P.

Aunt Peggy's Sour Cream Mashed Potatoes

PREP: 10 minutes

COOK: 15 minutes

YIELD: 6 servings

Place potatoes in 4-quart saucepot and cover with water. Bring to a boil over high heat. Reduce heat to medium and cook 10 minutes or until potatoes are very tender; drain. Return hot potatoes to saucepot and add **SHEDD'S SPREAD COUNTRY CROCK® Calcium plus Vitamin D**; mash. Stir in sour cream. Season, if desired, with salt and black pepper.

Courtesy of Unilever

3 lbs. red potatoes, unpeeled and cut into 1-inch pieces

¼ cup **SHEDD'S SPREAD COUNTRY CROCK® Calcium plus Vitamin D**

½ cup sour cream

Salt and black pepper (optional)

Grilled Summer Squash

PREP: 10 minutes

COOK: 20 minutes

YIELD: 6 servings

2 tablespoons **ORGANIC VALLEY Salted Butter**

2 tablespoons olive oil

2 tablespoons fresh lemon juice

1 teaspoon chopped fresh parsley

7 or 8 medium fresh summer squash

Melt butter and mix with oil, lemon juice, and parsley. Cut squash in half lengthwise and brush all over with the butter mixture. Grill over medium-hot coals for 15 to 20 minutes, turning every few minutes, until tender when pierced.

Courtesy of Terra Brockman and The Land Connection (www.thelandconnection.org) for Organic Valley Family of Farms

Sautéed Swiss Chard with Garlic

1 tablespoon olive oil

2 cloves garlic

1 bunch washed and chopped fresh Swiss chard leaves (use a salad spinner to dry if needed)

3 tablespoons **WELCH'S White Grape Juice**

Salt to taste

Pinch of red pepper flakes

Fresh ground black pepper, to taste

PREP: 10 minutes

COOK: 8 minutes

YIELD: 3 servings

Heat oil in skillet with garlic. Cook for 1 minute. Add Swiss chard and cook for 1 minute. Add grape juice, salt, and pepper flakes. Cook for 3 to 5 minutes or until leaves are tender. Add fresh ground pepper. Remove from heat. Serve.

COOK'S TIP

Swiss chard is a very flavorful and hardy green leaf vegetable. The leaves are not as delicate as spinach leaves but they cook almost as quickly. Kale or escarole can be substituted as well. Tossing in some white beans works well with any of these green leafy vegetables.

Courtesy of Welch Foods Inc., A Cooperative

Maple Winter Squash

1 (12-oz.) box **BIRDS EYE®
Cooked Winter Squash**,
thawed

2 tablespoons butter, softened

2 tablespoons light brown
sugar

½ teaspoon maple extract

4 oatmeal cookies, crumbled

2 tablespoons melted butter

PREP: 10 minutes

COOK: 15 minutes

YIELD: 3 servings

Preheat oven to 350°F. In a bowl, stir together winter squash, softened butter, brown sugar, and maple extract. Transfer to small (8-inch-square or smaller) greased baking dish. Toss cookie crumbs with melted butter. Spread squash mixture in dish and top with cookie crumbs. Bake uncovered for 15 minutes.

Courtesy of Birds Eye Foods, Inc.

SWANSON® Moist & Savory Stuffing

PREP: 5 minutes

COOK: 10 minutes

YIELD: 8 servings

Heat the broth, black pepper, celery, and onion in a 2-quart saucepan over medium-high heat to a boil. Reduce the heat to low. Cover and cook for 5 minutes or until the vegetables are tender. Add the stuffing and mix lightly.

VARIATIONS

• **CRANBERRY & PECAN STUFFING:** Stir ½ cup each dried cranberries and chopped pecans into the stuffing mixture.

• **SAUSAGE & MUSHROOM STUFFING:** Add 1 cup sliced mushrooms to the vegetables during cooking. Stir ½ lb. cooked and crumbled pork sausage into the stuffing mixture.

SERVING SUGGESTION: Serve with a store-bought rotisserie chicken or turkey breast and steamed whole green beans.

Courtesy of Campbell Soup Company

1 ¾ cups **SWANSON®
Chicken Broth (Regular,
Natural Goodness™, or
Certified Organic)**

Generous dash ground black pepper

1 stalk celery, coarsely chopped (about ½ cup)

1 small onion, coarsely chopped (about ¼ cup)

4 cups **PEPPERIDGE FARM®
Herb Seasoned Stuffing**

Holiday Vegetable Stuffing

PREP: 10 minutes

COOK: 15 minutes

YIELD: 8 servings

Heat the butter in a saucepot over medium heat. Add the mushrooms, carrots, and onion and cook until tender. Add the broth, water chestnuts, and spinach. Heat to a boil. Add the stuffing and stir lightly to coat.

Courtesy of Campbell Soup Company

2 tablespoons butter

2 cups sliced mushrooms

2 medium carrots, chopped

1 medium onion, chopped

1 ¾ cups **SWANSON® Vegetable Broth (Regular or Certified Organic)**

1 (8-oz.) can sliced water chestnuts, drained

2 cups coarsely chopped fresh spinach leaves

4 cups **PEPPERIDGE FARM® Herb Seasoned Stuffing**

Fruited Couscous

1 cup **TROPICANA Pure Premium® Orange Juice** or **DOLE® 100% Orange Juice**

2 teaspoons olive oil

½ teaspoon ground cinnamon

½ teaspoon ground coriander

¼ teaspoon salt

⅛ teaspoon cayenne pepper (optional)

½ cup dried fruit bits

¾ cup **NEAR EAST® Original Plain Couscous Mix**

¼ cup toasted slivered almonds (optional)

COOK: 10 minutes

YIELD: 4 servings

Combine juice, olive oil, cinnamon, coriander, salt, and cayenne pepper, if desired, in 1 ½-quart saucepan; mix well. Stir in fruit. Cover and bring to a boil. Stir in couscous. Cover and remove from heat. Let stand 5 minutes. Gently fluff couscous with fork. Sprinkle with almonds, if desired. Serve immediately.

TO MICROWAVE: Combine orange juice, olive oil, cinnamon, coriander, salt, and cayenne pepper, if using, in 1 ½-quart microwaveable casserole with lid; mix well. Stir in fruit. Cover. Microwave on high (100%) until boiling, about 4 minutes. Uncover; stir in couscous. Cover tightly. Let stand 5 minutes. Fluff with fork.

COOK'S TIP

Raisins, dried cranberries, or any combination of chopped dried fruits may be substituted for dried fruit bits.

Courtesy of Tropicana Products, Inc.

Couscous with Sun Gold Feta Sauce

1 cup couscous

1 pint **Sun Gold Cherry Tomatoes**

1 (4-oz.) container **ORGANIC VALLEY Feta Cheese Crumbles**

2 tablespoons chopped fresh dill or basil

2 tablespoons olive oil, divided

1 tablespoon lemon juice

Salt

Freshly ground black pepper

PREP/COOK: 20 minutes

YIELD: 4 servings

Prepare couscous according to package instructions. Meanwhile, slice the tomatoes in half and combine with feta, dill or basil, olive oil, and lemon juice. Add salt and pepper to taste. When couscous is ready, fluff it with a fork and top or toss it with the tomato mixture.

COOK'S TIP

Unlike most types of pasta, couscous (which is tiny grains of already cooked pasta) needs only brief rehydration to be fully "cooked." Just bring water to boil, add the couscous, cover it, and turn off the heat. Within a few minutes it's ready to be topped or tossed with any number of sauces.

Copyright by Terese Allen; courtesy of Organic Valley Family of Farms

Stovetop Macaroni & Cheese

COOK: 23 minutes

YIELD: 4 (1-cup) servings

Cook macaroni according to package directions. Drain. Combine cooked macaroni, fat-free half-and-half, and cheeses in 2-quart saucepan. Cook over medium heat, stirring occasionally, until cheese is melted, 6 to 8 minutes. To serve, spoon macaroni into serving dish; sprinkle with crushed croutons.

VARIATION

Stir in 1 cup cubed deli ham for a heartier meal.

Courtesy of Land O'Lakes, Inc.

6 oz. (1 ½ cups) uncooked dried elbow macaroni

1 cup **LAND O LAKES® Fat Free** or **Traditional Half & Half**

½ lb. sliced **LAND O LAKES® Deli Cheddar Cheese**, cut into strips

¼ lb. sliced **LAND O LAKES® Deli American Cheese**, cut into strips

½ cup coarsely crushed seasoned croutons

"Wheely" Easy Mac & Cheesy

2 cups (8 oz.) dry wagon wheel or rotelle pasta

1 cup frozen shelled edamame (shelled soybeans)

1 (12-fl. oz.) can **NESTLÉ® CARNATION® Evaporated Milk**

1 (8-oz.) package shredded Monterey Jack and Cheddar cheese blend or other cheese blend

½ teaspoon garlic powder

½ teaspoon ground black pepper

½ cup cherry or grape tomatoes, cut in half

PREP: 5 minutes

COOK: 15 minutes

YIELD: 4 servings

Prepare pasta according to package directions, adding edamame to boiling pasta water for last 2 minutes of cooking time; drain. Meanwhile, combine evaporated milk, cheese, garlic powder, and pepper in medium saucepan. Cook over medium-low heat, stirring occasionally, until cheese is melted. Remove from heat. Add pasta and edamame to cheese sauce; stir until combined. Add tomatoes; stir gently until combined.

COOK'S TIPS

• Look for edamame in the frozen food or organic section of your local store.

• Frozen peas can be used in place of edamame.

Courtesy of Nestlé USA

Whirled Peas Pasta

PREP: 5 minutes

COOK: 15 minutes

YIELD: 2 or 3 servings

Cook **ANNIE'S Organic Peace Pasta** according to package directions. Just before pasta is ready to drain, add peas; return to boil, then drain. Return drained pasta and peas to pot. Add butter, stirring to melt, over low heat. Whisk cheese packet contents with ½ cup milk, blending well. Mix sauce and pesto into pasta, add grated Parmesan, and remove from heat. Serve peacefully!

Courtesy of Annie's Homegrown

1 (6-oz.) box **ANNIE'S Organic Peace Pasta & Parmesan**

1 cup frozen petite organic peas

2 tablespoons organic butter

½ cup 1% organic milk

1 to 2 tablespoons pesto

½ cup freshly grated Parmesan

Funny Valentine Pasta

1 (6-oz.) box **ANNIE'S Shells & White Cheddar**

1 or 2 small cooked or canned beets, grated

½ cup crumbled sweet Gorgonzola or other mild blue cheese (optional)

Freshly ground pepper and salt to taste

PREP: 5 minutes

COOK: 15 minutes

YIELD: 2 or 3 servings

Cook **ANNIE'S Shells & White Cheddar** according to package directions, including the 2 tablespoons butter at end. Stir in the grated beets and blue cheese, if desired; heat over low flame, stirring, until hot and well blended. Season to taste and serve.

COOK'S TIP

To prepare fresh beets, wrap them in foil and cook in a 400°F oven until fork tender. Allow to cool, then peel and grate finely on cheese grater.

Courtesy of Annie's Homegrown

Penne with Zucchini and Oregano

PREP: 5 minutes

COOK: 15 minutes

YIELD: 4 servings

Heat olive oil in a large skillet over medium-high heat. Add zucchini and sauté until tender and browned. Stir in garlic and oregano and remove from heat. Add ½ cup Romano to warm pasta, tossing gently until cheese is melted. Add zucchini mixture to penne; garnish with additional grated Romano. Serve with freshly ground pepper.

VARIATION

Make a heartier dish with the addition of spicy sausage or strips of chicken breast. Bring up the spicy-heat level with ⅛ teaspoon crushed red pepper flakes.

Courtesy of Lundberg Family Farms

1 to 2 tablespoons olive oil

3 large zucchini, cut lengthwise, and then thinly sliced

6 cloves garlic, pressed

2 tablespoons minced fresh oregano

½ cup grated Romano or Parmesan, plus more for garnish

1 (12-oz.) box **LUNDBERG® Penne Brown Rice Pasta**, cooked al dente, drizzled with olive oil, and kept warm

Freshly ground black pepper

Broccoli & Noodles Supreme

COOK: 20 minutes

YIELD: 5 servings

Cook noodles according to package directions. Add broccoli for last 5 minutes of cooking time. Drain. Mix soup, sour cream, cheese, pepper, and noodle mixture in saucepan. Heat through.

Courtesy of Campbell Soup Company

3 cups uncooked medium egg noodles

2 cups fresh or frozen broccoli florets

1 (10 ¾-oz.) can **CAMPBELL'S® Condensed Cream of Chicken Soup (Regular or 98% Fat Free)**

½ cup sour cream

⅓ cup grated Parmesan

⅛ teaspoon ground black pepper

Mushroom Broccoli Alfredo

2 tablespoons butter or margarine

3 cups broccoli flowerets

3 cups sliced mushrooms

1 medium onion, chopped

½ teaspoon garlic powder or 2 cloves garlic, minced

1 (10 ¾-oz.) can **CAMPBELL'S® Condensed Cream of Mushroom Soup (Regular, 98% Fat Free, or 25% Less Sodium)**

⅓ cup milk

⅛ teaspoon ground black pepper

2 tablespoons grated Parmesan

4 cups hot cooked fettuccine or spaghetti

PREP: 10 minutes

COOK: 15 minutes

YIELD: 4 servings

Heat butter in skillet. Add broccoli, mushrooms, onion, and garlic powder. Cook until crisp-tender. Add soup, milk, pepper, and cheese. Heat through. Serve over fettuccine.

Courtesy of Campbell Soup Company

Alfredo Linguine

1 tablespoon **I CAN'T BELIEVE IT'S NOT BUTTER!® Spread**

½ cup chopped walnuts, plus more for garnish

1 large clove garlic, finely chopped

1 (15-oz.) jar **BERTOLLI® Creamy Alfredo Sauce**

8 oz. linguine, cooked and drained

Chopped fresh parsley (for garnish, optional)

PREP/COOK: 30 minutes

YIELD: 4 servings

Melt Spread in 2-quart saucepan over medium heat and cook walnuts 3 minutes or until golden. Stir in garlic and cook 30 seconds. Stir in sauce. Reduce heat to low and simmer, stirring occasionally, 3 minutes or until heated through. To serve, toss sauce with hot linguine. Sprinkle with additional chopped walnuts and garnish with chopped fresh parsley, if desired.

Courtesy of Unilever

BERTOLLI® Creamy Fettuccine Primavera

PREP: 5 minutes

COOK: 20 minutes

YIELD: 4 servings

Heat olive oil in 12-inch nonstick skillet over medium heat and cook vegetables and garlic, covered, 2 minutes or until vegetables are crisp-tender, stirring once. Stir in sauce and cook, covered, for 3 minutes or until heated through. Serve over hot fettuccine. Garnish with grated Parmesan and ground black pepper, if desired.

Courtesy of Unilever

2 tablespoons olive oil

3 cups assorted cut-up fresh vegetables (peas, red bell pepper, zucchini, and/or asparagus) or 1 (16-oz.) package frozen assorted vegetables, thawed and drained

1 tablespoon finely chopped garlic

1 (15-oz.) jar **BERTOLLI® Creamy Alfredo Sauce**

8 oz. fettuccine, cooked and drained

Grated Parmesan (for garnish, optional)

Ground black pepper (for garnish, optional)

Pasta Primavera

PREP: 10 minutes

COOK: 20 minutes

YIELD: 6 servings

Cook pasta according to package directions; drain and set aside. Heat oil in a large skillet and sauté garlic for 1 to 2 minutes. Add the broccoli, cauliflower, carrot, artichoke hearts, and sea salt. Sauté for 2 to 3 minutes. Add water; cover and steam 2 minutes. Turn off flame; add pepper, pasta, basil, and tomato. Toss thoroughly and serve.

Courtesy of Eden Foods

1 (12-oz.) package **EDEN ORGANIC Spelt Ziti Rigati**, or **EDEN ORGANIC Kamut & Buckwheat Rigatoni**

3 tablespoons **EDEN Extra Virgin Olive Oil**

2 cloves garlic, minced

2 cups small broccoli florets

2 cups small cauliflower florets

1 cup thinly sliced carrots

½ cup artichoke hearts, water-packed, drained, sliced in quarters

½ teaspoon **EDEN Sea Salt**

⅓ cup water or vegetable broth

¼ teaspoon freshly ground black pepper, or to taste

2 tablespoons finely chopped fresh basil

1 small organic tomato, cubed

Pasta with Capers, Olives, and Tomatoes

2 tablespoons **EDEN Extra Virgin Olive Oil**, divided

4 cloves garlic, minced

¼ teaspoon red pepper flakes

2 (14.5-oz.) cans **EDEN ORGANIC Diced Tomatoes, EDEN ORGANIC Diced Tomatoes with Basil,** or **EDEN ORGANIC Diced Tomatoes with Roasted Onion & Garlic**, drained, reserve ½ cup of tomato liquid

3 tablespoons capers, rinsed and drained

½ cup pitted black olives

¼ cup minced fresh parsley

EDEN Sea Salt (optional)

1 (14-oz.) package **EDEN ORGANIC Kamut Spaghetti**

PREP: 10 minutes

COOK: 20 minutes

YIELD: 7 servings

Heat 1 tablespoon of the olive oil in a medium skillet and sauté the garlic and red pepper for 2 minutes, stirring constantly. Add the tomatoes and liquid. Simmer about 10 minutes until thickened. Add the capers, olives, and parsley. Adjust the seasoning by adding sea salt, if desired. Cook 5 minutes. While the sauce is cooking, cook pasta according to package directions. When done, drain and toss with remaining 1 tablespoon of olive oil. Place in a serving dish. When the sauce is done, pour it over the pasta and toss.

Courtesy of Eden Foods

Whole Tomatoes, Mushrooms & Rigatoni

1 (12-oz.) package **EDEN ORGANIC Kamut & Buckwheat Rigatoni**

2 tablespoons **EDEN Extra Virgin Olive Oil**

1 cup chopped red onion

3 cloves garlic, minced

1 cup **EDEN Sliced Shiitake Mushrooms**, soaked 5 minutes in 1 cup cold water, reserving soaking water

1 (28-oz.) can **EDEN ORGANIC Whole Tomatoes with Basil**, undrained

¾ teaspoon **EDEN Sea Salt**, or to taste

⅛ teaspoon freshly ground black pepper, or to taste

2 tablespoons minced fresh parsley or 2 teaspoons dried parsley

PREP: 10 minutes

COOK: 20 minutes

YIELD: 6 servings

Cook pasta according to package directions, rinse, drain, and set aside. Heat oil in a large skillet and sauté the onion and garlic for 5 minutes. Add all remaining ingredients, including shiitake soaking water. Cover and bring to a boil. Reduce flame and simmer 5 minutes. Remove cover and mix in the pasta, stirring until hot. Serve.

Courtesy of Eden Foods

Italian Pasta with Tomato & Basil

PREP: 5 minutes

COOK: 15 minutes

YIELD: 4 servings

Mix tomatoes, ¾ cup of the cheese, basil, garlic, and oil. Add to hot pasta in large bowl; toss to coat. Sprinkle with remaining ¼ cup cheese.

Courtesy of Kraft Foods

3 cups chopped tomatoes

1 cup **KRAFT Shredded Parmesan, Romano, and Asiago Cheeses**, divided

1 tablespoon sliced fresh basil

1 clove garlic, minced

2 tablespoons olive oil

3 cups (8 oz.) bow tie pasta, cooked and drained

Spaghetti with Anchovies and Tomatoes

PREP: 10 minutes

COOK: 20 minutes

YIELD: 4 servings

Heat oil in a large skillet over medium heat. Add onion and garlic and sauté until onion is softened. Add anchovies, stirring for 1 minute. Add tomatoes, vinegar, and red pepper flakes and cook, stirring occasionally, until slightly thickened. Add capers, kalamata olives, and basil. Heat through. In a large bowl toss spaghetti with sauce and serve with Parmesan.

Courtesy of Lundberg Family Farms

2 tablespoons olive oil

½ large onion, finely chopped

2 garlic cloves, pressed

1 (2-oz.) can flat anchovy fillets, drained and minced

1 (28-oz.) can low-sodium diced tomatoes, undrained

1 tablespoon balsamic vinegar

¼ teaspoon crushed red pepper

2 tablespoons capers, rinsed and drained

¼ cup kalamata olives, drained and rinsed

¼ cup finely chopped fresh basil

1 (10-oz.) box **LUNDBERG® Spaghetti Brown Rice Pasta**, cooked, drained, and kept warm

Grated Parmesan

Penne with Spicy Sun-Dried Tomato Cream Sauce

1 tablespoon olive oil

4 garlic cloves, minced

1 cup oil-packed sun-dried tomatoes, drained and chopped

1 cup whipping cream or fat-free half-and-half

1 (7.25-oz.) jar roasted red peppers, drained and chopped

¼ teaspoon crushed red pepper

½ cup chopped fresh basil leaves

1 cup grated Parmesan

1 (12-oz.) box **LUNDBERG® Penne Brown Rice Pasta**, cooked and drained, reserving 1 cup cooking liquid

Salt and pepper

PREP: 10 minutes

COOK: 15 minutes

YIELD: 4 servings

Heat oil in medium saucepan over medium heat. Add garlic and sauté 1 minute. Add tomatoes, cream, red peppers, and crushed red pepper and simmer 2 minutes. Stir in basil. Add tomato/cream mixture and Parmesan to cooked penne and stir to coat. Add some reserved cooking liquid to pasta if dry. Season with salt and pepper.

VARIATIONS

Add cooked chicken or shrimp for a hearty variation. Sauté mushrooms and asparagus as other additions.

Courtesy of Lundberg Family Farms

Spiced Organic White Jasmine Rice with Peanuts

PREP: 5 minutes

BAKE: 25 minutes

YIELD: 4 to 6 servings

Heat olive oil in a heavy saucepan and stir in cumin seed, cloves, and bay leaf. Cook 5 to 10 seconds over moderate heat until cumin seed darkens slightly in color. Add red pepper flakes, onion, and garlic and stir until onion is softened. Add rice, salt, and water and bring to a boil; cover and simmer 20 minutes. Fluff with fork, remove bay leaf, and stir in peanuts.

Courtesy of Lundberg Family Farms

1½ tablespoons olive oil

2 teaspoons whole cumin seed

4 whole cloves

1 bay leaf

⅛ to ¼ teaspoon hot red pepper flakes

1 small onion, diced

2 garlic cloves, pressed

1 cup **LUNDBERG® Organic California White Jasmine Rice**

½ teaspoon salt (optional)

1 ½ cups water

¼ to ⅓ cup chopped roasted peanuts

White Jasmine Rice with Cranberries and Caramelized Onions

1 ½ cups chicken broth or water

1 cup **LUNDBERG® California White Jasmine Rice**

1 tablespoon butter

1 medium onion, sliced into thin wedges

1 teaspoon **LUNDBERG® Brown Rice Syrup**

½ cup dried cranberries

½ teaspoon finely grated orange zest

PREP: 5 minutes

COOK: 25 minutes

YIELD: 4 servings

Combine chicken broth and rice in a medium saucepan. Bring to boil. Reduce heat to low and cover. Simmer 20 minutes until liquid is absorbed and rice is tender. While rice is cooking, melt butter in a medium skillet over high heat. Add onion and rice syrup. Cook 5 minutes, until onions are soft and translucent. Reduce heat to low. Slowly cook onion, stirring often for 10 minutes, until caramelized. Stir in dried cranberries. Fold cranberry/onion mixture and orange zest into cooked rice.

Courtesy of Lundberg Family Farms

SUNKIST® Lemon and Pistachio Rice

3 tablespoons **SUNKIST® freshly squeezed lemon juice**

2 cups water or chicken broth

¼ teaspoon cinnamon

¼ teaspoon salt

¼ cup **SUNKIST® Pistachios**

½ cup golden raisins

2 cups instant rice

1 ½ teaspoons finely grated **SUNKIST® lemon zest**

PREP: 10 minutes

COOK: 12 minutes

YIELD: 4 servings

Combine lemon juice, water, cinnamon, salt, pistachios, and raisins and bring to a boil in a medium saucepan. Stir in rice, cover pan, and remove from heat. Let sit for 5 minutes or until liquid is absorbed. Fluff rice with fork and just before serving, stir in finely grated lemon zest.

Courtesy of Sunkist Growers, Inc.

Fiesta Broccoli Rice

PREP: 5 minutes

COOK: 20 minutes

YIELD: 4 servings

In a saucepan over medium heat, mix together prepared broccoli, rice, soup, and ranch dressing. Cook until heated through, 5 to 10 minutes. Season with salt and pepper.

Courtesy of Birds Eye Foods, Inc.

1 (12-oz.) package **BIRDS EYE® STEAMFRESH® Broccoli Cuts**, cooked according to package directions

1 (10-oz.) package **BIRDS EYE® STEAMFRESH® Long Grain White Rice**, cooked according to package directions

1 (10-oz.) can fiesta nacho cheese soup

1 tablespoon spicy ranch salad dressing

Salt and pepper

ORGANIC COUNTRYWILD® Rice with Red Cabbage

PREP: 5 minutes

COOK: 25 minutes

YIELD: 4 servings

Fry bacon in a large skillet. Drain off all but 1 tablespoon of fat. In same pan, sauté onion and cabbage until softened. Stir in vinegar. Add salt and pepper to taste. Chop bacon. Just before serving, stir cabbage mixture and bacon into rice.

Courtesy of Lundberg Family Farms

4 slices bacon

1 small onion, quartered and sliced thinly

2 cups thinly sliced red cabbage (about ⅙ head)

2 teaspoons red wine vinegar

Salt and pepper

2 (7.4-oz.) **LUNDBERG® HEAT & EAT ORGANIC COUNTRYWILD® Rice Bowls,** heated according to package directions

Pesto Glazed Vegetables and Rice

1 (1-lb.) bag **BIRDS EYE® Broccoli Stir-Fry**, skillet-cooked according to package directions

1 (10-oz.) bag **BIRDS EYE® STEAMFRESH® Whole Grain Brown Rice**, cooked according to package directions

⅓ cup prepared pesto

Salt and pepper

¼ cup shredded Parmesan

PREP: 10 minutes

COOK: 15 minutes

YIELD: 4 servings

To the skillet with prepared broccoli stir-fry, stir in the cooked brown rice and pesto. Cook over medium heat until heated through, 3 to 5 minutes. Season with salt and pepper and sprinkle with Parmesan before serving.

SERVING SUGGESTION

This rice dish would be great served with salmon.

Courtesy of Birds Eye Foods, Inc.

Moros y Cristianos Cuban Style Rice & Beans

1 cup **LUNDBERG® Long Grain White Rice**

1 (14 ½-oz.) can diced tomatoes with green chilies

1 ½ cups water

1 tablespoon apple cider vinegar

1 cup chopped onion

1 cup chopped green bell pepper

2 teaspoons chopped garlic

1 ½ teaspoons ground cumin

1 teaspoon dried thyme leaves

½ teaspoon crushed red pepper (optional)

1 bay leaf

1 tablespoon olive oil

1 (15-oz.) can black beans, drained

½ to 1 teaspoon salt (optional)

½ teaspoon black pepper

PREP: 5 minutes

COOK: 25 minutes

YIELD: 4 servings

Combine rice, diced tomatoes, water, and vinegar in a medium saucepan. Heat to boiling. Reduce heat and simmer, covered, until rice is tender, about 20 minutes. While rice is cooking, sauté onion, bell pepper, garlic, cumin, thyme, crushed red pepper, if using, and bay leaf in olive oil until onion is tender, about 5 minutes. Stir in beans and rice; cook until heated through, about 5 minutes. Season with salt, if using, and pepper.

Courtesy of Lundberg Family Farms

Pumpkin Confetti Rice

PREP: 10 minutes

COOK: 15 minutes

YIELD: 10 servings

Heat oil in large saucepan over medium heat. Add onion; cook, stirring occasionally, for 3 to 4 minutes or until soft. Add vegetables, pumpkin, broth, water, and thyme. Bring to a boil, stirring occasionally. Stir in rice, salt, black pepper, and cayenne pepper, if using; bring to a boil. Cover; reduce heat to low. Cook for 5 minutes. Remove from heat; let stand for 10 minutes or until liquid is absorbed. Fluff with fork before serving.

Courtesy of Nestlé USA

1 tablespoon olive oil

1 small onion, chopped

2 cups frozen mixed vegetable blend

1 cup **LIBBY'S® 100% Pure Pumpkin**

1 (14-oz.) can vegetable broth

¼ cup water

1 teaspoon dried thyme

2 cups uncooked instant brown rice

¼ teaspoon salt or more to taste

¼ teaspoon ground black pepper

Pinch cayenne pepper (optional)

Basmati Pilaf

PREP/COOK: 30 minutes

YIELD: 4 to 6 servings

Combine rice, stock, butter, and bay leaf in a medium pot with a tight-fitting lid. Bring to a boil. Cover with lid; reduce heat and simmer 20 minutes. While the basmati rice is cooking, heat the oil in a skillet, add onion, and sauté for 3 minutes. Add celery, raisins, ginger, cumin, coriander, and pepper. Cook an additional 2 minutes. Stir into the cooked rice. Add soy sauce and mix well. Remove the bay leaf before serving.

Courtesy of Lundberg Family Farms

1 cup **LUNDBERG® California White Basmati Rice**

1 ½ cups chicken stock or water

1 tablespoon butter

1 bay leaf

1 tablespoon olive oil

1 small onion, chopped

1 celery stalk, thinly sliced

2 tablespoons raisins

1 teaspoon peeled and finely chopped fresh ginger

1 teaspoon ground cumin

½ teaspoon ground coriander

¼ teaspoon ground black pepper

1 tablespoon soy sauce

Curried Rice, Beans & Vegetable Pilaf

PREP: 5 minutes

COOK: 25 minutes

YIELD: 4 servings

Place chutney and broth in blender. Puree and pour into a medium saucepan with lid. Add rice and curry powder; stir and bring to boil. Reduce heat to simmer, cover, and cook rice 20 minutes. While rice is cooking, heat oil in heavy large saucepan over medium heat. Sauté garlic for 30 seconds. Add beans, yam, raisins, spinach, and water. Cover and cook until vegetables are tender and liquid is absorbed, about 10 minutes. Gently stir vegetable-bean mixture into rice. Mound pilaf in a large bowl. Serve, passing yogurt separately.

VARIATION

Add sliced cooked chicken, sausage, or peeled fresh shrimp while the vegetables are cooking.

Courtesy of Lundberg Family Farms

⅓ cup mango chutney

1 (14-oz.) can canned chicken broth or water

1 cup **LUNDBERG® California White Basmati Rice**

1 tablespoon curry powder

1 tablespoon olive oil

4 cloves garlic, pressed

1 (15-oz.) can kidney beans or white cannellini beans, rinsed and drained

½ yam, peeled and cut into ½-inch dice (about 1 cup)

½ cup raisin or currents

4 cups bagged fresh baby spinach, bok choy, or collard greens, chopped

½ cup water

Plain yogurt

Three-Pepper Oat Pilaf

½ cup chopped red bell pepper

½ cup chopped yellow bell pepper

½ cup chopped mushrooms

½ cup sliced green onions

2 garlic cloves, minced

1 tablespoon olive oil

1 ¾ cups **Old Fashioned QUAKER®
Oats**, uncooked

2 egg whites or 1 egg, lightly beaten

¾ cup chicken broth

2 tablespoons minced fresh basil
leaves or 2 teaspoons dried basil

½ teaspoon salt

¼ teaspoon black pepper

PREP: 16 minutes

COOK: 14 minutes

YIELD: 6 servings

In 10-inch nonstick skillet, cook peppers, mushrooms, green onion, and garlic in oil over medium heat, stirring occasionally, until vegetables are crisp-tender, about 2 minutes. In large bowl, mix oats and egg whites until oats are evenly coated. Add oats to vegetable mixture in skillet. Cook over medium heat, stirring occasionally, until oats are dry and separated, 5 to 6 minutes. Add broth, basil, salt, and pepper. Continue cooking, stirring occasionally, 2 to 3 minutes or until liquid is absorbed. Serve immediately.

Courtesy of The Quaker Oats Company

Quick Mushroom Risotto

PREP: 15 minutes

COOK: 15 minutes

YIELD: 7 servings

Place the shiitake, maitake, and water in a small saucepan and bring to a boil without a cover. Reduce the flame to medium and simmer about 7 minutes or until all of the water has evaporated and the mushrooms are tender. When the mushrooms are almost ready, heat the oil in a medium saucepan and sauté the garlic and onions for 1 minute. Add the red pepper and sauté another minute. Add the mushrooms, rice and garbanzo beans, sea salt, black pepper, and basil. Cover and heat over a medium-low flame until the rice is hot, about 5 minutes.

Courtesy of Eden Foods

½ cup **EDEN Sliced Shiitake Mushrooms**

½ cup **EDEN Maitake Mushrooms**

1 cup water

1 tablespoon **EDEN Extra Virgin Olive Oil**

1 clove garlic, minced

½ cup diced onions

¼ cup diced red bell pepper

30 oz. **EDEN ORGANIC Rice & Garbanzo Beans**

2 pinches **EDEN Sea Salt**

⅛ teaspoon freshly ground black pepper, or to taste

¼ teaspoon dried basil or 1 teaspoon minced fresh basil

Butternut Squash and Sage Risotto

2 cups butternut squash cut into ¼-inch dice

6 tablespoons olive oil, divided

Salt and pepper to taste

1 cup finely diced onion

2 cups uncooked Arborio rice

2 cups dry white wine, divided

4 cups vegetable or chicken stock, divided

2 cups **STONYFIELD FARM Plain Yogurt**

10 to 12 large sage leaves

1 cup grated Parmesan, divided

PREP: 10 minutes

COOK: 20 minutes

YIELD: 6 servings

Preheat oven to 350°F. Toss cubed butternut squash with 1 tablespoon of the olive oil and salt and pepper to taste. Roast for 15 minutes. Remove from oven and set aside. In the meantime, over medium heat, sauté onion with remaining 5 tablespoons olive oil for 3 minutes. Add rice, stirring continuously for 2 minutes. Stir in 1 cup of the white wine and continue cooking and stirring until wine is absorbed. Add 1 cup of the stock, stirring until absorbed. Gradually stir in the remaining wine and stock, alternating until all liquid is absorbed. Gradually add roasted squash, yogurt, sage, and ½ cup of the Parmesan, gently stirring until well mixed. Remove from heat; cover for 5 minutes. Garnish with remaining Parmesan.

Courtesy of Stonyfield Farm

Desserts

Blueberry Lemon Parfaits

BUTTER NUT CRUNCH

2 tablespoons **LAND O LAKES®**
Butter

¼ cup brown sugar, firmly packed

⅓ cup slivered almonds, coarsely chopped

¼ cup uncooked old-fashioned oats

LEMON CREAM

1 ½ cups whipping cream

½ cup lemon curd

BERRIES

1 pint fresh blueberries

PREP: 15 minutes

COOK: 5 minutes

YIELD: 6 servings

FOR THE BUTTER NUT CRUNCH: Line a 15 x 10 x 1-inch jelly roll pan with aluminum foil; set aside. Melt butter in 10-inch skillet until sizzling; add brown sugar. Cook, stirring constantly, over medium-high heat until bubbling, 1 minute. Add almonds and oats; stir. Pour into prepared pan; cool completely. Break into chunks; store in container with tight-fitting lid until ready to assemble parfaits.

FOR THE LEMON CREAM: Beat whipping cream in chilled medium bowl until soft peaks form, scraping bowl often. Add lemon curd; continue beating until stiff peaks form.

TO ASSEMBLE PARFAITS: Layer ½ cup lemon cream, ⅓ cup berries, and 2 heaping tablespoons butter nut crunch in each of six (8- to 10-oz.) plastic cups or dessert glasses.

VARIATIONS

• Substitute pecans or walnuts for the almonds.

• Substitute fresh raspberries or small blackberries for the blueberries.

COOK'S TIP

Prepare up to 1 hour ahead. Cover each glass with plastic food wrap; refrigerate.

Courtesy of Land O'Lakes, Inc.

Fruity Parfaits

PREP: 20 minutes

YIELD: 6 servings

Spoon ¼ cup yogurt into bottoms of four parfait glasses. Sprinkle 1 tablespoon graham cracker crumbs over yogurt in each glass. Top crumbs with ¼ cup diced fruit. Top fruit with ¼ cup applesauce. Repeat layers. Cover and chill until ready to serve.

Courtesy of Mott's, LLP

2 cups fruit-flavored lowfat yogurt

½ cup graham cracker crumbs

2 cups diced fresh fruit

2 cups **MOTT'S Natural Apple Sauce**

Tropical Yogurt Parfait with Organic Short Grain Brown Rice

1 **LUNDBERG® Heat & Eat Organic Short Grain Brown Rice Bowl**, chilled

1 (8-oz.) container pineapple or pineapple coconut yogurt

¾ cup crushed pineapple, well drained

2 bananas, sliced, reserve a few slices (for garnish)

PREP: 20 minutes

YIELD: 4 to 5 servings

Combine all ingredients. Spoon into individual parfait glasses. Top with reserved banana slices.

Courtesy of Lundberg Family Farms

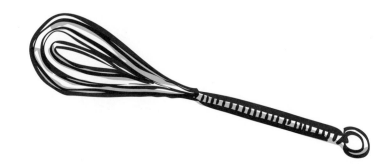

Sunrise Sundae

PREP: 5 minutes

YIELD: 3 servings

Spoon alternating layers of granola, yogurt, and fruit in three tall glasses.

COOK'S TIP

For easy variety, use the 6-pack assorted cereals and other **DEL MONTE Fruits**.

Courtesy of Del Monte Foods

1 ½ cups lowfat granola

1 (8-oz.) container plain or vanilla lowfat yogurt

1 (15 ¼-oz.) can **DEL MONTE® Fruit Cocktail in Heavy Syrup**, drained

Summer Fruit with Honey-Velvet Sauce

½ cup **HELLMANN'S®** or **BEST FOODS® Real Mayonnaise**

¼ cup honey

Grated zest of 1 lemon (about 1 ½ teaspoons)

4 cups mixed fresh fruit such as sliced peaches, blueberries, blackberries, and/or raspberries

¼ cup sliced almonds, toasted

PREP: 20 minutes

YIELD: 4 servings

In small bowl, combine **HELLMANN'S®** or **BEST FOODS® Real Mayonnaise**, honey, and lemon zest; set aside. In four serving dishes, evenly divide fruit. To serve, drizzle with honey sauce and top with almonds.

Courtesy of Unilever

Dipped Fruit

PREP: 5 minutes

COOK: 2 minutes

CHILL: 30 minutes

YIELD: 3 dozen

1 (11.5- to 12-oz.) package **NESTLÉ® TOLL HOUSE® Semi-Sweet Chocolate, Milk Chocolate**, or **Premier White Morsels** (1 ¾ to 2 cups)

2 tablespoons vegetable shortening

36 bite-size pieces fresh fruit such as strawberries, oranges, kiwifruit, bananas, or melons, rinsed and patted dry

Line baking sheet with wax paper. Microwave morsels and vegetable shortening in uncovered, microwave-safe bowl at medium-high (70%) power for 1 minute; stir. The morsels may retain some of their original shape. If necessary, microwave at additional 10- to 15-second intervals, stirring just until melted; cool slightly. Dip fruit about halfway into melted morsels; shake off excess. Place on prepared baking sheet; refrigerate until set.

VARIATION

For a fancy drizzle, place ½ cup **NESTLÉ® TOLL HOUSE® Premier White or Semi-Sweet Chocolate Morsels** or **Baking Bars** broken into pieces in a small, heavy-duty plastic bag. Microwave at medium-high (70%) power for 1 minute; knead. Microwave at additional 10- to 15-second intervals, kneading until smooth. Cut tiny corner from bag; squeeze to drizzle over fruit. Refrigerate until set.

Courtesy of Nestlé USA

Chocolate-Dipped Strawberries

PREP: 30 minutes

CHILL: 10 minutes

YIELD: about 16 servings

Gently rinse strawberries and let them dry on paper towels. Line a large tray with waxed paper. Place chocolate and butter in a double boiler over simmering water; heat until ingredients have melted. Remove from heat and stir until smooth. Dip strawberries into the chocolate one at a time, leaving upper third of each berry uncoated. If desired, dip again (tips only) into pecans. Place dipped berries on lined tray. Chill in refrigerator to let the chocolate set, at least 10 minutes. Keep the berries chilled until ready to serve. Excess melted chocolate can be refrigerated and melted again for later use.

Copyright by Terese Allen; courtesy of Organic Valley Family of Farms

Up to 2 quarts whole, stem-on fresh organic strawberries

8 oz. semisweet organic chocolate, cut into small pieces (or substitute chocolate chips)

4 tablespoons **ORGANIC VALLEY Butter**, cut into small pieces

Finely chopped pecans (optional)

Grilled Fruit with Apple-Maple Syrup

½ cup **Apple NESTLÉ® JUICY JUICE® All Natural 100% Juice**

¼ cup pure maple syrup

4 slices ripe pineapple, peeled

2 peaches, cut in half, pits removed

4 scoops **Vanilla DREYER'S** or **EDY'S® SLOW CHURNED® Light Ice Cream**

PREP: 10 minutes

COOK: 10 minutes

YIELD: 4 servings

Combine **JUICY JUICE®** and syrup in small saucepan over medium heat. Bring to a boil; reduce heat to low and cook for 5 minutes or until slightly thick. Remove from heat and cool slightly. Preheat grill. Brush fruit lightly with a small amount of syrup. Grill fruit, brushing occasionally with additional syrup, for 2 to 3 minutes per side or until nicely browned. Remove fruit to individual dishes and top each with a scoop of ice cream. Drizzle with remaining syrup.

Courtesy of Nestlé USA

Easy Baked Apples

PREP: 5 minutes

COOK: 5 minutes

YIELD: 4 servings

4 medium apples, cored

¼ cup dark brown sugar, firmly packed

¼ cup chopped walnuts

½ teaspoon ground cinnamon

4 teaspoons **PROMISE® activ® Buttery Spread**

Arrange apples in microwave-safe pie plate and cover with waxed paper. Microwave at high 3 minutes. Meanwhile, in small bowl, combine brown sugar, walnuts, and cinnamon. Evenly stuff into apples, then evenly top apples with **PROMISE® activ® Buttery Spread.** Cover with waxed paper and microwave at high 2 minutes or until apples are tender and sauce is boiling. Let stand 5 minutes. To serve, spoon sauce over apples.

TO COOK IN OVEN: Preheat oven to 425°F. Arrange apples in 9-inch pie plate. Add ¼ cup water; set aside. Stuff apples as above. Bake 20 minutes or until apples are tender.

Also terrific with **PROMISE® activ® Light Spread.**

Courtesy of Unilever

Easy Fruit Tarts

Vegetable cooking spray

12 wonton skins

2 tablespoons apple jelly or apricot fruit spread

1 ½ cups sliced or cut-up fruit such as **DOLE®** Bananas, Strawberries, Nectarines, Red or Green Seedless Grapes, Raspberries, or Blueberries

1 cup nonfat or lowfat yogurt, any flavor

PREP: 20 minutes

COOK: 8 minutes

YIELD: 12 servings

Preheat oven to 375°F. Spray vegetable cooking spray into 12 muffin cups. Press one wonton skin into each muffin cup, allowing corners of wontons to extend over edges of muffin cups. Bake 6 to 8 minutes or until lightly browned. Carefully remove wonton cups to wire rack; cool. Cook and stir jelly in small saucepan over low heat until jelly melts. Brush bottoms of cooled wonton cups with melted jelly. Place 2 fruit slices in each cup; spoon rounded tablespoon of yogurt over fruit. Garnish with additional fruit slice, if desired. Serve immediately.

Courtesy of Dole Food Company

Beautifully Easy Fruit Tart

PREP: 15 minutes

COOK: 15 minutes

YIELD: 9 servings

Preheat oven to 400°F. Unroll pastry on baking sheet. Fold over edges of pastry to form ½-inch rim; press firmly together to seal. Prick pastry sheet with fork. Bake 10 to 15 minutes or until puffed and golden brown. Cool completely. Place on serving tray. Add milk to dry pudding mix in large bowl. Beat with wire whisk 2 minutes or until well blended. Gently stir in whipped topping. Spread onto center of pastry. Arrange fruit in rows over pudding mixture. Mix preserves and water; brush over fruit. Drizzle with melted chocolate. Let stand until chocolate is firm. Serve immediately or cover and refrigerate until ready to serve. Store leftovers in refrigerator.

Courtesy of Kraft Foods

1 sheet (½ of a 17.3-oz. package) frozen puff pastry, thawed

1 cup cold milk

1 (3.4-oz., 4-serving) package **JELL-O Vanilla Flavor Instant Pudding**

1 cup **COOL WHIP Whipped Topping**, thawed

1 cup quartered strawberries

1 (11-oz.) can mandarin oranges, drained

1 kiwifruit, peeled, sliced, and halved

3 tablespoons apricot preserves

2 teaspoons water

1 (1-oz.) square **BAKER'S White Chocolate**, melted

Harvest Spice Peach Crisp

2 (15-oz.) cans **DEL MONTE® Harvest Spice Sliced Yellow Cling Peaches**, drained

½ cup flour

⅓ cup brown sugar, firmly packed

⅓ cup old-fashioned oats

⅓ cup walnuts, chopped

⅓ cup butter or margarine, softened

Ice cream or whipped cream (optional)

PREP: 10 minutes

BAKE: 20 minutes

YIELD: 6 servings

Preheat oven to 425°F. Place fruit in an 8-inch square baking dish. Combine flour, sugar, oats, and walnuts. Mix in butter until crumbly; sprinkle evenly over fruit. Bake for 15 to 20 minutes or until topping is golden. Serve with ice cream or whipped cream, if desired.

Courtesy of Del Monte Foods

Blueberry Crisp with Organic Short Grain Brown Rice

PREP: 10 minutes

COOK: 20 minutes

YIELD: 8 servings

Preheat oven to 375°F.

FOR THE FILLING: Combine rice, blueberries, and brown sugar in a large bowl. Coat 8 individual custard cups or a 2-quart baking dish with cooking spray. Place rice mixture in cups or baking dish; set aside.

FOR THE TOPPING: Combine flour, walnuts, brown sugar, and cinnamon in bowl. Cut in margarine with pastry blender until mixture resembles coarse meal. Sprinkle over rice mixture. Bake 15 to 20 minutes or until thoroughly heated. Serve warm.

Courtesy of Lundberg Family Farms

FILLING

2 **LUNDBERG® Heat & Eat Organic Short Grain Brown Rice Bowls**

3 cups fresh blueberries

3 tablespoons brown sugar, firmly packed

Vegetable cooking spray

TOPPING

¼ cup whole wheat flour

¼ cup chopped walnuts

¼ cup brown sugar, firmly packed

1 teaspoon ground cinnamon

3 tablespoons margarine or butter

Fruit Pizza

1 (18-oz.) package refrigerated sliceable sugar cookies

2 cups **COOL WHIP Whipped Topping**, thawed

2 cups assorted fruit, such as bananas, strawberries, grapes, nectarines, and kiwifruit, cut into slices

PREP: 12 minutes

BAKE: 18 minutes

YIELD: 16 (1-slice) servings

Preheat oven to 350°F. Press dough evenly into 12-inch pizza pan. Bake 15 to 18 minutes or until golden brown. Cool in pan on wire rack. Remove crust from pan; place on serving plate. Spread with whipped topping; top with fruit. Serve immediately or cover and refrigerate until ready to serve. Cut into 16 slices to serve. Store leftover pizza in refrigerator.

Courtesy of Kraft Foods

Cheesecake and Fruit Dessert Pizza

1 (18-oz.) package refrigerated sugar cookie dough

1 (8-oz.) package cream cheese, softened

¼ cup sugar

1 (11- or 15-oz.) can **DOLE®
Mandarin Oranges**, drained

2 **DOLE Kiwi Fruit**, peeled, sliced

¾ cup sliced **DOLE Strawberries**

½ cup **DOLE Raspberries**
(optional)

Mint leaves (for garnish, optional)

PREP: 15 minutes

COOK: 15 minutes

YIELD: 12 servings

Preheat oven to 350°F. Press cookie dough on bottom of lightly greased 12-inch pizza pan. Bake 11 to 15 minutes or until light brown. Cool to room temperature. Beat cream cheese and sugar in medium bowl until smooth and blended. Stir in ½ cup mandarin oranges. Spread over crust. Cover; refrigerate until ready to serve. Arrange kiwi, strawberries, raspberries, if using, and remaining mandarin oranges over cream cheese before serving. Garnish with mint leaves, if desired.

Courtesy of Dole Food Company

Easy No-Bake Peanut Butter Cheesecake

PREP: 25 minutes

COOK: 5 minutes

FREEZE: 4 to 6 hours

YIELD: 12 servings

FOR THE CHOCOLATE CRUMB CRUST: Stir together all ingredients in medium bowl until blended. Press firmly onto bottom of 9-inch springform pan.

FOR THE CHEESECAKE: Beat cream cheese with lemon juice in large bowl until fluffy. Combine peanut butter chips and sweetened condensed milk in medium saucepan. Cook over low heat, stirring constantly, until chips are melted and mixture is smooth; add to cream cheese mixture, beating until well blended. Beat whipping cream in small bowl until stiff. Fold into cream cheese mixture. Pour over crust. Cover; freeze 4 to 6 hours or until firm. Remove sides of pan. Garnish with sliced fresh fruit, if desired.

Courtesy of The Hershey Company

CHOCOLATE CRUMB CRUST

1 ¼ cups graham cracker crumbs

¼ cup **HERSHEY'S Cocoa**

¼ cup confectioners' sugar

¼ cup (½ stick) butter or margarine, melted

CHEESECAKE

1 (8-oz.) package cream cheese, softened

1 tablespoon lemon juice

1 (10-oz.) package (1 ⅔ cups) **REESE'S Peanut Butter Chips**

1 (14-oz.) can sweetened condensed milk (not evaporated milk)

1 cup cold whipping cream, whipped

Sliced fresh fruit (for garnish, optional)

Decadent Drizzled Cheesecake

PREP: 18 minutes

COOK: 12 minutes

CHILL: 2 hours

YIELD: 24 servings

Preheat oven to 325°F. For crust, combine 1 cup **SKIPPY® Peanut Butter**, ¼ cup of the sugar, egg, honey, 1 teaspoon of the vanilla, and salt in medium bowl until smooth. Evenly press into bottom of 13 x 9-inch baking dish. Bake 12 minutes or until golden; cool. Meanwhile, beat cream cheese, remaining ¼ cup sugar, and remaining 3 teaspoons vanilla in mixing bowl with electric mixer until blended. Slowly add heavy cream and continue beating on medium-high speed 2 minutes or until smooth and fluffy. Spread over cooled crust. Microwave remaining ¼ cup peanut butter in small microwave-safe bowl at high 15 seconds or until melted. Drizzle over cream cheese mixture. Chill 2 hours or until set. To serve, cut into squares.

Courtesy of Unilever

1 ¼ cups **SKIPPY® Creamy Peanut Butter** or **SKIPPY® SUPER CHUNK® Peanut Butter**, divided

½ cup sugar, divided

1 egg, slightly beaten

2 tablespoons honey

4 teaspoons vanilla extract, divided

¼ teaspoon salt

2 (8-oz.) packages cream cheese, softened

1 cup heavy or whipping cream

BREYERS Cherry Cheesecake

1 cup graham cracker crumbs

¼ cup **I CAN'T BELIEVE IT'S NOT BUTTER!® Spread**, melted

3 tablespoons plus ⅔ cup sugar

2 (8-oz.) packages cream cheese, softened

½ teaspoon vanilla extract

1 (1.5-quart) container **BREYERS® All Natural Vanilla Ice Cream**

1 (21-oz.) can cherry pie filling *or* your favorite pie filling

PREP: 20 minutes

FREEZE: 5 hours

YIELD: 16 servings

In medium bowl, combine graham cracker crumbs, **I CAN'T BELIEVE IT'S NOT BUTTER!® Spread**, and 3 tablespoons of the sugar; press into 9-inch springform pan. Freeze 15 minutes. Meanwhile, in large bowl of an electric mixer, beat cream cheese, remaining ⅔ cup sugar, and vanilla until smooth; set aside. Spoon **BREYERS® All Natural Vanilla Ice Cream** into springform pan, pressing to form an even layer. Evenly spread on cream cheese mixture. Cover and freeze 5 hours or overnight. Freeze serving platter 30 minutes before serving. Top cheesecake with cherry pie filling. Dip knife or metal spatula in hot water, then wipe dry and run around edge of cake to loosen. Remove ring from pan. On chilled serving platter, arrange cake.

VARIATION

For an Ice Cream Chocolate Cherry Cheesecake, use chocolate cookie crumbs and **BREYERS® All Natural Chocolate Ice Cream**.

Courtesy of Unilever

BREYERS Ice Cream Flag Cake

PREP: 30 minutes

FREEZE: 2 hours

YIELD: 24 servings

Cut containers from **BREYERS® All Natural Chocolate Ice Cream** with scissors. Arrange ice cream on its side, then cut each block lengthwise into 4 slices. Arrange 4 ice cream slices in 13 x 9-inch baking dish, pressing to form an even layer. Top with assorted fruit, then remaining 4 ice cream slices, pressing to form an even layer. Cover and freeze at least 2 hours or until ready to serve. Top with whipped cream, smoothing with spatula just before serving. Arrange berries in flag pattern, with blueberries in upper left corner and 7 raspberry "stripes."

Courtesy of Unilever

2 (1.5-quart) containers **BREYERS® All Natural Chocolate Ice Cream** and/or **BREYERS® All Natural Vanilla Ice Cream**, divided

4 cups assorted sliced fresh fruit

1 (7-oz.) can whipped cream or 2 cups thawed frozen whipped topping

50 fresh blueberries

2 pints raspberries or 1 quart strawberries, sliced

DOLE Golden Layer Cake

PREP: 20 minutes

CHILL: 30 minutes

YIELD: 12 servings

Combine undrained pineapple, whipped topping, and dry pudding mix. Let stand 5 minutes. Cut cake lengthwise in thirds. Drizzle with liqueur. Spread one-third pudding mixture over bottom layer of cake. Top with second layer. Repeat layering, ending with pudding. Chill 30 minutes or overnight. Sprinkle with toasted sliced almonds and garnish with pineapple slices, if desired.

Courtesy of Dole Food Company

1 (20-oz.) can **DOLE Crushed Pineapple**, undrained

1 ½ cups frozen whipped topping, thawed

1 (4-serving) package instant vanilla pudding mix

1 (16-oz.) pound cake

⅓ cup almond-flavored liqueur or ⅓ cup pineapple juice and ½ teaspoon almond extract

Toasted sliced almonds

Pineapple slices (for garnish, optional)

Right-Side-Up Fruit Cake

1 (10-oz.) package **SIMPLY ORGANIC Banana Bread Mix**

¾ cup rolled oats

2 eggs

1 cup water

2 (15-oz.) cans sliced and drained pineapple

PREP: 10 minutes

BAKE: 20 minutes

YIELD: 12 servings

Preheat oven to 350°F. In a medium mixing bowl, add **SIMPLY ORGANIC Banana Bread Mix** and oats. Add eggs and water. Stir until moistened. Pour into a lightly greased 11 x 7-inch baking pan. Dice pineapple and layer onto batter. Bake for 15 to 20 minutes or until center tests done with a toothpick or knife.

COOK'S TIP

Use the drained pineapple juice instead of water, adding water if needed to measure 1 cup.

VARIATION

Substitute pears or peaches for the pineapple.

Courtesy of Simply Organic

Grilled Pound Cake with Berries and Spiced Lime Sauce

PREP: 10 minutes

COOK: 5 minutes

YIELD: 4 servings

Combine sugar, cornstarch, and spice in saucepan and blend well. Add water and lime juice. Whisk mixture until smooth, and cook over medium heat until boiling and thickened. Remove from heat and stir in butter and vanilla. Grill or toast cake slices and place on each of four serving plates. Top with fresh berries and spoon some sauce over cake to serve.

3 tablespoons sugar

1 tablespoon cornstarch

½ teaspoon cinnamon or pumpkin pie spice

⅓ cup water

¼ cup fresh-squeezed **SUNKIST® lime juice**

1 tablespoon butter

½ teaspoon vanilla extract

4 (1-inch-thick) slices pound cake or angel food cake

1 cup fresh **SUNKIST® Berries**

Toasted Pound Cake with Ice Cream & Bananas

PREP: 20 minutes

BAKE: 15 minutes

CHILL: 30 minutes

YIELD: 12 servings

Preheat oven to 350°F. Blend **SHEDD'S SPREAD COUNTRY CROCK® Spread** with pumpkin pie spice; evenly spread ¼ cup Spread mixture on both sides of cake slices. Arrange cake slices on cookie sheet and bake 15 minutes or until toasted; set aside and keep warm. Combine bananas, brown sugar, and remaining ½ cup Spread mixture in microwave-safe shallow dish. Microwave at high, gently stirring once, 2 minutes or until heated through. Arrange warm cake on serving plates, then top with **BREYERS® All Natural Vanilla Ice Cream** and banana mixture.

Courtesy of Unilever

¾ cup **SHEDD'S SPREAD COUNTRY CROCK® Spread**

½ teaspoon pumpkin pie spice or ground cinnamon

1 prepared pound cake, cut into 8 slices

3 bananas, sliced diagonally

2 tablespoons light brown sugar, firmly packed

2 cups **BREYERS® All Natural Vanilla Ice Cream**

Cinnamon Apple Cake à la Mode

4 slices pound cake

1 (21-oz.) container **SHEDD'S COUNTRY CROCK® Side Dishes Deluxe Cinnamon Apples**, heated according to package directions

4 scoops **BREYERS® All Natural Vanilla Ice Cream** (about 2 cups)

Chocolate or caramel ice cream toppings (optional)

PREP: 10 minutes

YIELD: 4 servings

On four dessert plates, arrange cake, then top with **SHEDD'S COUNTRY CROCK® Side Dishes Deluxe Cinnamon Apples** and **BREYERS® All Natural Vanilla Ice Cream**. Drizzle with chocolate or caramel ice cream toppings, if desired.

Courtesy of Unilever

Raspberry Mango Grilled Shortcake

PREP: 20 minutes

GRILL: 3 minutes

YIELD: 4 servings

Heat gas grill on medium or charcoal grill until coals are ash white. Slice half of pound cake into 8 slices. Reserve remaining pound cake for another use. Brush both sides of each slice of cake with melted butter. Place cake onto grill. Grill, turning once, until golden brown, 2 to 3 minutes. Immediately sprinkle with cinnamon-sugar. Combine mango and raspberries in small bowl. Beat whipping cream and sugar together in another small bowl until soft peaks form. For each shortcake, place one grilled cake slice onto serving plate. Spoon ¼ cup fruit over cake. Top with 2 tablespoons whipped cream. Repeat layers. Serve immediately.

1 (10.75-oz.) frozen pound cake, thawed

2 tablespoons **LAND O LAKES® Butter**, melted

4 teaspoons purchased cinnamon-sugar mixture

1 ripe mango, peeled, cut into bite-size pieces

1 cup fresh raspberries

½ cup whipping cream

1 tablespoon sugar

COOK'S TIPS

- To make cinnamon sugar, mix 3 ½ teaspoons sugar and ½ teaspoon ground cinnamon in a small bowl.

- Create a parfait-style dessert by layering pieces of grilled cake with whipped cream and fruit in tall stemmed glasses.

Courtesy of Land O'Lakes, Inc.

Pineapple Summer Shortcakes

1 (8-oz.) can **DOLE® Pineapple Chunks** or **Pineapple Slices**

1 (3-oz.) package cream cheese, softened

1 tablespoon honey

½ teaspoon grated lemon zest

1 teaspoon lemon juice

1 (4-oz.) package individual shortcakes or 5 oz. (½ of a 10-oz. package) frozen prepared pound cake, thawed and sliced

Assorted sliced fresh fruit, such as **DOLE® Strawberries**, **Nectarines**, **Raspberries**, and **Blueberries**

PREP: 15 minutes

YIELD: 4 servings

Drain pineapple; reserve 1 tablespoon juice. Beat together cream cheese, honey, lemon zest, lemon juice, and reserved pineapple juice in small bowl until blended and smooth. Spoon filling evenly into center of shortcakes or over pound cake slices. Arrange pineapple and fruit over filling.

Courtesy of Dole Food Company

Black & White Cupcakes

2 cups sugar

1 ¾ cups all-purpose flour

¾ cup **HERSHEY'S Cocoa**

2 teaspoons baking soda

1 teaspoon baking powder

1 teaspoon salt

1 cup buttermilk or sour milk*

2 eggs

1 cup boiling water

½ cup vegetable oil

1 teaspoon vanilla extract

Vanilla Frosting
(recipe to right)

"Perfectly Chocolate" Chocolate Frosting (recipe to right)

*To sour milk, use 1 tablespoon white vinegar plus milk to equal 1 cup.

PREP: 15 minutes

BAKE: 15minutes

YIELD: 2 ½ dozen

Preheat oven to 350°F. Line 30 muffin cups (2 ½ inches in diameter) with paper bake cups. Combine dry ingredients in large bowl. Add buttermilk, eggs, water, oil, and vanilla; beat on medium speed of mixer 2 minutes (batter will be thin). Fill cups two-thirds full with batter. Bake 15 minutes or until wooden pick inserted in center comes out clean. Remove cupcakes from pan. Cool completely before frosting.

VANILLA FROSTING: Beat ¼ cup (½ stick) softened butter, ¼ cup shortening, and 2 teaspoons vanilla extract. Add 1 cup confectioners' sugar; beat until creamy. Add 3 cups confectioners' sugar alternately with 3 to 4 tablespoons milk, beating to spreading consistency. Makes about 2⅓ cups.

"PERFECTLY CHOCOLATE" CHOCOLATE FROSTING: Melt 1 stick (½ cup) butter or margarine; stir in ⅔ cup **HERSHEY'S Cocoa**. Add 3 cups confectioners' sugar alternately with ⅓ cup milk and 1 teaspoon vanilla extract, beating to spreading consistency. Makes about 2 cups.

Courtesy of The Hershey Company

Ice Cream Bar Cupcakes

1 (18-oz.) box chocolate cake mix

1 cup **HELLMANN'S®** or **BEST FOODS®** Real Mayonnaise

1 cup water

3 eggs

1 teaspoon ground cinnamon (optional)

BREYERS® All Natural Ice Cream

Ice cream bar toppings, such as chopped nuts, sprinkles, marshmallows, crushed candy bars or cookies, chocolate chips, hot fudge, melted **SKIPPY® Peanut Butter**, and cherries

PREP: 5 minutes

COOK: 20 minutes

YIELD: 2 dozen

Preheat oven to 350°F. Lightly grease and flour two 12-cup muffin pans or line with paper cupcake liners; set aside. In large bowl, with electric mixer at low speed, beat cake mix, **HELLMANN'S®** or **BEST FOODS®** Real Mayonnaise, water, eggs, and cinnamon, if using, for 30 seconds. Beat at medium speed, scraping sides occasionally, 2 minutes. Evenly spoon batter into prepared pans. Bake 20 minutes or until toothpick inserted in centers comes out clean. On wire rack, cool 10 minutes; remove from pans and cool completely. Serve with your favorite ice cream bar toppings.

Courtesy of Unilever

Spice and Cream Mini Cakes

PREP: 5 minutes

BAKE: 25 minutes

YIELD: 1 dozen

Preheat oven to 350°F. Lightly grease a 12-cup muffin pan or use paper liners. In a medium mixing bowl, add all ingredients and mix well. Pour into muffin pan and bake 20 to 25 minutes or until center tests done with a toothpick or knife. Do not underbake.

Courtesy of Simply Organic

COOK'S TIP

Decorate each as a tree ornament for Christmas!

1 (11.6-oz.) package **SIMPLY ORGANIC Carrot Cake Mix**

¼ cup applesauce

½ cup light sour cream

½ cup water

Dark Molten Chocolate Cakes

1 (6-oz.) package (6 squares) **BAKER'S Bittersweet Chocolate**

10 tablespoons butter

1 ½ cups confectioners' sugar, plus more for garnish

½ cup flour

3 whole eggs

3 egg yolks

Raspberries (for garnish, optional)

PREP: 15 minutes

BAKE: 15 minutes

YIELD: 12 servings, ½ cake each

Preheat oven to 425°F. Grease six 6-oz. custard cups or soufflé dishes. Place on baking sheet. Microwave chocolate and butter in large microwaveable bowl on medium (50%) 2 minutes or until butter is melted. Stir with wire whisk until chocolate is completely melted. Add sugar and flour; mix well. Add whole eggs and egg yolks; beat until well blended. Divide batter evenly into prepared custard cups. Bake 14 to 15 minutes or until cakes are firm around the edges but still soft in the centers. Let stand 1 minute. Run small knife around cakes to loosen. Carefully invert cakes onto dessert dishes. Sprinkle lightly with additional confectioners' sugar and garnish with raspberries, if desired. Cut in half. Serve warm.

Courtesy of Kraft Foods

Chocolate Lava Cakes

PREP: 15 minutes

COOK: 13 minutes

CHILL: 1 hour

YIELD: 2 servings

Line bottom of two (4-oz.) ramekins or custard cups with a round of waxed paper, then grease; set aside. In medium microwave-safe bowl, microwave **I CAN'T BELIEVE IT'S NOT BUTTER!® Spread** and chocolate at high 40 seconds or until chocolate is melted; stir until smooth. With wire whisk, beat in granulated sugar, flour, and salt until blended. Beat in egg, egg yolk, and vanilla. Evenly spoon into prepared ramekins. Refrigerate 1 hour or until ready to bake. Bake in a preheated 425°F oven for 13 minutes or until edges are firm but centers are still slightly soft; do not overbake. Cool on wire rack for 5 minutes. To serve, carefully run sharp knife around cake edges. Unmold onto serving plates, then remove waxed paper. Sprinkle with confectioners' sugar and serve immediately.

COOK'S TIP

If you don't have ramekins, you can use a 12-cup muffin pan instead. Line the bottom of 4 muffin cups with waxed paper, then grease. Evenly spoon in batter. Refrigerate as above. Bake at 425°F for 9 minutes or until edges are firm but centers are still slightly soft; do not overbake. Cool on wire rack for 5 minutes. To serve, carefully run sharp knife around cake edges and gently lift out of pan. Do not turn pan upside-down to unmold. Arrange cakes, bottom side up, on serving plates, two cakes per serving. Remove waxed paper and sprinkle with confectioners' sugar as above.

Courtesy of Unilever

3 tablespoons **I CAN'T BELIEVE IT'S NOT BUTTER!® Spread**

1 ½ oz. bittersweet or semi-sweet chocolate, cut in pieces

¼ cup granulated sugar

3 tablespoons all-purpose flour

Pinch salt

1 large egg

1 large egg yolk

⅛ teaspoon vanilla extract

Confectioners' sugar

Apple Pie with Peanut Butter Crumble

1 (21-oz.) can apple pie filling

1 cup uncooked quick oats

1 cup all-purpose flour

1 cup light brown sugar, firmly packed

⅓ cup **SKIPPY® Creamy Peanut Butter**

6 tablespoons **I CAN'T BELIEVE IT'S NOT BUTTER!® Spread**

Vanilla ice cream (optional)

PREP: 10 minutes

COOK: 20 minutes

YIELD: 8 servings

Preheat oven to 375°F. In 9-inch pie plate, evenly spread pie filling; set aside. In medium bowl, combine oats, flour, and brown sugar. With pastry blender or two knives, cut in **SKIPPY® Creamy Peanut Butter** and **I CAN'T BELIEVE IT'S NOT BUTTER!® Spread** until mixture is size of small peas. Sprinkle crumb mixture over pie filling. Bake 20 minutes or until apples are heated through and topping is golden brown. Serve warm or cool. Top with vanilla ice cream, if desired.

Courtesy of Unilever

Cherry Dream Pie

3 egg yolks

1 (14-oz.) can sweetened condensed milk (not evaporated milk)

⅓ cup lemon juice

1 (6-oz.) prepared graham cracker pie crust

1 (21-oz.) can **COMSTOCK®** or **WILDERNESS® Cherry Pie Filling,** chilled

Whipped topping (optional)

PREP: 10 minutes

BAKE: 8 minutes

CHILL: 3 hours

YIELD: One (9-inch) pie

Preheat oven to 350°F. In medium bowl, beat egg yolks; stir in sweetened condensed milk and lemon juice. Pour into crust; bake 8 minutes. Cool. Chill 3 hours or overnight. Prior to serving, top with **COMSTOCK®** or **WILDERNESS® pie filling**. Garnish with whipped topping, if desired. Store leftovers covered in refrigerator.

Courtesy of Birds Eye Foods, Inc.

Cherry Vanilla Ribbon Pie

PREP: 20 minutes

CHILL: 2 ¼ hours

YIELD: One (9- or 10-inch) pie

In large mixer bowl, beat cream cheese until fluffy; gradually beat in sweetened condensed milk until smooth. On low speed, beat in water and pudding mix until smooth. Chill 10 minutes. Fold in whipped cream. Spread half the pudding mixture into prepared piecrust; top with half of the **COMSTOCK®** or **WILDERNESS® Cherry Pie Filling**. Repeat. Chill 2 hours or until set. Store leftovers covered in refrigerator.

Courtesy of Birds Eye Foods, Inc.

1 (8-oz.) package cream cheese, softened

1 (14-oz.) can sweetened condensed milk
(not evaporated milk)

¾ cup cold water

1 (4-serving) package instant vanilla pudding mix

1 cup whipping cream, whipped

1 (9- or 10-inch) baked piecrust

1 (21-oz.) can **COMSTOCK®** or **WILDERNESS® Cherry Pie Filling**, chilled

CARNATION Key Lime Pie

1 (14-oz.) can **NESTLÉ® CARNATION® Sweetened Condensed Milk**

½ cup (about 3 medium limes) fresh lime juice

1 teaspoon grated lime zest

1 (9-inch) prepared graham cracker crust

2 cups frozen whipped topping, thawed

8 thin lime slices (for garnish, optional)

PREP: 5 minutes

CHILL: 2 hours

YIELD: 8 servings

Beat sweetened condensed milk and lime juice in small mixer bowl until combined; stir in lime zest. Pour into crust; spread with whipped topping. Refrigerate for 2 hours or until set. Garnish with lime slices, if desired.

Courtesy of Nestlé USA

Tropical Pineapple Pie

PREP: 20 minutes

FREEZE: 8 hours

YIELD: 10 servings

In medium mixing bowl, combine cheesecake mix, fruit filling, nuts, coconut, and rum. Pour into crust. Freeze 8 hours or until firm. Thaw 5 to 10 minutes at room temperature before serving. Cut into slices and serve.

Courtesy of Birds Eye Foods, Inc.

1 (3.4-oz.) package instant cheesecake mix, prepared according to package directions

1 (21-oz.) can **COMSTOCK® or WILDERNESS® Pineapple Fruit Filling**

¼ cup chopped pecans

¼ cup shredded coconut

½ teaspoon rum extract

1 (9-inch) prepared graham cracker crust

Banana Cream Sundae Pie

¾ quart (½ of a 1.5-quart container) **BREYERS® All Natural Banana Cream Pie Ice Cream**, slightly softened

1 (9-inch) graham cracker crust

¾ cup **SKIPPY® Creamy Peanut Butter** or **SKIPPY® SUPER CHUNK® Peanut Butter**, melted

2 bananas, sliced

¼ cup hot fudge topping, heated

PREP: 30 minutes

FREEZE: 4 ½ hours

YIELD: 12 servings

Spread half of the **BREYERS® All Natural Banana Cream Pie Ice Cream** in graham cracker crust, then top with ½ cup melted **SKIPPY® Peanut Butter** and half of the bananas. Freeze 30 minutes or until firm. Evenly top with remaining ice cream, then bananas; drizzle with hot fudge topping and remaining peanut butter. Cover and freeze 4 hours or until ready to serve. Let stand 10 minutes before serving.

Courtesy of Unilever

Lemon Cream Cheese Pie

PREP: 25 minutes

BAKE: 5 minutes

CHILL: 2 hours

YIELD: 8 servings

FOR THE CRUST: Preheat oven to 375°F. Combine cookie crumbs and melted butter in small bowl; press onto bottom and up sides of ungreased 9-inch glass pie pan. Bake for 5 to 6 minutes or just until set. Cool completely.

FOR THE GLAZE: Combine all glaze ingredients in 1-quart saucepan. Cook over medium-low heat, stirring constantly, until mixture is thickened and comes to a boil, 4 to 6 minutes. Refrigerate while making filling.

FOR THE FILLING: Combine sugar, cream cheese, and lemon zest in medium bowl. Beat at medium speed until creamy. Beat whipping cream in another medium bowl until stiff peaks form; gently stir into cream cheese mixture. Spoon into cooled crust. Make deep swirls in cream cheese mixture with back of teaspoon. Spoon glaze mixture over cream cheese mixture. Refrigerate until set, at least 2 hours.

COOK'S TIP

To make it easier to squeeze fresh lemon juice, first heat the lemon in microwave oven at high (100%) for about 20 seconds.

Courtesy of Land O'Lakes, Inc.

CRUST

1 ¼ cups gingersnap cookie crumbs

¼ cup **LAND O LAKES® Butter**, melted

GLAZE

⅓ cup water

¼ cup sugar

3 tablespoons lemon juice

1 tablespoon freshly grated lemon zest

1 ½ teaspoons cornstarch

FILLING

⅓ cup sugar

1 (8-oz.) package cream cheese, softened

1 tablespoon freshly grated lemon zest

½ cup whipping cream

Banana Split Pie

1 (9-inch) graham cracker or chocolate cookie crust

4 bananas, peeled and thinly sliced

1 (1.5-quart) container **BREYERS® All Natural Vanilla, Chocolate, Strawberry Ice Cream**

½ cup pineapple or caramel ice cream topping

½ cup strawberry ice cream topping

¼ cup chocolate syrup

1 cup sweetened whipped cream or whipped topping

Maraschino cherries (for garnish)

PREP: 20 minutes

FREEZE: 1 hour

YIELD: 12 servings

Line bottom of crust with half of the bananas. Scoop half of the **BREYERS® All Natural Vanilla, Chocolate, Strawberry Ice Cream** into crust, then drizzle with half of each ice cream topping and chocolate syrup; repeat layers. Freeze 1 hour or until firm. Just before serving, top with whipped cream and garnish with cherries.

VARIATION

Try your favorite ice cream toppings, such as walnut or caramel sauce.

Courtesy of Unilever

Black Forest Ice Cream Pie

PREP: 10 minutes

FREEZE: 4 hours

YIELD: 12 servings

Remove lid from hot fudge topping. Microwave hot fudge topping at high (100%) for 30 seconds or until pourable. Reserve ¼ cup topping. Spread remaining topping into crust and freeze 10 minutes. Scoop **BREYERS® All Natural Cherry Vanilla Ice Cream** onto topping. Freeze 4 hours or until firm. Just before serving, microwave reserved topping at high for 10 to 20 seconds or until it can be drizzled; drizzle over ice cream. Garnish with whipped cream and cherries.

Courtesy of Unilever

1 (11.75-oz.) jar hot fudge topping

1 (9-inch) chocolate graham cracker crust

1 (1.5-quart) container **BREYERS® All Natural Cherry Vanilla Ice Cream**, slightly softened

9 dollops sweetened whipped cream (for garnish)

9 maraschino cherries (for garnish)

Rocky Road Ice Cream Pie

1 (1.5-quart) container **BREYERS® All Natural Rocky Road Ice Cream**, slightly softened

1 (9-inch) chocolate graham cracker crust

2 cups sweetened whipped cream

¼ cup chocolate syrup

Toasted chopped walnuts (for garnish, optional)

Mini marshmallows (for garnish, optional)

PREP: 10 minutes

FREEZE: 4 hours

YIELD: 12 servings

Scoop **BREYERS® All Natural Rocky Road Ice Cream** into crust; freeze 4 hours or until firm. Just before serving, top with whipped cream and drizzle with syrup. Garnish with toasted chopped walnuts and mini marshmallows, if desired.

COOK'S TIP

Don't have **BREYERS® All Natural Rocky Road Ice Cream**? Use **BREYERS® All Natural Chocolate Ice Cream** and stir in ¾ cup chopped toasted walnuts and ¾ cup mini marshmallows. Top as above.

Courtesy of Unilever

Easy Chocolate Peppermint Pie

PREP: 10 minutes

FREEZE: 6 to 8 hours

YIELD: 6 to 8 servings

Remove wrappers from peppermint patties; cut into quarters. Place peppermint pieces and milk in medium microwave-safe bowl. Microwave at medium (50%) 1 minute; stir. Microwave at medium an additional 30 seconds to 1 minute or just until candy is melted and smooth when stirred. Cool slightly. Fold whipped topping into melted mixture; spoon into crust. Cover; freeze 6 to 8 hours or until firm. Garnish with additional whipped topping and peppermint pieces, if desired.

Courtesy of The Hershey Company

12 small (1 ½-inch) **YORK Peppermint Patties**

¼ cup milk

1 (8-oz.) container frozen nondairy whipped topping, thawed (do not use "extra creamy" or "light" whipped topping)

1 (9-inch) packaged crumb crust

Additional whipped topping (for garnish, optional)

Additional **YORK Peppermint Patties** (for garnish, optional)

Eggless No-Bake Pumpkin Pie

PREP: 20 minutes

COOK: 7 minutes

CHILL: 1 hour

YIELD: 8 servings

Soak agar flakes in ¼ cup boiling water for 20 minutes. Combine **EDENSOY**, maple syrup, and dissolved agar in a medium saucepan and bring to a boil. Turn down heat and simmer until agar has completely melted, 3 to 4 minutes. Add pumpkin, salt, and spices. Blend well in a food processor. Pour into crust and chill 1 hour or until firm.

COOK'S TIP

If using a fresh piecrust, bake crust until done and allow to cool before pouring in pumpkin filling.

Courtesy of Eden Foods

3 tablespoons **EDEN Agar Agar Flakes**

¼ cup boiling water

1 ¼ cups **EDENSOY Vanilla** or **EDENSOY Extra Vanilla**

⅔ cup organic maple syrup

2 cups unsweetened pumpkin purée

¼ teaspoon **EDEN Sea Salt**

½ teaspoon ground cinnamon

¼ teaspoon ground nutmeg

¼ teaspoon ground cloves

½ teaspoon ground ginger

1 (8-inch) organic graham cracker piecrust

Quick Creamy Chocolate Pudding

PREP: 5 minutes

COOK: 25 minutes

CHILL: 2 hours

YIELD: 4 or 5 servings

2/3 cup sugar

1/4 cup **HERSHEY'S Cocoa**

3 tablespoons cornstarch

1/4 teaspoon salt

2 1/4 cups milk

2 tablespoons butter or margarine

1 teaspoon vanilla extract

Whipped topping (for garnish, optional)

Stir together sugar, cocoa, cornstarch, and salt in medium saucepan; gradually stir in milk. Cook over medium heat, stirring constantly, until mixture boils; boil and stir 1 minute. Remove from heat; stir in butter and vanilla. Pour into individual dessert dishes. To avoid a skin from forming on top, press plastic wrap directly onto surface; serve warm or refrigerate at least 2 hours. Garnish with whipped topping, if desired.

TO MICROWAVE: Stir together sugar, cocoa, cornstarch, and salt in large microwave-safe bowl; gradually stir in milk. Microwave at high (100%) 7 to 10 minutes or until mixture comes to full boil, stirring every 2 minutes. Stir in butter and vanilla. Pour into dishes and serve as directed above.

Courtesy of The Hershey Company

Tapioca Pudding

2/3 cup pearl tapioca, soaked for 2 hours

1/2 cup maple syrup

1/4 teaspoon salt

3 3/4 cups milk

1 tablespoon **FRONTIER** arrowroot

1 teaspoon **FRONTIER** vanilla extract

1/2 cup **FRONTIER** coconut

1/2 cup walnuts

PREP: 5 minutes

COOK: 12 minutes

YIELD: 8 servings

Combine the first four ingredients in a double boiler. Cook while stirring over rapidly boiling water for 7 minutes. Remove 1 cup of the hot liquid and blend with the arrowroot powder. Return liquid to the pot and stir. Cook 5 minutes or until tapioca is clear. Remove from heat. Stir in vanilla, coconut, and walnuts.

Courtesy of Frontier Natural Products Co-op

Stovetop Rice Pudding

2 cups cooked organic short grain brown rice

1 ½ cups **EDENSOY Light Vanilla** or **EDENSOY Extra Vanilla**

½ cup **EDEN ORGANIC Dried Wild Blueberries** or **EDEN ORGANIC Dried Cranberries**

2 tablespoons **EDEN ORGANIC Barley Malt Syrup** or organic maple syrup

1 teaspoon pure vanilla extract

⅛ teaspoon ground cinnamon

½ teaspoon freshly grated lemon zest

PREP: 5 minutes

COOK: 25 minutes

YIELD: 4 servings

Place the cooked rice, **EDENSOY**, dried fruit, and barley malt syrup in a saucepan. Cover and bring almost to a boil. Reduce the flame to medium-low and simmer 15 to 20 minutes or until creamy. Remove the cover, and add the vanilla, cinnamon, and grated lemon zest. Cover and simmer another 5 minutes.

Courtesy of Eden Foods

Lemon Blueberry Bliss

PREP: 20 minutes

COOK: 10 minutes

YIELD: 8 servings

Combine sugar, eggs, egg yolks, lemon juice, and lemon zest in a 2-quart saucepan. Cook over medium-low heat until thick and creamy, 8 to 10 minutes, stirring constantly. Remove from heat; stir in butter and rice. Cool. Fold in 1 cup of the whipped cream, reserving rest for garnish. Alternate layers of blueberries and rice pudding in parfait glasses. Garnish with whipped cream and blueberries.

Courtesy of Lundberg Family Farms

1 cup sugar

2 large eggs plus 2 egg yolks

2/3 cup lemon juice

1 tablespoon finely grated lemon zest

1/2 cup butter, softened

3 cups cooked **LUNDBERG® California White Arborio Rice**

2/3 cup whipping cream, whipped

1 cup blueberries

Banana Kiwi Pudding

1 ⅓ cups cooked **LUNDBERG®
California White Arborio Rice**

1 ⅓ cups skim milk

1 teaspoon vanilla extract

Low-calorie sugar substitute to
equal 2 tablespoons sugar

1 ripe banana

¼ cup whipping cream, whipped

2 kiwifruit, sliced (for garnish)

PREP: 20 minutes

COOK: 10 minutes

YIELD: 4 servings

Cook rice and milk in 2-quart saucepan over medium
heat until thick and creamy, 5 to 8 minutes, stirring
frequently. Remove from heat; cool. Stir in vanilla and
sugar substitute. Just before serving, mash banana; fold
banana and whipped cream into pudding. Garnish with
kiwifruit slices.

Courtesy of Lundberg Family Farms

Quick Indian Pudding

PREP: 5 minutes

COOK: 10 minutes

YIELD: 3 servings

Whisk together **EDENBLEND** or **EDENSOY**, barley malt syrup,
maple syrup, ginger, and salt. Place in a heavy saucepan over
high heat. Bring almost to a boil. Reduce heat to medium.
Sprinkle in polenta while whisking constantly to avoid lumping.
Cook over low heat, whisking frequently, until cornmeal tastes
cooked and mixture thickens to porridge consistency, 3 to 4
minutes. Stir in additional maple syrup, if more sweetener is
desired. Ladle mixture into individual ramekins or small dessert
bowls and set a walnut half in the center. Serve warm or at
room temperature.

COOK'S TIP

This Indian pudding tastes best the day it's made.

Courtesy of Eden Foods

3 cups **EDENBLEND** or
EDENSOY Extra Original

¼ cup **EDEN ORGANIC
Barley Malt Syrup**

¼ cup organic maple syrup,
plus more to taste, if desired

1 ¼ teaspoons ground ginger

⅛ teaspoon **EDEN Sea Salt**

½ cup organic quick cooking
yellow polenta

3 to 4 tablespoons walnut
halves

Cocoa Cappuccino Mousse

PREP: 15 minutes

COOK: 10 minutes

CHILL: 2 hours

YIELD: 8 servings

1 (14-oz.) can sweetened condensed milk (not evaporated milk)

⅓ cup **HERSHEY'S Cocoa**

3 tablespoons butter or margarine

2 teaspoons powdered instant coffee or espresso, dissolved in 2 teaspoons hot water

2 cups cold whipping cream

Combine sweetened condensed milk, cocoa, butter, and coffee in medium saucepan. Cook over low heat, stirring constantly, until butter melts and mixture is smooth. Remove from heat; cool. Beat whipping cream in large bowl until stiff. Gradually fold chocolate mixture into whipped cream. Spoon into dessert dishes. Refrigerate until set, about 2 hours. Garnish as desired.

Courtesy of The Hershey Company

Coconut Mousse

¼ cup **LAND O LAKES®** **Butter**, softened

1 (8-oz.) package cream cheese, softened

⅔ cup sugar

2 cups whipping cream

½ cup sweetened flaked coconut

½ teaspoon coconut extract or vanilla

Toasted sweetened flaked coconut (optional)

PREP: 10 minutes

YIELD: 6 servings

Place butter and cream cheese in large bowl. Beat at medium speed, scraping bowl often, until creamy. Add sugar; continue beating until well mixed. Increase speed to high. Beat, gradually adding whipping cream, until stiff peaks form. Gently stir in flaked coconut and coconut extract by hand. To serve, divide mixture evenly among six individual serving dishes. Cover; refrigerate until serving time. Sprinkle with toasted coconut, if desired.

Courtesy of Land O'Lakes, Inc.

Mmmmm . . . Pumpkin Mousse

1 (3.4-oz.) box vanilla instant pudding and pie filling mix

¼ teaspoon pumpkin pie spice or ground cinnamon

1 (5-fl. oz.) can **NESTLÉ® CARNATION® Evaporated Fat Free Milk**

1 cup **LIBBY'S® 100% Pure Pumpkin**

1 ½ cups fat-free frozen whipped topping, thawed

PREP: 20 minutes

YIELD: 6 (½-cup) servings

Combine pudding mix and pie spice in medium bowl. With whisk, add evaporated milk; mix until well blended. Add pumpkin and mix. Gently fold in whipped topping into pudding mixture. Spoon into serving dishes. Top with additional whipped topping and pie spice, if desired. Serve immediately or cover and refrigerate.

Courtesy of Nestlé USA

REESE'S Chewy Chocolate Pan Cookies

PREP: 10 minutes

BAKE: 20 minutes

YIELD: 4 dozen

Preheat oven to 350°F. Grease a 15 x 10 x 1-inch jelly roll pan. Beat butter and sugar in large bowl until light and fluffy. Add eggs and vanilla; beat well. Stir together flour, cocoa, baking soda, and salt; gradually blend into butter mixture. Stir in peanut butter chips. Spread batter in prepared pan. Bake 20 minutes or until set. Cool completely in pan on wire rack; cut into bars.

Courtesy of The Hershey Company

1 ¼ cups (2 ½ sticks) butter or margarine, softened

2 cups sugar

2 eggs

2 teaspoons vanilla extract

2 cups all-purpose flour

¾ cup **HERSHEY'S Cocoa**

1 teaspoon baking soda

½ teaspoon salt

1 (10-oz.) package (1 ⅔ cups) **REESE'S Peanut Butter Chips**

No-Bake Chocolate Peanut Butter Bars

2 cups peanut butter, divided

¾ cup (1 ½ sticks) butter, softened

2 cups confectioners' sugar, divided

3 cups graham cracker crumbs

1 (12-oz.) package (2 cups) **NESTLÉ® TOLL HOUSE® Semi-Sweet Chocolate Mini Morsels**, divided

PREP: 15 minutes

CHILL: 1 hour

YIELD: 5 dozen

Grease a 13 x 9-inch baking pan. Beat 1 ¼ cups of the peanut butter and butter in large mixer bowl until creamy. Gradually beat in 1 cup of the confectioners' sugar. With hands or wooden spoon, work in remaining confectioners' sugar, graham cracker crumbs, and ½ cup of the morsels. Press evenly into prepared baking pan. Smooth top with spatula. Melt remaining peanut butter and remaining morsels in medium, heavy-duty saucepan over lowest possible heat, stirring constantly, until smooth. Spread over graham cracker crust in pan. Refrigerate for at least 1 hour or until chocolate is firm; cut into bars. Store in refrigerator.

Courtesy of Nestlé USA

Sugar Spritz Cookies

PREP: 10 minutes

BAKE: 20 minutes

YIELD: 3 dozen

Preheat oven to 325°F. Mix cookie dough and food coloring in medium bowl. Fill cookie press with dough following manufacturer's directions. Press dough onto baking sheets. Sprinkle with candies and sprinkles. Bake for 8 to 10 minutes or until very light golden brown around edges. Cool on baking sheets for 2 minutes; remove to wire racks to cool completely.

COOK'S TIP

If dough becomes too soft to use in the cookie press, refrigerate for about 5 minutes or until slightly firm before continuing.

Courtesy of Nestlé USA

1 (16.5-oz.) package **NESTLÉ® TOLL HOUSE® Refrigerated Sugar Cookie Bar Dough**, softened

Assorted food coloring, candies, and sprinkles (optional)

Cookie press

Chocolatey Chocolate Chip Cookie Cups

PREP: 5 minutes

BAKE: 11 minutes

COOL: 5 minutes

YIELD: 2 dozen

1 (16.5-oz.) package **NESTLÉ® TOLL HOUSE® Refrigerated Chocolate Chip Cookie Bar Dough**

1 cup **NESTLÉ® TOLL HOUSE® Peanut Butter & Milk Chocolate Morsels**

Preheat oven to 350°F. Grease 24 mini-muffin cups or line with paper cupcake liners. Place squares of dough into prepared muffin cups; press down lightly in center to make a well. Bake for 9 to 11 minutes or until edges are set. Cool in pans on wire racks for 5 minutes; remove to wire racks to cool completely. Microwave morsels in small, heavy-duty plastic bag at medium-high (70%) power for 30 seconds; knead until smooth. Microwave at additional 10- to 15-second intervals, kneading until smooth. Cut tiny corner from bag; squeeze chocolate into each cup.

VARIATION

For extra-chocolatey chocolate chip cookie cups, substitute 1 cup **NESTLÉ® TOLL HOUSE® Semi-Sweet Chocolate Morsels** for **Peanut Butter & Milk Chocolate Morsels**.

Courtesy of Nestlé USA

No-Bake Cookies

3 tablespoons butter

⅓ cup evaporated milk

⅓ cup peanut butter

1 (10.6-oz.) package **SIMPLY ORGANIC Cocoa Cayenne Cupcake Mix**

Sugar for rolling (about ⅓ cup)

Hot fudge or melted white chocolate

PREP: 10 minutes

CHILL: 1 hour

YIELD: 1 dozen

Over low heat, melt butter, milk, and peanut butter in a medium saucepan. In a large mixing bowl, combine Cocoa Cayenne Cupcake Mix with melted mixture. Stir until completely moist. Form into 1-inch balls, lightly roll in sugar, and place on pan. Refrigerate 1 to 3 hours. Place cookies in a bowl and drizzle with hot fudge or melted white chocolate.

Courtesy of Simply Organic

Oatmeal Cookies

PREP: 12 minutes

BAKE: 14 minutes

YIELD: About 2 dozen (2 ½- to 3-inch) cookies

Preheat oven to 350°F. Lightly grease (or line with parchment) two light-colored baking sheets. Beat together butter, shortening, sugars, vanilla, cinnamon, nutmeg, salt, and vinegar till fairly smooth; a few tiny bits of butter may still show. Beat in the egg, again beating till smooth. Add the baking soda and flour, beating till well incorporated. Add the oats and raisins, if using, stirring to combine. Drop the dough in 1 ¼-inch balls onto prepared baking sheets; if you're measuring, this is about 2 level tablespoons (using a tablespoon measure, not a dinner spoon). Space the cookies 2 inches apart; they'll spread. Bake for 12 to 14 minutes, reversing the pans halfway through (top rack to bottom, bottom to top). For softer cookies, bake the lesser amount of time; for crunchier, the longer amount. At 12 minutes, a few of the cookies on the edge should just barely be showing a pale brown around their edges. At 14 minutes, they should be starting to color all over. Remove the cookies from the oven, and let them cool right on the pan.

COOK'S TIPS

• Be sure to use quick oats from a canister, not instant breakfast oatmeal or old-fashioned oats. Quick oats will yield the correct texture and spread.

• While it's easier to beat butter that's at cool room temperature, it's not necessary to wait for it to warm up if you've taken it straight from the fridge. You'll just need to beat it a bit longer.

• For round, symmetrical cookies, be sure to leave 2 inches between them on all sides. This is sufficient room so that they won't spread and touch one another.

• If your baking sheets are dark/black, shorten the baking time by a minute or so. If you use air-insulated cookie sheets (which we don't recommend), increase the baking time by a couple of minutes.

Courtesy of King Arthur Flour

¼ cup (½ stick) unsalted butter

¼ cup vegetable shortening

½ cup light brown sugar

¼ cup granulated sugar

1 teaspoon vanilla extract

1 ¼ teaspoons ground cinnamon

⅛ teaspoon ground nutmeg

½ teaspoon salt

1 teaspoon cider or white vinegar

1 large egg

½ teaspoon baking soda

¾ cup **KING ARTHUR Unbleached All-Purpose Flour**

1 ½ cups quick-cooking rolled oats

1 cup golden raisins (optional)

3-Minute No-Bake Cookies

2 cups granulated sugar

8 tablespoons (1 stick) margarine or butter

½ cup lowfat milk

⅓ cup baking cocoa

3 cups **QUAKER® Oats** (quick or old-fashioned, uncooked)

PREP: 3 minutes

YIELD: about 2 dozen

In large saucepan, combine sugar, margarine, milk, and cocoa. Bring to boil over medium heat, stirring frequently. Continue boiling 3 minutes, stirring frequently. Remove from heat. Stir in oats. If using old-fashioned oats, cool mixture in saucepan 5 minutes. Drop by tablespoonfuls onto waxed paper. Let stand until firm. Store tightly covered.

Courtesy of The Quaker Oats Company

Brownie Cookie Bites

PREP: 14 minutes

BAKE: 16 minutes

YIELD: 3 dozen

Preheat oven to 375°F. Lightly grease baking sheets; set aside. In medium bowl, combine flour, baking powder, and salt; set aside. In microwave-safe bowl, microwave 1 cup chips at high 45 seconds or until chips are melted; stir until smooth. In large bowl, with electric mixer on medium speed, beat eggs, sugar, **HELLMANN'S®** or **BEST FOODS® Canola Cholesterol Free Mayonnaise**, and vanilla. Beat in melted chocolate, then flour mixture just until blended. Stir in remaining chips and nuts. Drop mixture by rounded two-tablespoonfuls onto prepared baking sheets, 2 inches apart. Bake 8 minutes or until set. Remove cookies to wire racks and cool completely.

Courtesy of Unilever

2 cups all-purpose flour

½ teaspoon baking powder

¼ teaspoon salt

1 (12-oz.) package semisweet chocolate chips

2 eggs

¾ cup sugar

½ cup **HELLMANN'S®** or **BEST FOODS® Canola Cholesterol Free Mayonnaise**

1 teaspoon vanilla extract

1 cup chopped walnuts

Nuts for Apples Cookies

1 cup sugar

1 cup **MOTT'S Natural Apple Sauce**

½ cup chunky peanut butter

1 large egg

1 cup flour

1 cup rolled oats

1 cup shredded coconut, lightly toasted

½ cup raisins

1 teaspoon cinnamon

½ teaspoon baking soda

PREP: 15 minutes

BAKE: 15 minutes

YIELD: About 2 dozen

Preheat oven to 350°F. Combine sugar, applesauce, peanut butter, and egg in large bowl. Mix until smooth. Stir in remaining ingredients. Spoon dough by rounded tablespoons onto lightly greased baking sheet. Bake 15 minutes, until lightly browned. Allow to cool slightly before removing cookies to cool completely.

Courtesy of Mott's, LLP

Gingersnap Cookies

PREP: 10 minutes

BAKE: 15 minutes

YIELD: 2 dozen

Preheat oven to 350°F. Lightly oil two baking sheets. Mix all dry ingredients together. Mix all wet ingredients together. Combine dry and wet ingredients and mix well. Scoop out 1 tablespoon of cookie dough for each cookie and place 1 inch apart on the baking sheets. Bake 15 minutes, until lightly browned on the bottom. Remove and allow to cool on a wire rack.

Courtesy of Eden Foods

2 ½ cups organic whole wheat pastry flour

1 teaspoon nonaluminum baking powder

1 teaspoon baking soda

½ teaspoon **EDEN Sea Salt**

1 ¼ teaspoons ground ginger

¾ teaspoon ground cinnamon

¾ cup organic maple syrup

3 tablespoons **EDEN ORGANIC Barley Malt Syrup**

1 teaspoon pure vanilla extract

½ cup **EDEN Extra Virgin Olive Oil**

EDEN ORGANIC Safflower Oil

SKIPPY Quick Cookies

1 cup **SKIPPY® Creamy Peanut Butter** or **SKIPPY® SUPER CHUNK® Peanut Butter**

1 cup sugar

1 egg, slightly beaten

1 teaspoon vanilla extract

Sprinkles, chocolate chips, or chocolate candies (optional)

PREP: 10 minutes

BAKE: 8 minutes

YIELD: 2 dozen

Preheat oven to 325°F. Combine all ingredients in medium bowl. Shape dough into 1-inch balls. Arrange cookies on ungreased baking sheets 2 inches apart. Gently flatten each cookie and press crisscross pattern into top with fork. Bake 8 minutes or until lightly browned and slightly puffed. Immediately top with sprinkles, chocolate chips, or chocolate candies, if desired. Cool completely on wire rack before removing from baking sheets.

Courtesy of Unilever

Classic Peanut Butter Cookies

¼ cup vegetable shortening

½ cup granulated sugar

½ cup light brown sugar

1 large egg

1 teaspoon vanilla extract

¾ cup supermarket-style smooth peanut butter

1 ½ cups **KING ARTHUR Unbleached All-Purpose Flour**

1 teaspoon baking soda

½ teaspoon salt

2 to 3 tablespoons water

PREP: 15 minutes

BAKE: 20 minutes

YIELD: About 2 dozen

Preheat oven to 350°F. Lightly grease (or line with parchment) two baking sheets. Beat together the shortening, sugars, egg, vanilla, and peanut butter till smooth. Add the flour, baking soda, and salt to the peanut-butter mixture, beating gently till everything is well combined. Add enough water to make a cohesive dough. Drop the cookie dough by tablespoonfuls onto the prepared baking sheets (a tablespoon cookie scoop works well here), leaving 2 inches between them. Use a fork to flatten each cookie to about ½-inch thick, making a crosshatch design. Bake the cookies for 12 to 14 minutes, till they're barely beginning to brown around the edges; the tops won't have browned. Remove them from the oven and cool on a rack.

COOK'S TIP

This recipe was developed to use traditional supermarket-style peanut butter. If you use all-natural peanut butter, grind your own, or use lowfat or low-salt peanut butter, the cookies won't turn out as described.

Courtesy of King Arthur Flour

Banana Split

PREP: 20 minutes

YIELD: 3 servings

Scoop **BREYERS® All Natural Ice Cream** into serving dish. Add banana and topping, then sprinkle with walnuts. Top with whipped cream and a maraschino cherry, if desired.

Courtesy of Unilever

1 ½ cups (½ cup each serving) **BREYERS® All Natural Chocolate, Vanilla, and/or Strawberry Ice Cream**

1 banana halved lengthwise

6 tablespoons (2 each serving) hot fudge, pineapple and/or strawberry topping

1 tablespoon chopped walnuts

Whipped cream (optional)

3 maraschino cherries (optional)

Bananas Foster Sundaes

6 tablespoons **I CAN'T BELIEVE IT'S NOT BUTTER!® Spread**

3 tablespoons light brown sugar, firmly packed

2 tablespoons rum

2 medium bananas, sliced

2 cups **BREYERS® All Natural Vanilla Ice Cream**

¼ cup chopped walnuts or pecans

PREP: 15 minutes

COOK: 2 minutes

YIELD: 4 servings

In 1-quart saucepan, heat Spread, brown sugar, and rum over low heat, stirring frequently, until Spread and brown sugar are melted, about 1 minute. Let stand 5 minutes to cool; stir in bananas. Into four serving dishes, evenly scoop **BREYERS® All Natural Vanilla Ice Cream**, then top with sauce and walnuts.

Courtesy of Unilever

Ambrosia Sundaes

1 (11-oz.) can mandarin oranges, drained, or 1 large seedless orange, sectioned, outer membrane removed

¼ cup orange marmalade

2 tablespoons rum- or coconut-flavored rum

¼ cup flaked coconut, toasted if desired

2 cups **BREYERS® All Natural Vanilla Ice Cream**

PREP: 5 minutes

COOK: 5 minutes

YIELD: 4 servings

Cook oranges, marmalade, and rum in small saucepan until heated through. Scoop **BREYERS® All Natural Vanilla Ice Cream** into four goblets or dessert dishes, then top with warm orange mixture and coconut.

Courtesy of Unilever

Key Lime Ice Cream Treats

PREP: 5 minutes

COOK: 10 minutes

YIELD: 8 servings

½ cup Key lime juice

1 cup sugar

Pinch salt

4 cups **BREYERS® Smooth & Dreamy ½ the Fat Creamy Vanilla Ice Cream**

½ cup toasted flaked coconut

Combine Key lime juice, sugar, and salt in 2-quart nonstick saucepan. Bring to a boil over high heat, stirring constantly. Reduce heat to medium and simmer gently, stirring frequently, 7 minutes or until thickened. Cool to room temperature. Evenly scoop **BREYERS® Smooth & Dreamy ½ the Fat Creamy Vanilla Ice Cream** into eight bowls. Top with Key lime sauce, then coconut.

COOK'S TIP

Recipe can be halved.

Courtesy of Unilever

Caramel Apple Sundaes

1 tablespoon butter or margarine

1 tablespoon brown sugar

2 medium cooking apples, peeled, cored and thinly sliced (about 2 cups)

1 ½ pints (3 cups) vanilla ice cream

6 tablespoons caramel ice cream topping

12 **NABISCO Ginger Snaps**, coarsely broken

PREP: 15 minutes

COOK: 6 minutes

YIELD: 6 servings

Melt butter in large skillet on medium heat. Stir in brown sugar. Add apples; toss to coat. Cook 4 to 5 minutes or until apples are tender, stirring frequently. Scoop ice cream evenly into six dessert dishes; cover evenly with the warm apple mixture. Top each sundae with 1 tablespoon of the topping and about 2 tablespoons of the gingersnap pieces. Serve immediately.

Courtesy of Kraft Foods

SKIPPY Dippin' Sundaes

1 quart **BREYERS® Smooth & Dreamy ½ the Fat Creamy Vanilla Ice Cream**

½ cup **SKIPPY® Creamy Peanut Butter** or **SKIPPY® SUPER CHUNK® Peanut Butter**, melted

Your favorite sundae toppings

PREP: 5 minutes

YIELD: 8 servings

Scoop **BREYERS® Smooth & Dreamy ½ the Fat Creamy Vanilla Ice Cream** into eight dessert dishes. Drizzle with melted **SKIPPY®** peanut butter, then spoon on toppings.

Courtesy of Unilever

Easy Decadent Brownie Sundaes

PREP: 10 minutes

YIELD: 2 servings

Place brownies on two dessert plates or in bowls. Top with **BREYERS® All Natural Ice Cream**, then spoon on ice cream toppings. Garnish with whipped cream and cherries.

Courtesy of Unilever

2 store-bought or baked brownies

1 cup your favorite flavor **BREYERS® All Natural Ice Cream**

½ cup your favorite ice cream topping (chocolate syrup, caramel or hot fudge sauce, or wet walnuts)

¼ cup your favorite crunchy ice cream topping (walnuts, peanuts, sprinkles, or toasted coconut)

2 dollops sweetened whipped cream (for garnish)

2 maraschino cherries (for garnish)

My Heart Belongs to You Sundaes

PREP: 30 minutes

CHILL: 30 minutes

YIELD: 8 servings

Line baking sheet or jelly roll pan with waxed paper. Place cooling rack on prepared pan. Trim rounded portion from top of cake. Slice cake horizontally into two equal layers (each about ¾-inch thick). Using heart-shaped cookie cutter, cut heart shapes from cake. Place hearts on cooling rack. Set aside extra cake pieces for another use. Place chocolate chips and shortening in medium microwave-safe bowl. Microwave at medium (50%) 1 minute; stir. If necessary, microwave at medium an additional 15 seconds at a time, stirring after each heating, until chips are melted and mixture is smooth when stirred. Pour or spoon melted chocolate over and down sides of hearts. Refrigerate about 30 minutes or until chocolate is firm. For each sundae, place chocolate-covered heart on serving plate. Add scoop of ice cream and drizzle ice cream with strawberry syrup.

Courtesy of The Hershey Company

1 (10 ¾-oz.) frozen loaf pound cake, thawed

1 cup **HERSHEY'S Mini Chips Semi-Sweet Chocolate**, **HERSHEY'S SPECIAL DARK Chocolate Chips**, **HERSHEY'S Semi-Sweet Chocolate Chips**, or **HERSHEY'S Milk Chocolate Chips**

1 tablespoon shortening (do not use butter, margarine, spreads, or oil)

Vanilla ice cream

HERSHEY'S Strawberry Syrup

Pecan Pie Sundae Cups

PREP: 15 minutes

YIELD: 4 servings

Arrange waffle bowls on dessert plates, then spoon in 1 tablespoon caramel ice cream topping in each bowl. Evenly top with **BREYERS® All Natural Butter Pecan Ice Cream**, then sprinkle with pecans. Drizzle with hot fudge topping and remaining caramel topping.

Courtesy of Unilever

4 (3-inch) waffle or tulip bowls

⅓ cup caramel ice cream topping, divided

4 scoops (2 cups) **BREYERS® All Natural Butter Pecan Ice Cream**

¼ cup coarsely chopped candied or glazed pecans or walnuts

¼ cup hot fudge topping, heated

Black & White Ice Cream Sandwiches

8 (3-inch) soft baked sugar cookies, divided

4 small scoops (about 1 cup) **BREYERS® All Natural Vanilla Ice Cream**

4 small scoops (about 1 cup) **BREYERS® All Natural Chocolate Ice Cream**

½ cup sweetened whipped cream or thawed frozen whipped topping

1 to 2 tablespoons chocolate syrup

PREP: 10 minutes

FREEZE: 1 hour

YIELD: 4 servings

On bottom of four cookies, place 1 scoop each **BREYERS® All Natural Vanilla and All Natural Chocolate Ice Cream,** then gently press on remaining cookies, bottom-side down. Evenly top with whipped cream, then drizzle with chocolate syrup. Arrange ice cream sandwiches on baking sheet. Cover and freeze 1 hour or until ready to serve.

Courtesy of Unilever

Gingersnap Ice Cream Sandwiches

PREP: 20 minutes

FREEZE: 30 minutes

YIELD: 1 dozen

On bottoms of 12 cookies, place 1 scoop **BREYERS® All Natural Ice Cream,** then gently press on remaining cookies, bottom-side down. Roll sides of sandwiches in nuts. Arrange ice cream sandwiches on baking sheet. Cover and freeze 30 minutes or until ready to serve.

Courtesy of Unilever

24 (1 ¾-inch) gingersnap cookies, divided

12 small scoops (about 2 cups) your favorite **BREYERS® All Natural Ice Cream**

1 cup chopped nuts or crystallized ginger

Ginger Bites with Zesty Lemon Sorbet

PREP: 16 minutes

BAKE: 15 minutes

YIELD: 24 servings

1 (16.5-oz.) package **NESTLÉ® TOLL HOUSE® Refrigerated Sugar Cookie Bar Dough**

6 tablespoons finely chopped crystallized ginger

1 pint **Zesty Lemon HÄAGEN-DAZS® Fat Free Sorbet**

⅓ cup chopped pistachios

Preheat oven to 325°F. Break dough along prescored lines. Dip the top of each square in chopped ginger. Place 2 inches apart on ungreased baking sheets, ginger side up. Bake for 14 to 16 minutes or until golden around edges. Cool on baking sheets for 2 minutes; remove to wire racks to cool completely. Top each cookie with a small scoop of sorbet. Sprinkle with about ½ teaspoon chopped pistachios. Serve immediately.

Courtesy of Nestlé USA

Ice Cream Truffles

2 cups **BREYERS® All Natural Chocolate or your favorite flavor Ice Cream**

Ground nuts, finely chopped toasted coconut, chocolate cookie crumbs, and/or cocoa powder

PREP: 20 minutes

FREEZE: 30 minutes

YIELD: About 2 ½ dozen

Line a baking pan with wax paper. Scoop **BREYERS® All Natural Chocolate Ice Cream** by rounded tablespoonfuls and quickly roll into balls, then roll in nuts, coconut, cookie crumbs, or cocoa powder. Arrange truffles on prepared pan, cover, and freeze 30 minutes or until ready to serve.

Courtesy of Unilever

Bananas Foster à l'Orange

PREP: 15 minutes

COOK: 10 minutes

YIELD: 4 servings

Melt the butter in a medium-size skillet over low heat. Add brown sugar to melted butter, increase heat to medium, and stir to dissolve sugar. Let mixture cook about 1 minute. Add banana slices and stir to coat with sugar butter. Add the Moro orange juice, increase heat, and bring to a boil. Cook for 1 to 2 minutes to let juice mixture thicken slightly, then reduce heat. Pour 2 tablespoons of rum from bottle into a small container, and then add carefully to skillet. (It is safer not to pour rum directly from bottle into the hot pan.) Stir to combine and cook 1 minute. Place ice cream scoops in serving bowls. Divide and pour sauce over ice cream. Garnish with **SUNKIST® Honey Roasted Almond Accents** and serve immediately.

COOK'S TIPS

SUNKIST® Moro oranges are also called "blood" oranges because of their deep red-colored pulp. Serve this dessert in hollowed orange shells. Take orange halves that have been juiced and remove all pulp. Place 1 scoop of vanilla ice cream in each hollowed orange half and keep in freezer until ready to serve. Orange-flavored liqueur can be substituted for the dark rum, or if you prefer, the alcohol can be completely omitted.

Courtesy of Sunkist Growers, Inc.

2 tablespoons butter

2 tablespoons brown sugar

2 medium bananas, peeled, sliced ½-inch thick

¼ cup freshly squeezed **SUNKIST® Moro orange juice**

2 tablespoons dark rum

4 scoops vanilla ice cream

4 teaspoons **SUNKIST® Honey Roasted Almond Accents** (for garnish)

Warm Sugared Pineapple over Ice Cream

1 (20-oz.) can pineapple chunks in natural juice, drained

¼ cup light brown sugar, firmly packed

2 tablespoons orange liqueur (optional)

2 cups **BREYERS® All Natural Vanilla** or **Butter Pecan Ice Cream**

¼ cup slivered almonds, toasted if desired

PREP: 5 minutes

COOK: 2 minutes

YIELD: 4 servings

Cook pineapple, brown sugar, and liqueur, if using, in 10-inch nonstick skillet over medium heat 2 minutes or until sugar is melted and liquid is syrupy. **Scoop BREYERS® All Natural Vanilla Ice Cream** into four dessert dishes, then top with warm pineapple mixture and sprinkle with almonds.

Courtesy of Unilever

Easy Chocolate Fudge

PREP: 6 minutes

COOK: 5 minutes

CHILL: 2 hours

YIELD: 4 dozen

Line an 8- or 9-inch square baking pan with foil. Combine morsels and sweetened condensed milk in medium, heavy-duty saucepan. Warm over lowest possible heat, stirring until smooth. Remove from heat; stir in nuts and vanilla extract. Spread evenly into prepared baking pan. Refrigerate for 2 hours or until firm. Lift from pan; remove foil. Cut into 48 pieces.

Courtesy of Nestlé USA

1 (12-oz.) package (2 cups) **NESTLÉ® TOLL HOUSE® Semi-Sweet Chocolate Morsels**

1 (14-oz.) can **NESTLÉ® CARNATION® Sweetened Condensed Milk**

1 cup chopped walnuts

1 teaspoon vanilla extract

Creamy Double Decker Fudge

1 cup **REESE'S Peanut Butter Chips**

1 (14-oz.) can sweetened condensed milk (not evaporated milk), divided

1 teaspoon vanilla extract, divided

1 cup **HERSHEY'S SPECIAL DARK Chocolate Chips** or **HERSHEY'S Semi-Sweet Chocolate Chips**

PREP: 10 minutes

CHILL: 2 to 3 hours

YIELD: 4 dozen

Line an 8-inch square pan with foil. Place peanut butter chips and ⅔ cup of the sweetened condensed milk in small microwave-safe bowl. Microwave at medium (50%) 1 to 1½ minutes, stirring after 1 minute, until chips are melted and mixture is smooth when stirred. Stir in ½ teaspoon of the vanilla; spread evenly in prepared pan. Place remaining sweetened condensed milk and chocolate chips in another small microwave-safe bowl; repeat above microwave procedure. Stir in remaining ½ teaspoon vanilla; spread evenly over peanut butter layer. Cover and chill until firm. Remove from pan; place on cutting board. Peel off foil. Cut into squares. Store tightly covered in refrigerator.

COOK'S TIP

For best results, do not double this recipe.

Courtesy of The Hershey Company

Butterscotch Nut Fudge

PREP: 10 minutes

COOK: 5 minutes

CHILL: 3 hours

YIELD: About 5 dozen

Line an 8-inch square pan with foil, extending foil over edges of pan. Combine sugar, marshmallow creme, evaporated milk, and butter in heavy 3-quart saucepan. Cook over medium heat, stirring constantly, until mixture comes to full boil; boil and stir 5 minutes. Remove from heat; gradually add butterscotch chips, stirring until chips are melted. Stir in nuts and vanilla. Pour into prepared pan; cool. Refrigerate 2 to 3 hours. Remove from pan; place on cutting board. Peel off foil. Cut into squares. Store tightly covered in refrigerator.

COOK'S TIP

For best results, do not double this recipe.

Courtesy of The Hershey Company

1 ¾ cups sugar

1 (7-oz.) jar marshmallow creme

¾ cup evaporated milk

¼ cup (½ stick) butter

1 (11-oz.) package (1 ¾ cups) **HERSHEY'S Butterscotch Chips**

1 cup chopped salted mixed nuts

1 teaspoon vanilla extract

Fabulous Orange Fudge

2 cups sugar

5 ⅓ oz. evaporated milk

10 large marshmallows

¾ cup semisweet chocolate pieces

1 cup chopped walnuts

½ cup butter or margarine, cut into small pieces

Grated zest of 2 **SUNKIST®** **Oranges**

PREP: 15 minutes

COOK: 15 minutes

CHILL: 2 hours or until firm

YIELD: 25 pieces, about 2 lbs.

Butter an 8-inch square baking pan. In a saucepan, combine the sugar, evaporated milk, and marshmallows. Bring to a boil over medium heat, stirring to dissolve the sugar. Boil for 6 minutes, stirring constantly. Remove from heat and add remaining ingredients. Beat well until fudge thickens, about 5 minutes. Pour into prepared pan. Chill until firm and cut into squares.

Courtesy of Sunkist Growers, Inc.

Toasted Almond Truffles

½ cup **NESTLE® CARNATION® Evaporated Milk**

¼ cup granulated sugar

1 (11.5-oz.) package (1 ¾ cups) **NESTLÉ® TOLL HOUSE® Milk Chocolate Morsels**

½ to 1 teaspoon almond or vanilla extract

1 cup sliced almonds, finely chopped, toasted

PREP: 20 minutes

COOK: 5 minutes

CHILL: 1 hour 30 minutes

YIELD: 2 dozen

Combine evaporated milk and sugar in small, heavy-duty saucepan. Bring to a full rolling boil over medium-low heat, stirring constantly. Boil, stirring constantly, for 3 minutes. Remove from heat. Stir in morsels. Stir vigorously until mixture is smooth. Stir in almond extract. Refrigerate for 1 ½ to 2 hours. Shape into 1-inch balls; roll in nuts. Cover; refrigerate until ready to serve.

Courtesy of Nestlé USA

KISSES Candy Twists

PREP: 10–20 minutes, depending on quantity

BAKE: 3 minutes

YIELD: up to 2 dozen

Preheat oven to 350°F. Remove wrappers from chocolates. Place pretzels on ungreased baking sheet. Place one unwrapped chocolate on top of each pretzel. Bake 2 to 3 minutes or until the chocolate is soft, but not melting. Remove from oven; gently press decorative garnish on top of the soft chocolate piece. Cool and serve.

Courtesy of The Hershey Company

HERSHEY'S KISSES Brand Milk Chocolates

1 bag small pretzels (twisted)

Decorative garnishes such as **REESE'S MINI PIECES Candy, REESE'S MINI PIECES Peanut Butter Chips, HERSHEY'S Triple Chocolate Sprinkles, REESE'S Peanut Butter Sprinkles,** small holiday-themed candies, nut pieces, miniature marshmallows, candied cherry pieces

No-Bake Butterscotch Haystacks

PREP: 20 minutes

YIELD: 2 dozen

Line tray with wax paper. Place butterscotch chips, peanut butter chips, and shortening in medium microwave-safe bowl. Microwave at medium (50%) 1 minute; stir. If necessary, microwave at medium an additional 15 seconds at a time, stirring after each heating, just until chips are melted and mixture is smooth when stirred. Immediately add chow mein noodles; stir to coat. Drop mixture by heaping teaspoons onto prepared tray or into paper candy cups; let stand until firm. If necessary, cover and refrigerate until firm. Store in tightly covered container in refrigerator.

VARIATION

Chocolate Haystacks: Substitute 1 cup **HERSHEY'S SPE-CIAL DARK Chocolate Chips**, **HERSHEY'S Semi-Sweet Chocolate Chips**, or **HERSHEY'S Milk Chocolate Chips** for butterscotch chips. Proceed as directed above with peanut butter chips, shortening, and chow mein noodles.

Courtesy of The Hershey Company

1 cup **HERSHEY'S Butterscotch Chips**

½ cup **REESE'S Peanut Butter Chips**

1 tablespoon shortening (do not use butter, margarine, spread, or oil)

1 (3-oz.) can (1 ½ cups) chow mein noodles, coarsely broken

NESTLÉ Graham Dippers

Wax paper

3 to 4 tablespoons candy sprinkles, **NESTLÉ® TOLL HOUSE® Semi-Sweet Chocolate Mini Morsels**, or chopped nuts

⅓ cup **NESTLÉ® TOLL HOUSE® Premier White Morsels** or **Semi-Sweet Chocolate Mini Morsels**

16 honey or cinnamon graham sticks

PREP: 15 minutes

COOK: 1 minute

CHILL: 10 minutes

YIELD: 8 (2-stick) servings

Line tray with wax paper. Place candy sprinkles on plate or in shallow bowl. Melt ⅓ cup morsels according to package directions in small bowl. Dip one graham stick halfway into melted morsels, then into candy sprinkles. Transfer to prepared tray. Repeat with remaining graham sticks. Refrigerate for 10 minutes or until set. Store in airtight container at room temperature for up to 1 week.

Courtesy of Nestlé USA

Chocolate-Dipped Snacks

PREP: 20 minutes

CHILL: 30 minutes

YIELD: About ½ cup chocolate coating

Cover tray with wax paper. Place chocolate chips and shortening in small microwave-safe bowl. Microwave at medium (50%) 1 minute; stir. If necessary, microwave at medium an additional 15 seconds at a time, stirring after each heating, just until chips are melted and mixture is smooth when stirred. Cool slightly. Dip two-thirds of each snack or fruit into chocolate mixture. Shake gently to remove excess chocolate. Place on prepared tray. Refrigerate, uncovered, about 30 minutes or until coating is firm. Store in airtight container in cool, dry place.

Courtesy of The Hershey Company

½ cup **HERSHEY'S Milk Chocolate Chips**

½ cup **HERSHEY'S SPECIAL DARK Chocolate Chips** or **HERSHEY'S Semi-Sweet Chocolate Chips**

1 tablespoon shortening (do not use butter, margarine, spread, or oil)

Cookies, dried apricots, miniature pretzels, or potato chips

Peanut Butter Bumble Bees

¼ cup (½ stick) butter or margarine, softened

1 cup creamy peanut butter

1 cup confectioners' sugar

1 ½ cups **HONEY MAID Graham Cracker Crumbs** or finely crushed **HONEY MAID Honey Grahams**

1 (1-oz.) square **BAKER'S Semi-Sweet Chocolate**

⅓ cup **PLANTERS Sliced Almonds**, toasted

PREP: 30 minutes

YIELD: 2 ½ dozen

Beat butter, peanut butter, and confectioners' sugar in large bowl with electric mixer on medium speed until well blended. Add cracker crumbs; mix well. Shape tablespoonful of butter mixture into 1-inch oval to resemble body of bumble bee. Repeat with remaining butter mixture for additional "bees." Melt chocolate as directed on package. Drizzle chocolate in lines on top of bees to resemble bees' stripes. Insert almonds into both sides of each body for "wings." Store in refrigerator up to 3 days.

Courtesy of Kraft Foods

Snowman Cups

PREP: 15 minutes

YIELD: 10 (½-cup) servings

Beat milk and pudding mixes with whisk 2 minutes. Let stand 5 minutes. Stir in 1 cup of the cookie crumbs. Spoon remaining cookie crumbs into bottoms of 10 (6- to 7-oz.) paper or plastic cups; cover with pudding mixture. Drop spoonfuls of **COOL WHIP Whipped Topping** onto desserts to resemble snowmen. Decorate with gels for the eyes, noses, and scarves.

Courtesy of Kraft Foods

1 quart (4 cups) cold milk

2 (3.9-oz.) packages **JELL-O Chocolate Instant Pudding**

20 **OREO Cookies**, crushed, divided

2 cups **COOL WHIP Whipped Topping**, thawed

Assorted decorating gels

HERSHEY'S Hugs & Kisses Crescents

PREP: 10 minutes

BAKE: 10 minutes

YIELD: 8 crescents

Preheat oven to 375°F. Separate dough into 8 triangles. Remove wrappers from chocolates. Place two chocolates at wide end of each triangle; place an additional chocolate on top of other two pieces. Starting at wide end, roll to opposite point; pinch edges to seal. Place rolls, pointed side down, on ungreased cookie sheet. Curve into crescent shape. Bake 10 minutes or until lightly browned. Cool slightly; sift with confectioners' sugar. Serve warm. Leftover crescents can be reheated in microwave for a few seconds.

Courtesy of The Hershey Company

1 (8-oz.) package refrigerated crescent dinner rolls

24 **HERSHEY'S KISSES Brand Milk Chocolates** or **HERSHEY'S HUGS Brand Candies**

Confectioners' sugar

Confetti Bars

1 (16.5-oz.) package **NESTLÉ® TOLL HOUSE® Refrigerated Chocolate Chunk Cookie Bar Dough**

2 cups miniature marshmallows

1 ½ cups (about 4 oz.) milk chocolate–covered pretzels broken into pieces

3 tablespoons rainbow sprinkles

¼ cup **NESTLÉ® TOLL HOUSE® Semi-Sweet Chocolate Mini Morsels** (optional)

PREP: 10 minutes

COOK: 14 minutes

YIELD: 2 dozen

Preheat oven to 350°F. Grease a 13 x 9-inch baking pan. Place whole bar of dough in prepared pan. Allow to soften for 5 to 10 minutes. Using fingertips, pat dough gently to cover bottom. Bake for 11 to 13 minutes or until edges are golden brown. Sprinkle marshmallows over cookie; bake for an additional 1 to 2 minutes, or until marshmallows are puffed. Distribute pretzels, sprinkles, and morsels, if using, over marshmallows; press down lightly. Cool completely in pan on wire rack. Cut into bars with wet knife.

Courtesy of Nestlé USA

Candy Bars

1 (11-oz.) package (1 ⅔ cups) **NESTLÉ® TOLL HOUSE® Butterscotch Flavored Morsels**

4 cups toasted rice cereal

2 (11.5-oz.) packages **NESTLÉ® TOLL HOUSE® Milk Chocolate Morsels**, divided

COOK: 4 minutes

CHILL: 30 minutes

YIELD: 2 dozen

Grease a 13 x 9-inch baking pan. Microwave butterscotch morsels in large, microwave-safe bowl on medium-high (70%) power for 1 minute; stir. Microwave at additional 10- to 20-second intervals, stirring until smooth. Stir in cereal and 1 cup of the milk chocolate morsels. Press evenly into prepared baking pan. Microwave remaining milk chocolate morsels in small, microwave-safe bowl on medium-high (70%) power for 1 minute; stir. Microwave at additional 10- to 20-second intervals, stirring until smooth. Spread evenly over mixture in pan. Refrigerate until firm. Cut into bars.

Courtesy of Nestlé USA

Peanut Butter Rice Crispy Treats

PREP: 10 minutes

COOK: 10 minutes

YIELD: 9 servings

Spray an 8 x 8-inch square baking pan with nonstick spray. Whisk the peanut butter and rice syrup in a saucepan on moderate-low heat to the point of boiling. In a large bowl, mix crumbled rice cakes and almonds. Coat crumbles with rice syrup and peanut butter mixture. Press the crumbles mixture into prepared pan. Allow to cool and cut into squares.

VARIATION

Use any flavor of **LUNDBERG® Rice Cakes**: Honey Nut, Apple Cinnamon, Buttery Caramel, Cinnamon Toast, Caramel Corn, or Brown Rice.

Courtesy of Lundberg Family Farms

1 cup peanut butter

1 cup **SWEET DREAMS® Rice Syrup**

4 cups crumbled **LUNDBERG® rice cakes** (or 4 cups puffed rice cereal)

1 cup raw almonds, finely chopped

Peanut Butter S'mores

PREP: 10 minutes

YIELD: 9 servings

Spread 1 teaspoon of the peanut butter onto each of 9 graham squares. Top each with about 1 tablespoon of the chopped cookies, 1 teaspoon of the fudge sauce, and 3 or 4 marshmallows. Cover each with second graham square to make 9 s'mores. Place 4 or 5 of the s'mores on microwave-safe plate. Microwave at high 10 to 15 seconds or until marshmallows begin to melt. Repeat with the remaining s'mores. Serve warm.

Courtesy of Kraft Foods

3 tablespoons creamy peanut butter

9 **HONEY MAID Honey Grahams**, broken crosswise in half (18 squares)

7 **OREO Cookies**, coarsely chopped (about ⅔ cup)

3 tablespoons hot fudge ice cream topping

½ cup **JET-PUFFED Miniature Marshmallows**

NESTLÉ® TOLL HOUSE® Cookie S'mores

48 graham cracker squares, divided

1 (16.5-oz.) package **NESTLÉ® TOLL HOUSE® Refrigerated Chocolate Chip Cookie Bar Dough**

12 large marshmallows, cut in half

PREP: 5 minutes

BAKE: 15 minutes

COOL: 2 minutes

YIELD: 2 dozen

Preheat oven to 350°F. Line baking sheet with foil. Arrange 24 graham cracker squares on prepared baking sheet; set aside. Bake cookie dough on another baking sheet according to package directions. Cool for 2 minutes on baking sheet. Remove cookies from baking sheet and place one warm cookie on each graham cracker square on foil. Top each cookie with one marshmallow half. Bake for 1 to 2 minutes or until marshmallows are soft. Immediately top s'mores with remaining graham cracker squares.

This first-prize winner was created by Mardell Ramey of Reynoldsburg, Ohio; courtesy of Nestlé USA

Blooming Ice Pop Parfaits

1 cup sliced banana

2 cups your favorite **BREYERS® All Natural Ice Cream**

½ cup crushed chocolate wafer cookies

4 **POPSICLE® SCRIBBLERS®**, unwrapped

4 gummy worm candies

PREP: 15 minutes

FREEZE: 30 minutes

YIELD: 4 servings

Divide banana evenly among four small ramekins or custard cups. Top evenly with **BREYERS® All Natural Ice Cream**, then sprinkle with cookie crumbs. Freeze 30 minutes or until firm. Garnish with **POPSICLE® SCRIBBLERS®** and gummy worms. Serve immediately.

VARIATION

To serve a crowd, line a clean, unused flowerpot with plastic wrap, then layer as above, adding additional ingredients as needed.

Courtesy of Unilever

Peanut Butter & Jelly Brownie Sundaes

PREP: 15 minutes

YIELD: 2 servings

In microwave-safe glass measuring cup, microwave **SKIPPY®** peanut butter until melted, about 20 seconds; stir. In another microwave-safe glass measuring cup, microwave jelly until melted, about 20 seconds; stir. In each of two dessert dishes, arrange 4 brownie squares, then top each with 1 scoop **BREYERS® All Natural Vanilla Ice Cream**. Evenly drizzle with half of the melted peanut butter, then half of the melted jelly; repeat layers.

COOK'S TIP

Use store-bought brownies or prepare your favorite recipe. Recipe can be doubled.

Courtesy of Unilever

¼ cup **SKIPPY® Creamy Peanut Butter**

¼ cup your favorite jelly

16 (1-inch) brownie squares

4 small scoops (about 1 cup) **BREYERS® All Natural Vanilla Ice Cream**

Mint Chip Spiders

1 (2.7-oz.) package round chocolate-covered cream-filled cakes

2 scoops **BREYERS® All Natural Mint Chocolate Chip Ice Cream**

1 tablespoon marshmallow cream or vanilla frosting

4 candy-coated chocolate candies

Chocolate syrup

PREP: 10 minutes

YIELD: 2 servings

For each "spider," cut cake in half crosswise. On two dessert plates, arrange bottom half cut-side-up. Top each with 1 scoop **BREYERS® All Natural Mint Chocolate Chip Ice Cream**, then remaining cake half, frosting-side up. Add two small dots of marshmallow cream and candies for "eyes." Drizzle chocolate syrup on plate for "legs." Serve immediately.

Courtesy of Unilever

Purple Cow

PREP: 2 minutes

YIELD: 1 serving

In a 12-oz. glass, combine two scoops of vanilla ice cream with chilled **Welch's Purple Grape Juice**.

Courtesy of Welch Foods Inc., A Cooperative

Vanilla ice cream

WELCH'S Purple Grape Juice

CONTRIBUTORS, THANK YOU!

Annie's Homegrown www.annies.com

Aimee Sands

Applegate Farms www.applegatefarms.com

Gina Asoudegan

Birds Eye Foods, Inc. www.birdseyefoods.com

Barbara Ilecki
Ashley Walters

**Cadbury Schweppes Americas Beverages
www.cadburyschweppes.com**

Chris Barnes
Cherie Schulman

**Campbell Soup Company
www.campbellsoup.com**

Kathryn Conrad
Jane Freiman
Bette Steele

Chelsea Milling Company www.jiffymix.com

Pam Balyeat
Sandy Schultz

Del Monte Foods, Inc. www.delmonte.com

Laura Ali
Lawrence A. Hawley
Leslie L. Macioce

Dole Food Company www.dole.com

Donna Skidmore

Eden Foods, Inc. www.edenfoods.com

Sue Becker
Wendy Esko
Celeste Kukla

Flowers Foods www.flowersfoods.com

Sherry Harper

**Frontier Natural Products Co-op
www.frontiercoop.com**

www.simplyorganicfoods.com

Steve Krusie

Hain Celestial Group www.hain-celestial.com

Lisa Lehndorff

H.J. Heinz Company, L.P. www.heinz.com

Sabrina Hudson
Jessica Jackson
Maria Talpas

The Hershey Company www.hersheys.com

Carol Danz
Sue Harris
Linda Stahl

**King Arthur Flour Company, Inc.
www.kingarthurflour.com**

Allison Furbish

Kraft Foods, Inc. www.kraftfoods.com

Basil Maglaris

Land O' Lakes, Inc. www.landolakes.com

Barb Bickle
Cindy Manwarren
Pat Weed

Lundberg Family Farms www.lundberg.com

Yvonne Garrett
Janet A. Souza
Kateland Weighall

National Pork Board www.theotherwhitemeat.com

Carma Rogers

Nestlé USA www.nestleusa.com

Christine Garboski

Amy Hiestand

Newman's Own Organics
www.newmansownorganics.com

Nell Newman

Sally Shepard

Organic Valley Family of Farms/Cropp
Cooperative www.organicvalley.coop

Angie Scotland

Perdue Farms, Inc. www.perdue.com

Lisa Doyle

Cyndy Glover

Quaker Oats Company www.quakeroats.com

Marisa Gottlieb

Monique Jacobson

Jennifer Leemis

Smithfield Foods www.smithfieldfoods.com

Eric Esch

Michelle Lieszkovszky

Stonyfield Farm www.stonyfield.com

Carol Billings

Elizabeth Baron

Lisa Kinzel

Sunkist Growers, Inc. www.sunkist.com

Angela Della Ripa

Tropicana Products, Inc. www.tropicana.com

Jacqlyn Coleman

Janet Silverberg

Unilever Group of Companies www.unilever.com

Anna Marie Cesario

Lauren Dellabella

June Kuruc

Sarah G. Page

Welch Foods, Inc. www.welchs.com

Carolyn Boyle

Teleia Farrell

Darlene Hollywood

COMPANY TRADEMARKS

ANNIE'S HOMEGROWN® is a registered trademark of Annie's, Inc.

APPLEGATE FARMS® is a registered trademark of Applegate Farms.

BIRDS EYE®, STEAMFRESH®, COMSTOCK®, and WILDERNESS® are registered trademarks of Birds Eye Foods, Inc.

MOTT'S® is a registered trademark of Cadbury Schweppes Americas Beverages.

CAMPBELL'S®, HEALTHY REQUEST®, PEPPERIDGE FARM®, SWANSON®, PACE®, and PREGO® are registered trademarks, and NATURAL GOODNESS™ is a trademark of CSC Brands LP.

"JIFFY"® is a registered trademark of Chelsea Milling Company.

COLLEGE INN®, CONTADINA®, DEL MONTE®, DEL MONTE® Orchard Select®, DEL MONTE® FreshCut®, and DEL MONTE® SunFresh® are registered trademarks of Del Monte Foods, Inc.

DOLE® and Tropical Gold® are registered trademarks of Dole Food Company.

EDEN®, EDEN FOODS®, EDEN ORGANIC®, EDENBLEND®, and EDENSOY® are registered trademarks of Eden Foods, Inc.

NATURE'S OWN® and COBBLESTONE MILL® are registered trademarks of Flowers Bakeries Brands, Inc.

SIMPLY ORGANIC® is a registered trademark and FRONTIER NATURAL PRODUCTS CO-OP™ is a trademark of Frontier Natural Products Co-op.

HAIN®, SPECTRUM®, WESTSOY®, HAIN PURE FOODS®, ARROWHEAD MILLS®, SPECTRUM NATURALS®, and GARDEN OF EATIN'® are registered trademarks of Hain Celestial Group.

HEINZ®, CLASSICO®, LEA & PERRINS®, and WYLER'S® are registered trademarks of H.J. Heinz Company and its affiliated companies.

HERSHEY'S®, HERSHEY'S KISSES®, HERSHEY'S MINI KISSES®, HERSHEY'S SPECIAL DARK®, HERSHEY'S HUGS®, MOUNDS®, REESE'S®, REESE'S MINI PIECES®, HEATH®, and YORK® are registered trademarks, and HERSHEY'S Mini Chips™ is a trademark of The Hershey Company.

KING ARTHUR® is a registered trademark of King Arthur Flour Company, Inc.

KRAFT®, MIRACLE WHIP®, GOOD SEASONS®, GREY POUPON®, RITZ®, KNUDSEN®, BREAKSTONE'S®, OREO®, BAKER'S®, COOL WHIP®, HONEY MAID®, JELL-O®, NABISCO®, PLANTERS®, PHILADELPHIA®, PREMIUM®, A.1. ORIGINAL STEAK SAUCE®, OSCAR MAYER®, ATHENOS®, SHAKE 'N BAKE®, OVEN FRY®, BULL'S EYE®, PLANTERS COCKTAIL®, KRAFT FREE®, KOOL-AID®, JET-PUFFED®, and HOFFMAN'S® are registered trademarks of Kraft Foods, Inc.

LAND O LAKES® and Fresh Buttery Taste® Spread are registered trademarks of Land O'Lakes, Inc.

LUNDBERG®, LUNDBERG FAMILY FARMS®, LUNDBERG HEAT & EAT ORGANIC COUNTRYWILD®, and SWEET DREAMS® are registered trademarks of Lundberg Family Farms.

"THE OTHER WHITE MEAT"® is a registered trademark of the National Pork Board.

INDEX